D1531369

don't click on the blue e!

on the

switching to firefox

Scott Granneman

Beijing • Cambridge • Farnham • Köln • Paris • Sebastopol • Taipei • Tokyo

Don't Click on the Blue E!
by Scott Granneman

Published by O'Reilly Media, Inc., 1005 Gravenstein Highway North,
Sebastopol, CA 95472.

O'Reilly books may be purchased for educational, business,
or sales promotional use. Online editions are also available for most titles
(*safari.oreilly.com*). For more information, contact our corporate/institutional
sales department: (800) 998-9938 or *corporate@oreilly.com*.

Editor:	Brian Jepson
Production Editor:	Mary Brady
Cover Designer:	Scott Idleman/Blink
Interior Designer:	Marcia Friedman
Printing History:	April 2005: First Edition.

 This book uses RepKover,™ a durable and flexible lay-flat binding.

ISBN: 0-596-00939-9
[M]

Table of Contents

PREFACE

The reviews are in, and Firefox is a winner:

InformationWeek, November 19, 2004
> "Firefox 1.0 is the first Web browser since October, 1997, that deserves serious consideration by the entire world of desktop computer users… I'm not going back to Internet Explorer 6.0."
>> *http://www.informationweek.com/story/showArticle. jhtml?articleID=53700761*

eWeek, November 9, 2004
> "…the free, open-source Firefox is the best stand-alone Web browser option available today and is generations ahead of Microsoft's IE."
>> *http://www.eweek.com/article2/0,1759,1722326,00.asp*

CNET, November 12, 2004
> "Mozilla Firefox 1.0 is the dream Internet browser you've been looking for."
>> *http://reviews.cnet.com/Mozilla_Firefox_1_0/4505-9241_7-31117280.html*

Wired News, November 11, 2004
> "The browser is an absolute joy to use—smart, fast and very user-friendly…"
>> *http://www.wired.com/news/technology/0,1282,65668,00.html*

Firefox was officially released in early November 2004, but even before that, the word was out: this was a web browser that was definitely worth downloading and investigating. Now that Firefox has reached 1.0, the world can use it, and people are finding out that Firefox benefits just about everyone:

Everyday users
> As I discuss in the first chapter of this book, Internet Explorer just doesn't cut it any more. It's buggy, insecure, and out of date, and it lacks features that Firefox has had since its beginning. Firefox is well-coded: if bugs are found, they're fixed at an incredible rate of speed. Firefox is secure: it doesn't engage in the risky behaviors that make IE so dangerous. Firefox is fresh, new, and hip: since it's an open source project, it's constantly being updated and improved by a team of developers all over the world. Firefox is feature-rich: it's probably the easiest browser in the world to use, but if you want to add a feature that you think is missing, it's incredibly easy to do so (as you'll see in Chapter 4).

Power users

If you're a member of this exalted group, you're in luck—you get all the benefits listed above, and more. Power users will find that Firefox is amazingly customizable, with all sorts of hidden extra goodies that are available to those who know where to look. Want to get to the good stuff? Jump ahead to Chapters 4 and 5—they're going to make you very, very happy.

Businesses

Maybe they haven't told you yet, but trust me, your IT people are sick of having to deal with IE. The constant updates for the security issue du jour, the general flakiness, the spyware deposited on employee PCs every day—it all adds up to a never-ending headache. Your IT department can't just get rid of IE completely—Microsoft has seen to that—but by switching to Firefox, they'll definitely reduce the problems they have to face with IE, so they can go back to dealing with Bob in Accounting.

Web developers

Firefox is the browser of choice for most web developers. It has features that make web work fun and easy, and its ability to render correctly HTML, CSS, and other web technologies is a boon when creating web pages.

Programmers

A recent article on CNET (*http://news.com.com/Firefox+fortune+hunters/ 2100-1032_3-5455173.html*) discussed how many programmers are starting to make good livings creating custom software that is based on Firefox. Why? Firefox has an architecture that makes it easy to add features, or even base whole programs on it; the installed base of users is constantly growing; and the browser is cross-platform, running on Windows, Mac OS X, and Linux. This is great news for developers.

The Internet

Thanks to Firefox, there's competition in the web browser space again, which is a good thing, even for people who don't use Firefox. Now that Microsoft is starting to feel some heat from Firefox, they'll (hopefully) start improving their moribund browser. Meanwhile, AOL is using Firefox as the basis for a new, rejuvenated Netscape. Web developers are being encouraged to create web sites not just for IE, but for a wider variety of web users. Firefox is helping to make the Web and the Internet a better place, and that alone is one heck of a benefit.

This book is a guide to using Firefox and a celebration of all the wonderful things it can do. I know Firefox isn't perfect, but it's the best web browser available today—and, more importantly, the people behind Firefox are working to make it better every day.

Audience for This Book

This book is aimed at Windows users who are thinking about replacing the Blue E (Internet Explorer) and want to know how to install, configure, and use the Firefox web browser to its fullest capabilities.

If you're not the most sophisticated computer user in the world, don't worry. You should be able to follow along with everything just fine, and you're going to learn some neat tricks that you'll really enjoy.

If you're the kind of person who people call for computer help, you can probably skip the second chapter, but I guarantee that you will find plenty of great information in this book that you can use to make your own—and others'—browsing experiences better.

Finally, if you helped create Firefox, let me know if I got anything wrong, OK? : –)

Organization of This Book

Here's a brief overview of what's in the book:

Chapter 1, *The Problem with the Blue E*,
> This chapter justifies the first part of the book's title, explaining just what is wrong with the Blue E—Internet Explorer—and why other options are better.

Chapter 2, *Installing and Configuring Firefox*
> Chapter 2 walks you through the process of downloading and configuring Firefox. Even if you've done this before on your own, you'll still find some useful tips here.

Chapter 3, *Firefox Features*
> This chapter gives a whirlwind tour of the Firefox browser and its awesome features.

Chapter 4, *Killer Firefox Add-Ons*
> One of Firefox's best aspects is its add-ons: the plug-ins, themes, and extensions that are available. Want to make something great even better? Read this chapter.

Chapter 5, *Advanced Firefox*

OK, power users (and power-user wannabes), this chapter is for you. Read this to learn all the cool advanced stuff that you can do with Firefox.

Appendix A, *Other Web Browsers*

Firefox isn't the only web browser in the world—it's just the best. If you're interested in finding out the basics of some other good browsers, look here.

Appendix B, *Firefox Options*

In Chapter 2, I touch only on the essential things you need to do to configure Firefox. For the complete list of all configuration possibilities, check out this Appendix.

Conventions Used in This Book

The following typographical conventions are used in this book:

Italic

Used for new terms where they are defined, URLs, filenames, file extensions, directories, commands, and options. For example, a path in the filesystem will appear in the text as *C:\Windows*.

Constant width

Used for HTML tags and to show the contents of files and the output from commands.

Constant width bold

Used for emphasis in code examples and for text that should be typed literally by the user.

Menus/navigation

Menus and their options are presented in the text as File → Open, Edit → Copy, and so on. Arrows are also used to signify navigation paths when using window options; for example, Control Panel → Add/Remove Programs → Internet Explorer → Remove means that you should launch the Control Panel, click the icon for Add/Remove Programs, select Internet Explorer, and then click Remove (if only Microsoft really made it that easy!).

Pathnames

Pathnames are used to show the location of a file or application in the filesystem. Folders are separated by backward slashes. For example, if you're told to "launch the Firefox application (*C:\Program Files\Mozilla Firefox*)," that means you can find the Firefox application in the *Mozilla* subfolder of the *Program Files* folder.

Note

This signifies a tip, suggestion, or general note.

Warning

This indicates a warning or caution.

We'd Like to Hear from You

Please address comments and questions concerning this book to the publisher:

> O'Reilly Media, Inc.
> 1005 Gravenstein Highway North
> Sebastopol, CA 95472
> (800) 998-9938 (in the U.S. or Canada)
> (707) 829-0515 (international/local)
> (707) 829-0104 (fax)

To comment or ask technical questions about this book, send email to:

> *bookquestions@oreilly.com*

We have a web site for the book, where we'll list examples, errata, and any plans for future editions. The site also includes a link to a forum where you can discuss the book with the author and other readers. You can access this site at:

> *http://www.oreilly.com/catalog/bluee/*

For more information about books, conferences, Resource Centers, and the O'Reilly Network, see the O'Reilly web site at:

> *http://www.oreilly.com*

Safari Enabled

 When you see a Safari® Enabled icon on the cover of your favorite technology book, it means the book is available online through the O'Reilly Network Safari Bookshelf.

Safari offers a solution that's better than e-books. It's a virtual library that lets you easily search thousands of top tech books, cut and paste code samples, download chapters, and find quick answers when you need the most accurate, current information. Try it for free at *http://safari.oreilly.com.*

Acknowledgments

I'd like to first thank Ben Goodger, The Mozilla Foundation, and the other amazing developers and workers who envisioned and have contributed to Firefox, one of the finest open source projects of all time, and certainly the best web browser ever.

This book couldn't have been written without the help and support of the following:

- My agent Laura, who never gave up on me through a lot of craziness.

- My editor Brian Jepson, who has been helpful in a thousand different ways.

- My mother Betty Sue and my stepfather Ray, who let me stay at their home in tiny Arrow Rock, Missouri, where I could write in peace.

- David Hartley, who let me use his wireless connection and his phone at his office in Marshall, Missouri.

- Washington University in St. Louis, home of Windows XP machines and super-fast Net connections.
- The fine folks at Kayak's and the St. Louis Bread Company, where a lot of this book was written. If you're looking for great coffee and free WiFi in St. Louis, go there!
- Jerry Bryan, for his invaluable help editing and correcting my writing (especially the "you've got" problem).
- Ben Jones, who looked over several chapters and asked lots of good questions.
- Jans Carton, my Mac guru, for answering questions about Mac OS X browsers and providing the Mac screenshots.
- Craig Buchek, for his detailed technical review.
- My patient wife Denise, for her understanding, support, and editing help.
- And finally, our cute lil' shih-tzu Libby, who was always available to make me laugh.

This book was written on an IBM ThinkPad running Libranet Linux. I had to use Microsoft Word, but it ran beautifully under Codeweavers' CrossOver Office. See *http://www.libranet.com* and *http://www.codeweavers.com* for more info.

1 + ! THE PROBLEM WITH THE BLUE E

On July 6, 2004, US-CERT (the United States Computer Emergency Readiness Team, a partnership between the U.S. Department of Homeland Security and public and private sectors that protects the nation's Internet infrastructure) released a security report in response to a frightening new security attack.

The infection began on June 24, 2004, when a menace named Download.Ject first made its appearance. Criminals secretly compromised the machines hosting the web sites of several banks, stores, auction sites, and search engines, by taking advantage of a hole in Microsoft's web server software. After taking over the servers, the crooks placed programming code on them so that if you requested a web page from one of the sites, a program was insidiously installed on your computer. This powerful little program could not only place a back door on your computer that would allow hackers to take it over and control it without your knowledge, but could also install keylogging software that would capture passwords and credit card numbers as you typed them.

I left out one important detail, however: in order to be the victim of this infection, you had to be using Microsoft's web browser, Internet Explorer (IE). If you were using any other web browser, you were perfectly safe. The contagion couldn't affect you.

US-CERT offered several recommendations in its report, but the last caught the eyes of system administrators and users all over the world: "Use a different web browser." That's right—the computer security experts at the Department of Homeland Security were advising people to use something other than IE, because Microsoft's web browser was that dangerous.

That's pretty bad. How did we get to this point, where the browser employed by almost 90% of all web users enables gangsters across the world to steal your credit card details with ease? Are there any safe alternatives to IE, or are we stuck with this deeply flawed software?

To answer those questions, we need to take a look at the history of web browsers.

Long, Long Ago...in Internet Time

Before the Web was developed, there were several ways to communicate over the Internet, including the still ubiquitous *email,* *Telnet* (used to log into machines remotely and run programs on a command line), *Usenet* (otherwise known as newsgroups), and *FTP* (which allows people to download software and other items). There was even something called *Gopher*, which allowed users to navigate through folders arranged in an outline-like structure to find the desired information. All of these Internet technologies (with the exception of email) lacked something that would have made their use more widespread, be it ease of use, simplicity, or a sufficiently wide assortment of available resources.

Tim Berners-Lee, a scientist at CERN (the Conseil Européen pour la Recherche Nucleaire, or European Organization for Nuclear Research, a European physics lab), developed the World Wide Web in 1990 as a means for scientists to share narrative documents without having to worry about operating systems or word-processing software. Documents (and soon, images) were stored on *web servers*, computers that patiently listen for requests for particular pages or pictures and then respond with the asked-for items. The software making the requests became known as a *web browser*, the idea being that using the Web was so easy that a user could simply browse for the desired information.

The beginning of it all

The world's first web server—which ran on a computer running the operating system NeXT—was located at *http://info.cern.ch* (which is no longer available), and the first really useful web pages contained the CERN phone book. (The first web page is still available, at *http://www.w3.org/History/19921103-hypertext/hypertext/WWW/TheProject.html.*) The server opened to visitors on December 25, 1990. The first web server in the United States was located at the Stanford Linear Accelerator Center (SLAC) in California, where it made available a large collection of physics paper abstracts.

The first web browsers were simple, crude affairs, although they were amazing at the time. You could actually connect easily to other computers and view information that people had made available—and, even more amazing, you could use hyperlinks to jump from resource to resource! The Web was initially developed on computers made by NeXT (the company Steve Jobs started after he was forced out of Apple in 1985), and since NeXT machines could display icons, menus, and pictures, the first web browser could also display both text and images. Figure 1-1 shows it in action.

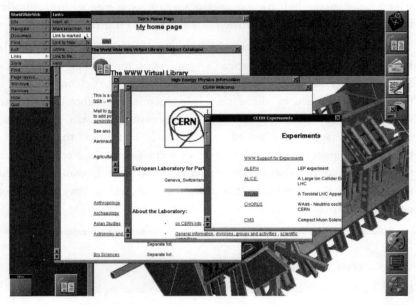

FIGURE 1-1. The Web didn't look bad on a NeXT machine in 1990
(photo from http://www.w3.org/History.html, courtesy of T. Berners-Lee).

Confusingly, Berners-Lee gave the first browser he developed the same name as the thing it was viewing; in other words, you used World-WideWeb to view the World Wide Web! However, since most people weren't using NeXT machines in those days, Berners-Lee also decided to release a text-only browser that would work with almost any computer, and over Telnet, then one of the main ways people accessed the Internet. Figure 1-2 shows what this early web browser—known as the CERN *line-mode* browser—looked like (although the browser in the picture is viewing a very modern web page at *http://www.wikipedia.org*).

```
        Main Page
                From Wikipedia, the free encyclopedia.




Welcome[1] to Wikipedia[2], a free-content[3] encyclopedia in ma
ny languages[4]. In this English edition,
started in January 2001, we are working on 396548 articles[5].
Visit our Community Portal[6] to find out how
you can edit any article[7],
or experiment in the sandbox[8].[9] (http://en.wikipedia.org/w/w
iki.phtml?title=Main_Page&action=purge)

Other languages[10]
Sister projects[11]
No tables[12]
FAQ[13]
Browse[14]: Culture[15] | Geography[16] | History[17] | Life[18]
 | Mathematics[19] | Science[20] | Society[21] | Technology[22]
1-260, Top, Up, BOttom, Down or <RETURN> for more,
Quit, or Help: █
```

FIGURE 1-2. The line-mode browser, the first text-only browser for the Web.

This was not a graphical browser at all; instead, it was all text, all the time. To move from link to link, you had to type in a number at the bottom of the screen and then press Enter. There was no idea of a home page, or bookmarks, or any of the other browser features that we now take for granted. But folks who knew about the Web at this time found the line-mode browser, and the CERN WorldWideWeb browser if they could run it, a revelation.

Hypertextual

Text-based browsers are still around and are still used by a lot of people, but they've come a long way since the line-mode browser. I take a look at one of the most popular text-only browsers—Lynx—in Appendix A.

Some people who encountered the Web in its infancy were inspired to write their own web browsers. In those first few years, Tony Johnson developed Midas, and Pei-Yuan Wei created Viola (shown in Figure 1-3) in 1991. Both could display graphics, tables, and forms, but both ran solely on Unix machines, which somewhat limited their popularity (remember, Windows 3.0/3.1 was Microsoft's operating system at the time, and Unix machines were still light years ahead of computers running Windows).

FIGURE 1-3. Viola, one of the first graphical browsers.

In April 1993, Berners-Lee made a decision so far-reaching that it is directly responsible for the book you are reading now: he convinced CERN to certify that the Web and all associated CERN code should be released into the public domain. In other words, no one would own the Web, and there would be no tolls charged to anyone who wanted to use the Web or develop technologies to work with it.

Berners-Lee—and CERN—thus chose not to profit directly from the Web, which was an amazingly generous, thoughtful, and visionary act. If CERN had insisted on licensing the technology, it never would have spread like it did. We would today have islands of disconnected webs accessible only by separate groups of subscribers, instead of the universal availability that lays open the Web to all of us.

Mosaic

Also in April 1993, the National Center for Supercomputing Applications (NCSA) at the University of Illinois at Urbana-Champaign released Mosaic 1.0 for the Unix operating system (1.0 for Windows and Mac OS appeared in December). This was the big one, the software that finally began to make the Web popular. As you can see in Figure 1-4, Mosaic looks a lot like the web browsers we use today, with menus, buttons, images that appeared inside the web page instead of in a separate window (yes, that is how browsers had displayed images prior to Mosaic), and an address bar.

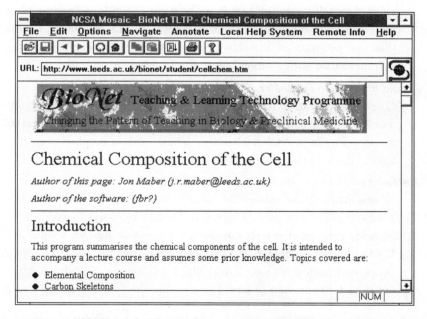

FIGURE 1-4. NCSA Mosaic for Windows (image courtesy of The University of Manchester).

And who were the main coders behind Mosaic? An employee of the NCSA named Eric Bina and a young intern named Marc Andreessen, who was still an undergraduate at the University of Illinois. Andreessen was responsible for several features that you can't see in Figure 1-4, and those were the things that really made Mosaic special. For instance, Mosaic was the first browser that was easy for "normal" Internet users (although "normal" in 1993 was pretty advanced compared to the general population) to download, install, and use. Further, Andreessen was careful to actually support Mosaic's users: he listened to their requests and complaints and improved the browser accordingly, and he provided support if users needed it. The result? Mosaic was the most user-friendly web browser available in the early 1990s, the one that was "good enough" and easy enough to appeal to most users.

Mosaic got a lot of press, and the word spread fast among Net users: if you wanted to enjoy the online world in a whole new way, get Mosaic on your computer. The following selections from newsgroup postings of the time give you an idea of the breathless wonder and excitement that Mosaic engendered in its users:

Richard Melick on November 17, 1993

"I got Mosaic up and running last night on my PC at home and I wanted to tell everyone that it looks great! NCSA has provided us with a peek of the future of the Internet with this product... I think that this program is a real winner! I would recommend it to any Windows user with a direct link to the Internet."

Arnold Bloemer on December 10, 1993

"If you're not using Mosaic for X version 2.0, upgrade immediately! You'll be glad you did. Kudos to Eric Bina and Marc Andreessen, the developers of NCSA Mosaic... Their work is helping to revolutionize the way that people 'view' the Net."

Joe Kohn on March 8, 1994

"I saw Mosaic the other day for the first time, and it completely knocked my socks off... I was just floored by what I saw... With Mosaic, you could search the net by using your mouse. I want it... It's kind of incredible that I've been using the net for probably 2 years, and seeing Mosaic, it was like I was seeing something different than I'd ever seen before. I was seeing the future. I haven't seen

anything so that completely impressed me in a long long time...
maybe never. I want Mosaic, and I want it now!"

Nenette Alejandria on March 24, 1994

"I REALLY love Mosaic!! I've been downloading tons of stuff from
everywhere! As Aimee said, it is pretty amazing! Words don't do
justice. I recommend that you all try it sometime."

Mosaic was a phenomenal success, and it helped to popularize the still-
young World Wide Web. In just a few months, traffic on the Net
devoted to the Web jumped over 10,000%, as more than a 1,000 copies
of Mosaic were downloaded every day (that might seem like a small
number now, but remember how small the online population was in
1993–4).

Time capsule

For a fantastic artifact of the time, read *Wired* magazine's October
1994 article "The (Second Phase of the) Revolution Has Begun,"
available at *http://www.wired.com/wired/archive/2.10/mosaic_pr.html*. It
begins like this: "Don't look now, but Prodigy, AOL, and Compu-
Serve are all suddenly obsolete—and Mosaic is well on its way to
becoming the world's standard interface." In 1994, this looked like
the truth.

Netscape

Jim Clark, the highly successful founder of Silicon Graphics, Inc. (SGI),
saw commercial possibilities in Mosaic and the Web, so in April 1994 he
created Mosaic Communications Corporation (after wooing Marc
Andreessen and several other former employees of NCSA), intending to
create, market, and sell web browsers, web servers, and associated services and software. On October 13, 1994, the fledging company released
the first public beta of its new browser, called Mosaic Netscape. The
browser was available at no cost to individuals and academic users and
at a cost of $99 per user to businesses (that seems like a crazy price now,
but remember that this was 1994, when the Web was new and before
Microsoft had made free browsers the norm). The University of Illinois

complained, however, that it held a trademark on "Mosaic," forcing Clark and Andreessen to change the name of their company to Netscape Communications Corporation in November 1994.

Stealing the spotlight

Netscape and Internet Explorer soon took all the attention away from Mosaic-so much so that NCSA stopped all development on Mosaic in January 1997, long after the browser had stopped being widely used.

The newly renamed company proceeded in its goal: to write a web browser from scratch, something that would be better than Mosaic, something that would crush Mosaic like Godzilla crushed Tokyo. The codename of this new browser? Mozilla, a combination of "Mosaic-killer" and "Godzilla." To commemorate the new name, whimsical illustrations of a green lizard began making an appearance around the Web.

Netscape released its web browser, officially named Navigator 1.0 but commonly known simply as Netscape, in December 1994, and it took off like a rocket (see Figure 1-5 for a screenshot of that first official release).

Netscape was a better browser than Mosaic and was available for an amazing variety of operating systems, including Windows, Mac OS, Linux, OS/2, Solaris, BSD, IRIX, AIX, and HP-UX. The company and its browser were featured in countless articles and news stories as the Internet and the Web became household words; in fact, for many people, Netscape *was* the Internet. Soon Netscape Navigator held over 90% of the market share for web browsers, and users excitedly began to play with the betas of what would become Netscape Navigator 2.0. Netscape was on top of the world...

And then Microsoft entered the picture.

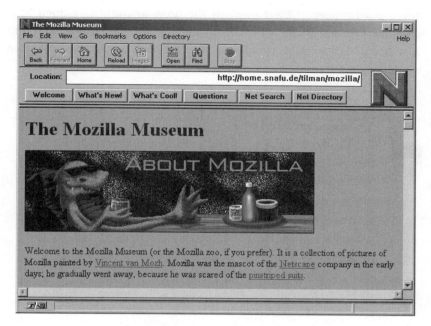

FIGURE 1-5. Netscape Version 1.0, from 1994.

Inflating the bubble

It's now accepted as almost a truism that Netscape's astoundingly successful IPO in August 1995 inaugurated the tech-stock bubble of the late '90s. Michael Malone, writing in *Forbes* on March 7, 2002, spoke for many when he stated that "Crucial to any tech boom is the appearance of the big, stimulus IPO. The last time around, it was Netscape, which went public to such a financial earthquake that it set the pattern for the thousand dot-coms that followed" (*http://www.forbes.com/columnists/2002/03/07/0307malone.html*).

Microsoft, IE, and the Browser Wars

Windows 95 (codenamed "Chicago" inside Microsoft) was far along in development by the fall of 1994. At that stage, the company was not planning to include a web browser as part of the operating system. By the start of 1995, however, Microsoft executives had decided that Netscape's web browser was a threat, and they decided to quickly develop a browser of their own. At the time, a company named Spyglass had licensed NCSA's Mosaic technology and trademarks, and it in turn licensed that same technology to Microsoft as the base of what would become Internet Explorer.

Traces of history

To this day, if you open IE and go to Help → About Internet Explorer, it still says "Based on NCSA Mosaic… Distributed under a licensing agreement with Spyglass, Inc."

The arrangement was that Microsoft would pay Spyglass a quarterly fee plus a percentage of the revenues Microsoft realized from selling the software. Since Microsoft ended up giving IE away for free, Spyglass saw only a fraction of what it had expected to make, taking in only around $400,000. Eventually, after Spyglass filed a lawsuit in 1997, Microsoft settled by paying the small company $8 million.

Still, even as late as June 1995, with the release date for Windows 95 getting closer and closer, Microsoft was not planning to include its browser as part of Windows. Instead, Internet Explorer was to be part of the "Microsoft Plus! for Windows 95" CD (or floppies), which was sold separately from Windows 95.

At that point, however, things changed at Microsoft. Netscape was now seen as too much of a threat, which had to be neutralized as quickly and as ruthlessly as possible; as one Microsoft exec is alleged to have said, the company decided to "cut off Netscape's air supply." First, there was the matter of price. Netscape's browser was available for free to many classes of users, but businesses and others were expected to pay a fee for the software. While Microsoft had originally planned to charge for IE by including it on the Plus! offering, this idea was abandoned in favor of giving the browser away for free with the Windows operating system.

By the time Windows 95 shipped to computer companies such as Dell, IBM, and Compaq in July 1995, Internet Explorer 1.0 was included as part of the operating system (but on a separate disk). The browser was tied to the Windows OS, although hardware manufacturers could, technically, install—or remove—IE from Windows without changing how the rest of the OS worked, and users could remove it using the Add/Remove Programs control panel (IE 2.0, released in November 1995, offered the same functionality...or lack of it). You can see IE 1.0 in Figure 1-6.

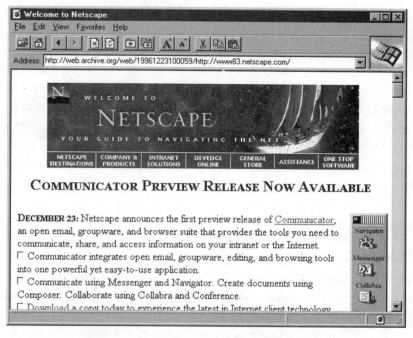

FIGURE 1-6. A Microsoft Internet Explorer 1.0 user contemplates the switch, circa 1996 (historical snapshot of Netscape.com, courtesy of the Internet Archive).

To prevent the hardware manufacturers from decoupling the new browser from the operating system, Microsoft decided to go a step further and tie the two together contractually. The licenses that Microsoft had computer companies agree to prohibited those companies from removing Internet Explorer from Windows 95. If the companies removed any of the icons or programs from the Windows desktop or Start menu, or gave consumers options for third-party programs while the computer was booting, they faced a dire consequence: Microsoft would terminate their licenses to sell Windows, or force them to pay retail prices, thus destroying their already-thin margins. With hardball tactics like this, it was essentially impossible for Dell, IBM, Gateway, and similar companies to remove Microsoft's web browser from the computers they shipped to consumers, or to promote Netscape's.

Compaq tested Microsoft's resolve in August 1995, when, after signing promotional deals with other ISPs, it began removing the IE icon from desktops and replaced it with an icon for Netscape Navigator. After making its displeasure known for months, Microsoft responded with a nuclear bomb: in a letter dated May 31, 1996, the company threatened to end Compaq's license to sell Windows 95 unless Compaq came to its senses and restored the IE icon. Within a month, the IE icon was back on Compaq desktops. At the time, Compaq sold more PCs than any other Microsoft partner—yet Microsoft was prepared to sacrifice that outlet for its software in order to both protect its web browser and damage its biggest competitor in the browser world.

As a kickback to Compaq for agreeing to comply with Microsoft's demands, Microsoft promised that Compaq's price for Windows would be less than that paid by any other hardware manufacturer. In addition, starting in March 1998, Microsoft waived any fees that Compaq would normally have to pay for Microsoft products on computers used by Compaq employees.

PC companies aroused Microsoft's wrath even if they just failed to use IE on their own corporate networks. Gateway used Netscape internally on its own computers, but in February 1997, Microsoft let Gateway know that this was a source of friction between the companies and that Microsoft would gladly help cover Gateway's expenses if it decided to switch over to IE. Gateway refused; consequently, Gateway paid a higher price for Windows than any of its competitors.

Behind the Browser Wars

So why did Microsoft embark on this campaign to decimate Netscape (and every other web browser, for that matter)—a course of action that was found by the courts to be an illegal leveraging of its monopoly? Why did it play hardball with the companies who provided Windows to consumers and businesses on the machines they bought—actions that were also found to be illegal? And why did big companies like IBM and Dell accede to Microsoft's demands?

Tightening the noose

Microsoft later decided to make it virtually impossible for the IBMs and Dells of the world (as well as users) to remove IE from its operating system technically, as well as legally. Windows 98 users were stuck with IE, which increased the likelihood that they would use it and decreased the incentives for computer manufacturers to include other web browsers (such as Netscape) that they would have to support. In a blatant declaration of intent, Microsoft VP Brad Chase wrote in an email to his bosses, "We will bind the shell to the Internet Explorer, so that running any other browser is a jolting experience."

At the time of Netscape's rise, although Windows was the most widely used desktop operating system, the browser was becoming more important than the OS. If users spent most of their computer time using a web browser, it didn't really matter what operating system they were running. And Netscape ran on many operating systems besides Windows, including Mac OS, Unix, and an upstart OS known as Linux. To protect the Windows desktop from becoming marginalized, it was in Microsoft's interest to make it as difficult as possible for consumers to run any browser other than Internet Explorer. The company knew that the vast majority of consumers had limited technical knowledge and either could not or would not download additional software onto their computers. The browser that was on the computer when the consumer first booted the machine was the one that was almost certainly going to be used. Therefore, Microsoft needed to exert control over the companies selling those computers, so that Netscape wasn't an option for consumers and IE became their only choice.

Hardware manufacturers might not have liked Microsoft's policies, but they ultimately had no choice but to give in. If a consumer has just purchased a new PC from Gateway and has a problem with the software on it, he will call Gateway for help, not Microsoft. That call will cost Gateway money. If there are two web browsers preinstalled on that computer, Gateway will have to spend additional money to make sure that both browsers work with everything on the machine, and it faces the possibility of more calls for help and higher support costs. It's therefore in Gateway's financial interests to include only one browser on its machines…and Microsoft forcibly limited Gateway's browser choices to one: IE.

The PC companies really had no choice. If they lost their licenses to sell Windows, they would quite simply go out of business. This was the big stick that Microsoft held, and it wielded it with ruthless efficiency. It didn't matter to Microsoft that its partners in the computer business had already spent millions customizing their machines with tutorials and other tools to support Netscape and would lose those investments. It also didn't matter to Microsoft that its decision to postpone the release of Windows 98 solely so that IE 4 could be inextricably bound to the operating system—even though there was no technical reason for doing so—meant that those same companies stood to lose millions more in sales during the busy back-to-school and Christmas seasons (in fact, one email from company VP Paul Maritz said that the integration of browser and OS was "the only thing that makes sense even if OEMs suffer").

Ultimately, Microsoft's strategy to promote its own web browser by leveraging its operating system monopoly worked. By the beginning of 1998, Microsoft executive Joachim Kempin reported to management that out of 60 sources for computers, Netscape could now be found on only 4. And on those four, Netscape was provided in a way that made it hard for consumers to find, install, and use it (on a separate CD-ROM, for instance).

Netscape didn't just roll over and play dead in the face of Microsoft's assaults, however. It fought back, and thus began what became known as the *browser wars*, the struggle between Microsoft and Netscape for ownership of the Web. Unfortunately, facing Microsoft's enormous cash reserves, its monopoly in the desktop market, and its desire to defend and extend that monopoly by any means necessary, Netscape never had a chance.

The browser wars were not good for anyone—especially not for web users. Microsoft and Netscape released new versions of their browsers as fast as possible, each trying to outdo the other. The aim was to stay ahead of the competition by constantly developing and incorporating new features, but unfortunately these advancements came at the expense of stability and security. Netscape, for instance, decided not just to offer the web browser—Navigator—as a separate download, but also to combine Navigator with an email program, an address book, a web page editor, and more, creating a suite known as Netscape Communicator. The result? An already big, and increasingly buggy, program got bigger and buggier.

In addition, both companies felt at the time that they had to lock developers and consumers into using their products as much as possible, and the way to achieve this was by extending the basic language of the Web—HTML, or Hypertext Markup Language—with all sorts of proprietary extensions that only worked, or worked best, with one particular web browser. Netscape, for example, introduced the abomination known as the <BLINK> tag, which made text literally blink off and on in a painful approximation of the Las Vegas Strip, while Microsoft countered with the annoying and widely vilified <MARQUEE> tag, which caused text to scroll by in an everlasting stream that quickly proved both impossible to read and terribly distracting if you were trying to read something else.

Finally, after three years of back-and-forth combat, Netscape saw the handwriting on the wall: it was getting beaten. Microsoft's web browser was free and bundled with every copy of Windows shipped on a new PC, making it especially easy for businesses to adopt IE en masse. The market share for Netscape's browser was decreasing at a rapid clip, and it reported its first losing quarter at the end of 1997, which led to layoffs at the beginning of 1998. Something had to happen, or the Netscape browser was doomed.

A Long Shot That Paid Off

Netscape's responded to its dilemma in two ways over the course of 1998, and both shocked the world. First, in January 1998, Netscape announced that it was open sourcing the programming code to its web browser, making it available to anyone in the world to work on collaboratively. By harnessing the collective work of brilliant programmers all over the world, Netscape hoped to leap past Microsoft and ultimately win the browser war—and produce much better software while it was at it.

Nowadays, as the open source movement continues its inexorable march toward ubiquity and Microsoft is beginning to feel the pressure of a rival that it cannot buy out, frighten, or cow into submission, Netscape's move (like so many of its other actions throughout its history), seems prophetic and forward thinking. Netscape was the first big company to embrace open source by opening its code, but it was certainly not the last.

The name of this new open source project? Mozilla. The Mozilla browser was to be the result of Netscape's release of its code, and it was overseen by the newly formed Mozilla Organization (*http://www.mozilla.org*). The Mozilla Organization was up and running by March 1998, and work immediately began on a new open source web browser.

In late 1998, the second big announcement was made: AOL was purchasing Netscape for $4.2 billion. Netscape was absorbed into AOL's corporate culture, causing many of the old-timers–among them Marc Andreessen–to leave.

However, neither action stopped Internet Explorer from continuing to gain market share throughout the rest of the decade and into the new century. Today, the vast majority of web surfers use Microsoft's browser. I won't say it's the *preferred* browser of most users, though, because most people have no idea that alternatives exist. To the vast majority of Windows users, the Internet is that blue "e" on the desktop. Netscape? A name from the distant past, something that no one uses anymore. Mozilla? Isn't he the monster in those cheesy Japanese movies?

A funny thing happened once Microsoft achieved dominance on the Web, though: it got complacent, lazy, and slow, and its poor choices about architecting a web browser–choices that were first made nearly a decade earlier–began to catch up with it. IE began to ossify, and, amazingly, users began to notice (of course, it's hard *not* to notice when your brand spanking new PC slows to a crawl due to an infestation of worms, viruses, and other nasties caused by simply using your web browser...and this happens regularly). It's now starting to look as though the browser war that Microsoft appeared to have won was actually just one battle, with the next still to be fought. Let's look at the reasons why, and at how a new web browser offers up a more-than-compelling alternative.

Internet Explorer's Stagnation

Microsoft claimed during its antitrust trial in the late 1990s that it was fighting for "innovation." Innovation, huh? Table 1-1 takes a look at a list of IE versions, the dates they were released, and the Windows versions that accompanied them.

TABLE 1-1. See a pattern in IE releases?

IE version	Date released	Windows version
1.0	August 1995	Windows 95
2.0	November 1995	Windows NT 4.0
3.0	August 1996	Windows 95 OSR 2
4.0	October 1997	Windows 98
5.0	March 1999	Windows 98 SE & 2000
5.5	July 2000	Windows ME
6.0	October 2001	Windows XP
7.0	2006 (projected)	"Longhorn" (codename)

If you look at that chart, a pattern becomes obvious (one that has been repeated time and time again in Microsoft's history). In the early years, when there was competition in the browser market, Microsoft worked as hard and as fast as it could to release new versions of IE. Later, though…

In its first year of life, IE went through three versions (and, in another typical Microsoft pattern, it wasn't until the third release that the software was decent at all). Version 4, a major upgrade and the first time that IE really overtook Netscape in features and quality, appeared just a little over a year after the previous release.

Then the slowdown started. Moving from Versions 4 to 5 took almost a year and a half. Version 5 really was better than Version 4, with some interesting new features, improved stability, and better support for common web standards. But these new abilities shouldn't have taken over a year to add. So why the delay? IE was now being released along with the operating system, and as Microsoft's release cycles for Windows lengthened, so did those for the web browser that was now bolted onto the OS.

This pattern only worsened with later releases. IE 5.5 had nothing on IE 5 beyond a few bug fixes, but Microsoft had to have something to make Windows ME (otherwise considered one of the absolute worst versions of Windows ever released—and that's saying something!) appear new, fresh, and interesting. Consider Version 5.5 essentially a stopgap. IE 6 didn't appear until two-and-a-half years after IE 5, and it was essentially just a spiffed-up version of that release, made to look nice for Windows XP. Oh, sure, there were a few new gewgaws and a little bitty bit of better standards support—and golly, those icons sure were big and cartoony!—but IE 6 was hardly breaking new ground. If anything, it was treading water.

Another way to look at the slow stagnation of IE is through the lens of cash and manpower. When IE 1.0 appeared, a grand total of about six people worked on it at Microsoft. At that point, the company began to pour money into browser development, to the tune of more than $100 million every year, and developers were assigned to make a better browser—fast!

Just a year later, by the time IE 3.0 came out, the IE team consisted of 100 people. When IE 5.0 saw the light of day, that team had grown tenfold, to more than 1,000! That's right—1,000 people were working on IE at Microsoft in 1996, while Netscape's *total* employee count (including management, support staff, and, most importantly, programmers working on the browser and on other software projects) was just a little over that number.

And then what? Tony Chor, the Group Program Manager for Internet Explorer at Microsoft, explained what happened in a blog posting he wrote on April 13, 2004: "After IE 6 shipped in the fall of 2001, parts of the IE team went off to focus on different web browsing challenges...it's probably fair to say that we defocused on Internet Explorer proper."

This "defocusing" will be obvious to anyone who's used IE in the last few years. The browser hasn't really been updated in over three years, and its age is showing. Oh, sure, Windows XP Service Pack 2 (SP2) finally introduced pop-up blocking (which other browsers have offered for years and still do better and more easily than IE) and a few bits of security tightening, but on the whole, IE 6 is still the same ol' thing—and if you're not using Windows XP, you're out of luck entirely. Some of the other areas in which IE lags behind other, better web browsers include:

Tabbed browsing

Every other major web browser offers support for multiple tabs inside a browser window, so you can have several sites open at the same time without cluttering up your work environment with numerous windows. IE refuses to embrace this innovation (see Chapter 3 for more info).

Support for web standards

When IE 6 came out, its support for HTML, CSS, and other World Wide Web Consortium standards was great. However, other browsers have surpassed it, and now it's easily the worst of any major browser in use, causing headaches for web developers and users.

Incomplete support for PNG images

Web browsers have supported the GIF and JPEG image formats forever, but a new, better image format is now available: PNG (Portable Network Group, pronounced "ping"). The PNG format enables web developers to do amazingly cool things with graphics online. Unlike the other major browsers, IE offers only shoddy support for this important new format.

User control

Other browsers enable users to change font sizes to suit their eyes, no matter how the web developer set the original size. Not IE. Other browsers let users stop certain kinds of annoying behavior, such as scripts that disable right-clicking or resize windows. Not IE. Other browsers make it easy for users to block annoying ads or images they don't want to see. Not IE. I could go on, believe me.

Multiple built-in search engines

Other browsers provide built-in access to a variety of search engines—chiefly Google, but others are always available—so that you can find the info you want in the way you want it. Microsoft really, really wants you to use its own MSN search engine, so it pretends that others don't exist.

Security

This one is so bad that I'm devoting a later section in this chapter to it. Suffice it to say that if your PC has suffered through a spyware infestation, you undoubtedly have IE to blame. And that's just the start. In summary, Internet Explorer is a security disaster.

And you know the worst part of IE's decrepitude? That it's not going to be updated until the next version of Windows, codenamed "Longhorn," comes out. The current forecast is for 2006. Maybe. That's a long way off right now. Oh, and there's one little detail I forgot to mention: in order to get that new version of Internet Explorer, you're going to have to buy Longhorn when it comes out!

No More Free Lunch

What's that? The only way to get IE 7 (if it's called that) will be to buy an upgrade to Windows? Yup.

Up to now, it didn't matter if you were running a previous version of Windows—you could still download and install the latest version of IE. Heck, even Windows 98 users can run IE 6. That's no longer going to be the case, though.

On May 7, 2003, Brian Countryman, Microsoft's Internet Explorer Program Manager, announced that IE will no longer be distributed separately from Windows: "As part of the OS, IE will continue to evolve, but there will be no future standalone installations. IE6 SP1 is the final standalone installation." In essence, if you want the new IE, you'll have to shell out for a new copy of Windows.

Beating the retreat

Just a month after Countryman made his statement, the other shoe dropped: Microsoft announced that it was stopping all further development on the Mac OS version of IE. When IE 5 for Mac came out in 2001, it was probably the best web browser available on any operating system: the most innovative, with the best standards support, containing features that IE for Windows still does not have to this day. However, Microsoft had no financial imperative to continue developing IE for the Mac, so it was put down.

So what does this mean for users? Currently, if you have trouble viewing a web site because you're using an old version of IE, it's easy and free to upgrade to a new one. In the future, you'll have to head over to your local computer store and spend good money on a Windows upgrade or, even worse, a computer upgrade. Who the heck is going to do that just to see a web site with a new browser? Hardly anyone, unless the browser not only displays web pages but also washes your car, feeds your dog, and makes your morning cup of coffee.

Previously, new releases of IE have edged out older versions over time. By the end of 2004, IE 6 had been available as a free download for all versions of Windows for three years, and its use currently dominates among IE users, with only a few using IE 5 and hardly anyone still using IE 4. Upgrading a browser is one thing, but upgrading an OS is something of a completely different order. Windows XP has been out since 2001, and it took three times as long as Windows 98 to capture the earlier OS's place on one-third of all computers running Windows. People are upgrading their computers far more slowly now than they used to, either to save money or because the newest versions of Windows don't really seem to have new features that they absolutely must have. Microsoft's new scheme means that IE 6 will continue to be around for a long, long time, which means that all its bugs, all its security problems, and all its flaws are going to be issues for web developers and users for years to come—probably until at least 2010.

This is terrible news, but it's not surprising. Microsoft is a monopoly, and this is the logical end to its goals with IE. The new Justice Department in place after the 2000 Presidential election wasn't inclined to pursue further legal remedies against Microsoft for its illegal anticompetitive behavior (remember, the judge in the case determined it to be a *fact* that Microsoft illegally abused its monopoly, and that judgment still stands), so the company feels it has free rein to do what it wishes. Now it can leverage a browser update to sell more copies of its flagship operating system (in the case of IE for Mac, there was nothing to leverage, so why continue working on it?). The fact that these actions will mean that web site buyers, developers, and users will have to live for years to come with the browser described by noted web designer Bryan Bell as "the boat anchor being dragged behind the Internet" (*http://www.bryanbell.com/ 2003/06/18#a434*) means nothing to Microsoft.

IE and Windows: Joined at the Hip

Microsoft decided long ago to tightly integrate Internet Explorer with Windows, so that the two would be inseparably bonded together. I'm not just talking about making IE the default web browser for Windows.

No, Microsoft went far beyond that. Windows uses chunks of IE all over the operating system, even in programs in which you wouldn't expect to find a web browser's presence. For instance, these programs all require IE to work:

Windows Explorer

When you look at files on your computer, you're actually using IE to view your own filesystem.

Add/Remove Programs

When you open this control panel, IE is being used to display the list of programs you have installed on your PC.

Outlook and Outlook Express

Ever viewed an HTML-based email (an email message that looks like a web page)? Sure you have. Microsoft's email programs use IE to display HTML-based email.

Windows Media Player

WMP uses IE to show information about the songs, CDs, and movies you're listening to or viewing.

Windows Help and Support

If you use Windows Help, you're using IE–it's displaying the text and pictures you see in front of you.

MSN Explorer

Microsoft's ISP service, MSN, offers its own frontend to the Internet, called MSN Explorer. This is really just a highly customized version of IE.

Those are just some of the Microsoft programs that use IE. Lots of other third-party applications (including AOL, Winamp, Quicken, and RealPlayer) use pieces of it–called a *DLL,* or *Dynamic Link Library*–as well. Not only can you not remove Internet Explorer from your OS, but you really shouldn't remove it, or oodles of programs will break.

So IE is fused into Windows now, and there's no getting rid of it. If you use Windows, you will use IE, but you can lessen your danger greatly by not using the browser to access the Web (unless you absolutely must) and by avoiding Microsoft's email programs–instead, use a better, safer browser, like Firefox, and a better, safer email program, like Thunderbird (available at *http://www.mozilla.org/products/thunderbird/*). Simply using a different browser to surf the Web will go a long way toward improving the safety and security of your PC. Why is that? Let's take a look.

The Blue E: The Achilles Heel of Windows Security

Microsoft's decision to amalgamate its web browser and its operating system made it harder for the U.S. government to argue that the company should separate the two pieces of software, but the consolidation was technically unnecessary and has in fact been enormously problematic. If Microsoft wanted to provide a library that other third-party companies and programmers could use to web-enable their software, it could have done so without welding those libraries into every nook and cranny of Windows and its own software. Since everything *is* amalgamated, though, a vulnerability in the browser means that the operating system itself is threatened, and a problem in the OS can likewise affect the web browser. This has happened time and time again over the past several years, as Microsoft has been forced to issue security alert after security alert for attacks that can be triggered simply by reading email or listening to music using Windows Media Player.

Seeing is believing

If you find this hard to believe, see, for example, the Secunia advisories for "Microsoft Windows Media Player DHTML Local Zone Access" (*http://secunia.com/advisories/9957/*), "Windows Media Player Interaction with Local Zone8" (*http://secunia.com/advisories/9358/*), "Microsoft Outlook Express MHTML URL Processing Vulnerability" (*http://secunia.com/advisories/11067/*), and "Internet Explorer/Outlook Express Restricted Zone Status Bar Spoofing" (*http://secunia.com/advisories/11273/*). At the time of this writing—six months after it was reported—the last of these security issues still has not been fixed.

Sneaky, Malicious ActiveX Programs

Microsoft's *ActiveX* is another source of problems for IE. ActiveX is a technology that enables interactive programs, called *controls*, to load from web pages and run inside IE, with the same privilege levels as the user running the browser. In other words, if you're running as Administrator, and can therefore do whatever you want on your PC, any ActiveX control you load in IE has full access to your PC as well. Microsoft's solution? ActiveX controls must be marked "Safe For Scripting," which means that the ActiveX control is supposedly safe to run on your PC. Ah, but who determines that the ActiveX control is safe? Why, the guy who programmed the control!

Imagine that late one dark night you get a knock on your door. "Who is it?" you ask. "The police," says the voice outside. "What's your proof?" you ask. "Oh, I'm looking at my badge, and it clearly says I'm a policeman. So let me in!" says the voice.

You gonna let that person in?

Take a look at Figure 1-7. This fictional example is the kind of apparently safe, yet fraudulent, prompt that a hacker might display in IE when you visit a web page that is trying to load a dangerous ActiveX control onto your computer.

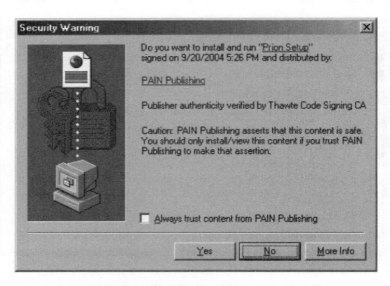

FIGURE 1-7. Do you trust PAIN and its Prion Setup control?

PAIN Publishing says that Prion Setup is safe. They assert it strongly. Heck, you can even check a box saying that you will always trust them. Go ahead and press Yes. Prion Setup installs on your PC, and now your computer has Mad Cow Disease. Oops.

That's the situation you're in with ActiveX controls. If an ActiveX control says it's safe, and you run it, it can do anything on the computer that you can. Sure, Windows XP's Service Pack 2 now prevents web sites from automatically installing ActiveX controls on your PC. However, by forcing ActiveX as the only solution for plug-ins and a major solution for other interactive programs, Microsoft has painted themselves into a corner, as the new SP2 settings will probably cause a lot of web sites to break due to reduced functionality. Furthermore, SP2 will still allow users to install malicious ActiveX controls if they're not careful, and, even worse, only XP users benefit from the new changes. Millions and millions of computers are still running Windows 2000, NT, ME, 98, and even 95, and those machines are still extremely vulnerable.

IE's Approach to Security

When Microsoft is pushed on its security record, it falls back on its notion of *security zones*, first introduced in IE 4, which you can see in Figure 1-8.

Essentially, all web sites are placed into one of four zones:

- Internet
- Local intranet
- Trusted sites
- Restricted sites

By default, all unplaced web sites are in the Internet zone, but you can specify that specific sites should have their permissions set by other zones. Out of the box, IE has default permissions set up for each zone— the settings for Trusted sites are far more lenient than for sites in the Internet zone, for example, while Restricted sites are allowed to do very, very little.

Zones have a couple of problems. First, Microsoft assumes that the average user is going to know what a zone is, and that he will take the trouble to insert a URL (assuming he even knows what a URL is) into the proper zones. Riiiight. Zones are too complicated for most folks to fig-

FIGURE 1-8. IE wants you to place all sites into four zones.

ure out and use. Other browsers make it real simple—a feature is either on or off—but while IE allows you to turn a feature on or off, it often adds a third choice, *prompt*, and you need to make your choices about all the features in 4 different zones, so 25 choices are actually 100. On top of that, if a bad guy emails you a web page and gets you to open it, it will run in the hidden *fifth* zone, My Computer or Local, which by default has almost all permissions enabled. In other words, that web page will have pretty much free rein on your computer. Uh-oh.

Worse than bad security is the time it can take Microsoft to fix holes when they're found. Secunia, a security research company, reports 70 advisories for IE 6 in 2003-2004, 35% of which are still unfixed at the time of this writing (*http://secunia.com/product/11/*). Remember the Download.Ject vulnerability that I discussed at the beginning of this chapter, in which IE users faced back doors and keyloggers being installed on their computers by compromised web servers? It was actually a bit more complicated than I explained then.

XP lockdown

Windows XP SP2 sharply restricts what web pages in the Local zone can do, to the point of annoying and/or confusing users (see the web pages *http://www.phdcc.com/xpsp2.htm* and *http://weblogs.asp.net/jgalloway/archive/2004/08/20/218123. aspx*). It's still possible for a bad guy to get around this new lockdown, however, and again, any Windows users not running XP are still in deep trouble.

SecurityFocus columnist Tim Mullen identified the real cause of that mess: "multiple vulnerabilities in IE, at least one spanning back months, which have remained un-patched by Microsoft" (*http://www.securityfocus. com/columnists/251*). Microsoft's initial fix came out over a week after the attack was discovered, but within a day or two security researchers had announced that its solution was ineffective and that IE was still vulnerable. It wasn't until a month later that Microsoft finally released a patch that solved the problem. So, in other words, while IE users remained vulnerable to a serious hole in their web browsers that exposed them to great harm, it took the most powerful software company in the world—a business employing more than 30,000 programmers—over a month to fix a severe problem with its browser.

Clearly, IE has a serious problem with security. One argument Microsoft and others use in an attempt to blunt criticism of IE's security record has to do with its ubiquity—namely, they claim that IE is attacked constantly because it is in such widespread use, and that if a different browser had IE's vast share of the market, that browser would also be the continual target of security attacks.

This argument is problematic. First, the assertion that ubiquity, or near ubiquity, automatically results in security attacks that expose vulnerabilities is quite simply untrue. For example, Apache is the world's most widely used web server software (with 68% of the market compared to Microsoft's 21%), and has been for several years, yet it has seen far fewer serious security holes and attacks than Microsoft's web server.

Second, the real reason that IE (and other Microsoft software) is so often attacked is because these attacks are so easy. Microsoft tends to allow marketing goals to govern the direction of software engineering—hence the decisions to tie the browser and the operating system together (not for a good technical reason, but instead to push IE and score points during the antitrust trial), and the constant rush to add more and more features to its software without first making sure that everything is locked down as much as possible. This is well known to those in the technology field as "Microsoft's dirty little secret," but it's a secret only to the wider public, who by and large have no knowledge of this consistent behavior on the part of Microsoft.

Nothing's perfect

I'm not asserting that other web browsers are perfect and without security issues. All software has bugs and security holes. Open source programs, however, and Firefox in particular, tend to have fewer security issues than Microsoft's software, and issues that are discovered tend to be fixed far, far faster than holes found in IE and its ilk. For an easy-to-follow example, see "Mozilla Vulnerability Timeline" at *http://www.sacarny.com/blog/index.php?p=104.*

Microsoft has said that it is attempting to change, and that security will become its highest priority as it goes forward. So far, the results have been mixed—and that's being kind. Security vulnerabilities continue to be discovered—and exploited by hackers—on a regular basis, while Microsoft's not-so-subtle message continues to be, "Upgrade! Upgrade! Upgrade to Windows XP, and then upgrade to Longhorn when that gets released in a few years! Upgrade, and all will be fixed!" This attitude conveniently ignores the fact that millions of people and businesses find older versions of Windows, which they paid good money for, otherwise satisfactory—especially since they could always download a free upgrade to the latest version of IE to acquire security patches as new holes were exposed. However, as discussed earlier in "No More Free Lunch," that's no longer going to be an option for IE users.

Surely there has to be a better way. Are we stuck with IE, and now with needing to purchase an entire operating system in order to upgrade it so we can avoid its security holes? Is there no alternative?

The Red Lizard and Its Children

Last time we looked at Netscape, back in 1998, it had just open sourced its code to form the foundations of a new web browser, to be called Mozilla. So what happened to Mozilla?

The code was opened, and lots of developers began poring over it. Very quickly, a big problem became obvious: the Netscape code that was supposed to be the base of Mozilla was a total mess. Netscape developers had worked frantically for years, pulling all-nighters fueled by pizza and cola, and the programming code consequently was enormous, complex, and unwieldy—what developers call "spaghetti code." After some time had been spent trying to rework the code, a decision was made: almost all of the old code had to be jettisoned, and the browser had to be rewritten from scratch, in a more structured, organized, and correct way.

Along the way, the Mozilla logo changed as well. In the early days of Netscape, Mozilla was a cartoonish green lizard. The new Mozilla was more serious, more purposeful, and definitely no cartoon. A new red lizard took the place of the old logo (you can see the original in Figure 1-5; the new one is shown in Figure 1-9), making it obvious that this was one project not to be trifled with.

FIGURE 1-9. The new Mozilla logos.

Time passed. Years, in fact. Every once in a while, a new test release of Mozilla was announced, prefaced by the letter "M" to indicate a new milestone release. M3, the first real milestone release under the new codebase, appeared on March 19, 1999, while the last release to start with an M, M18, came out on October 12, 2000. After that, a more conventional numbering scheme was used, beginning with 0.6 in December 2000.

Mozilla 0.6 was usable on the Linux operating system (I began using it at around that time on Linux, and while it was buggy, it worked). However, on Windows it was really problematic, with numerous and serious bugs, stability issues, and incomplete features. Unfortunately, AOL made a bad decision at that time. Netscape 4 was still the version in wide circulation, and that browser went all the way back to 1997–to the original code that the Mozilla project had rejected as impossible to use. AOL was getting a bit nervous: almost four years had passed, and Netscape was still at Version 4, while IE was already at Version 5.0. It was time for a new release of Netscape–now!

To understand the course AOL took, you must understand that since Mozilla is an open source project, no one "owns" its code. The code is available to anyone to use, as long as they follow the requirements of the software license that governs that code (the Mozilla Public License, or MPL). Essentially, anyone can grab the code for Mozilla, make some changes, and re-release the new browser; however, the program code, comprised of the original source plus any changes, must be released and made available to everyone else to use as well. For example, say I decide to release my own Mozilla. I download the code, make my changes, and release the newly rechristened Scottzilla. You can then take Scottzilla, change the code, and release it as Readerzilla, and so on. All this is legal, even encouraged.

So, AOL owned Netscape, but it realized that it needed to make a clean break from the past and Netscape 4. In addition, AOL wanted the new Netscape to have a higher version number than IE's 5.0. The solution? AOL took the M18 version of Mozilla (even though Mozilla developers themselves labeled the browser as not yet ready for general use), made some changes, added a bunch of AOL marketing junk, and released it as Netscape 6.0. Big mistake.

Netscape 6 was not ready for prime time, because Mozilla wasn't yet ready for prime time–especially for Windows, where a tremendous amount of work still needed to be done. The reviews for Netscape 6 were dismal–*InfoWorld*'s November 26, 2000 review was titled "Netscape strikes out with Navigator 6.0"–and many of Netscape's loyal users, who had been waiting years for a major upgrade to their favorite browser, were so disappointed that they finally gave up and switched to IE (which was a shame, since it wouldn't be long before Mozilla 1.0 was ready).

Work continued on Mozilla, and it steadily got better and better, with increased stability, innovative new features, and clever user-interface changes. By the time Version 0.9 was released, it was still buggy, but it was obvious that something great was taking shape. AOL, again displaying a bit of poor judgment but determined to put the debacle of Netscape 6.0 behind it, took Mozilla 0.9.2.1, tweaked it a bit, and released it as Netscape 6.1. Reviews were a bit better (*eWeek*'s was titled "Netscape 6.1 Delivers—Kind Of," which wasn't what one could call a ringing endorsement), but it was hardly a success.

Finally, the big day arrived: June 5, 2002, the day that Mozilla 1.0 was released to the world. Reviews were very positive, as this excerpt from the June 10, 2002 issue of *eWeek* demonstrates:

> Finally, Mozilla 1.0 is ready. The much-anticipated open-source browser has left the long road of beta testing and is finally ready for regular use, providing not only an easy-to-use and powerful browser but also a highly extensible Web platform.

> In eWeek Labs' tests of Mozilla 1.0, which was released last week and is available free at *www.mozilla.org*, we were impressed with almost all aspects of the browser, from its user configuration options to its usability features to its excellent mail client.

Mozilla is still very much active and in development today; at the time of this writing, 1.7.3 is the current release, with work progressing on 1.8. (Netscape versions based on Mozilla are also still being released; the current release is Netscape 7.2.) However, almost from the first release, a few valid complaints were made about Mozilla. Most importantly, Mozilla, though coded far better than Netscape, is still a large, monolithic product, with not only a browser but also an email program, an address book, and a web page editor in the package. Consequently, Mozilla is often slow to open, sometimes a bit slow to run, and certainly overrun with myriad configuration options that overwhelm a lot of users.

In response to these concerns, a new project was born. In the same way that Netscape's code was the basis for the new and better Mozilla project, Mozilla's code became the basis for a new and better project: Phoenix, a lighter, simpler to use product focused solely on browsing the Web. In September 2002, three months after Mozilla 1.0 was released,

Phoenix 0.1 became available for download. It was quite usable for a product only at Release 0.1, but that really wasn't surprising, as it was based on the stable and well-tested Mozilla 1.0.

Work continued on Phoenix, but then a bump in the road appeared. Phoenix Technologies, a company that makes the BIOS (the software that first loads when a computer boots) for a wide variety of manufacturers, complained that the name used for the web browser violated its trademarks. Consequently, the name of the Phoenix browser was changed to Firebird for the 0.6 release on May 17, 2003.

In a case of "out of the frying pan and into the fire," that name didn't work either. The Firebird project had been working for years on an open source database, and they weren't very happy that another open source project, this one backed by the well-known Mozilla Organization, had co-opted its name. It was time for another name change, and so, after careful searching and thought, Firefox became the new name of the 0.8 release, which took place on February 9, 2004.

As 2004 progressed, so did work on Firefox. The browser just kept getting better and better, and the hype really started to spread about this new, innovative browser—the one that would finally be able to take on Internet Explorer and win. In this case, however, there was some truth to the hype, as Firefox really was that good. The 1.0 release, on November 9, 2004, was greeted with celebration by Internet users all over the world, stories and reviews of praise in the media, and *ten million* downloads in a little over a month.

What's more, IE began to see its share of the browser market drop for the first time in, well, ever. In less than a month, IE dropped 5%, and Firefox filled in that gap. In other words, in less than 30 days, Firefox captured 5% of the usage on the Web, an astounding accomplishment. Clearly, there's a new browser on the scene—one that excites users because it offers something new: a secure, innovative, easy-to-use browsing experience. All hail Firefox!

Where to Learn More

If you're looking for more information about any of the topics covered in this chapter, the following sections will point you to some online resources that you may find helpful and interesting.

History of the World Wide Web

If you're interested in the history of the Web, you can still find the original document behind what became the World Wide Web online: Tim Berners-Lee's blueprint, titled "Information Management: A Proposal" and dated "March 1989, May 1990." You can also find another brief and interesting piece by Berners-Lee, titled "The World Wide Web: A very short personal history," as well as some interesting information about the original WorldWideWeb browser (it's absolutely astounding how ahead of its time the graphical version of that piece of software was).

Another good source of information is the text of a speech delivered in November 1995 by Robert Cailliau (a close collaborator of Berners-Lee and one of the other fathers of the Web), which covers in quick detail the prehistory (from 1945 to 1989) and early days of the Web (from 1989 to 1995). It's pretty engrossing for the insights it provides by someone who was there from the beginning.

"Information Management: A Proposal"
  http://www.w3.org/History/1989/proposal-msw.html

"The World Wide Web: A very short personal history"
  http://www.w3.org/People/Berners-Lee/ShortHistory

Tim Berners-Lee on WorldWideWeb
  http://www.w3.org/People/Berners-Lee/WorldWideWeb

Robert Cailliau's Speech
  http://www.netvalley.com/archives/mirrors/robert_cailliau_speech.htm

Vintage Browsers

You can still run the original line-mode browser today, but the vast majority of web pages look horrible in it. The World Wide Web Consortium has pages up with information about this browser, although a lot of the details are quite technical. Another web site, Funet.fi, provides some history and even a movie of the line-mode browser in action. Information about the Viola and Midas browsers is also available online.

The NCSA's web site contains a full history of all the features that the Mosaic browser introduced, and Gary Wolfe's October 1994 article in *Wired* gives some fascinating numbers about the growth of the Web as tracked against Mosaic's growing popularity. Finally, if you're looking for ecstatic comments from contemporary Mosaic users, they aren't hard to find using Google Groups.

Line-mode browser
   http://www.w3.org/LineMode/
   http://www.funet.fi/index/FUNET/history/internet/en/linemode.html

Viola
   http://www.xcf.berkeley.edu/~wei/viola/violaHome.html

Midas
   http://www-midas.slac.stanford.edu/midas_latest/introduction.html

NCSA's pages on Mosaic
   http://www.ncsa.uiuc.edu/Divisions/PublicAffairs/MosaicHistory/

Gary Wolfe's October 1994 article in Wired
   http://www.wired.com/wired/archive/2.10/mosaic_pr.html

Netscape

David Brody's early review of Mosaic Netscape, titled "Mosaic Netscape: One Small Step for the Web…," is a hoot, and "Origin of a Browser" is an excellent overview of the early Netscape years, including lots of screenshots and fascinating information. The Netscape Handbook, dating from 1995, can also still be found online; it's a charming historical document.

Another site that deserves a look is The Mozilla Museum. Mozilla was not just a codename for Netscape's early browsers; it was also a mascot, and you can see a huge number of humorous illustrations of Mozilla the lizard in action at the museum's web site.

David Brody's "Mosaic Netscape: One Small Step for the Web…"
   http://www.hnehosting.com/mirrors/Origin_of_a_Browser/5/a.html

"Origin of a Browser"
   http://www.hnehosting.com/mirrors/Origin_of_a_Browser/

The Netscape Handbook
   http://wp.netscape.com/home/online-manual.html

The Mozilla Museum
   http://home.snafu.de/tilman/mozilla/

Internet Explorer and the Browser Wars

Microsoft, of course, has an official IE web site. For a more balanced overview, though, look at the article on Internet Explorer at Wikipedia.

For more on Microsoft's actions in the 1990s as they developed Internet Explorer and competed (illegally) against Netscape, read all of District Court Judge Thomas Penfield Jackson's 1999 "Finding of Fact in U.S. v. Microsoft." Judge Jackson's Finding of Fact quotes Brad Chase's promise to make "running any other browser...a jolting experience." The infamous "cut off Netscape's air supply" quote is taken from the "Statement By Assistant Attorney General Joel Klein: Filing Of Antitrust Suit Against Microsoft: May 18, 1998."

For an unbiased account of the so-called "browser wars," see Wikipedia's article; for (slightly) biased accounts, there are several discussions by web developers online (understand that many web developers do *not* like IE, as it makes their lives difficult!). If you feel like spending money, you can buy an article on "A Brief History of the Browser Wars" for just $6.50 from Harvard Business Online.

Microsoft's official IE web site
   http://www.microsoft.com/ie/

Internet Explorer at Wikipedia
   http://en.wikipedia.org/wiki/Internet_Explorer

Judge Thomas Penfield Jackson's "Finding of Fact in U.S. v. Microsoft"
   http://www.usdoj.gov/atr/cases/f3800/msjudgex.htm

"Statement By Assistant Attorney General Joel Klein"
   http://www.techlawjournal.com/courts/dojvmsft2/80518klein.htm

Browser wars at Wikipedia
   http://en.wikipedia.org/wiki/Browser_wars

Browser wars: slightly biased accounts
   http://www.quirksmode.org/browsers/history.html
   http://www.yourhtmlsource.com/starthere/browserreview.html

"A Brief History of the Browser Wars"
   http://harvardbusinessonline.hbsp.harvard.edu/b02/en/common/item_detail.
   jhtml?id=703517

IE: Stagnation and Control

Information about the size of Microsoft's IE team and its changes over time was taken from the U.S. Department of Justice and News.com. Tony Chor's blog post admitting that Microsoft essentially disbanded the IE team when the company felt that it had "won" the browser wars can be found at Microsoft's Developer Network web site. Brian Countryman's statement that IE would no longer be available as a separate download is found at a Microsoft TechNet discussion called "Changes in Internet Explorer for Windows Server 2003."

Many excellent pieces were written about IE for Mac OS when Microsoft announced that it was ending development of the program. CNET quotes a Microsoft spokesperson on the decision in the aptly titled "Microsoft: No new versions of IE for Mac." Eric Meyer's "Hail and Farewell" provides a comprehensive overview of the features that made the browser ahead of its time, while Jon Rentzsch's "Losing Mac IE 6" lists who was really hurt by the decision and why. John Gruber's blog entry on "Internet Explorer" provides a thorough analysis of Microsoft's reasoning and also links to several good postings by others.

The best source I know of for web browser statistics and news is Chuck Upsdell's "Browser News." Statistics about operating system market share are, surprisingly, more difficult to find; however, WebSideStory released a press release on May 13, 2003 (titled "Windows XP Captures One-Third Of O/S Market On The Web") that provides some numbers.

Information about the size of Microsoft's IE team and its changes
> *http://www.usdoj.gov/atr/cases/f3800/msjudgex.htm#vd*
> *http://news.com.com/2009-1032-995681.html?tag=toc*

Tony Chor's blog post
> *http://channel9.msdn.com/ShowPost.aspx?PostID=2366#2366*

Brian Countryman in "Changes in Internet Explorer for Windows Server 2003"
> *http://www.microsoft.com/technet/community/chats/trans/ie/ie0507.mspx*

CNET's "Microsoft: No new versions of IE for Mac"
> *http://news.com.com/2100-1045_3-1017126.html*

Eric Meyer's "Hail and Farewell"
> *http://www.meyerweb.com/eric/thoughts/2003b.html#t20030614*

Jon Rentzsch's "Losing Mac IE 6"
   http://rentzsch.com/notes/losingMacIE6

John Gruber's "Internet Explorer"
   http://daringfireball.net/2003/06/internet_explorer

Chuck Upsdell's "Browser News"
   http://www.upsdell.com/BrowserNews/

WebSideStory's "Windows XP Captures One-Third Of O/S Market On The Web"
   http://www.websidestory.com/pressroom/pressreleases.html?id=193

ActiveX and Microsoft Security

Microsoft provides information about ActiveX on its own web site, and Google collects many different definitions of ActiveX in one place. For a few older but still relevant discussions of ActiveX, check out Paul Festa's 1998 article on CNET about the security issues associated with ActiveX and David Hopwood's "A Comparison between Java and ActiveX Security."

Internet Explorer's security zones can be confusing to understand and configure. Vic Laurie's web site is the best resource I've seen on IE's zones; in particular, his advice on the hidden fifth Local zone deserves your scrutiny. (Laurie's site also contains a good article on ActiveX.)

US-CERT's "Vulnerability Note VU#713878" covers the Download.Ject worm and containing its recommendation to use a browser other than Internet Explorer. Also, the British IT news site The Register ran an excellent series of articles on Download.Ject over the summer of 2004. For a good analysis of the Download.Ject worm and Microsoft's tepid response, written by someone I normally consider a Microsoft apologist, see Paul Thurrott's article.

If you're interested in checking out the numbers in the Apache/ Microsoft web server race (although Apache always, and I mean *always*, wins), check out the latest Netcraft web server survey.

A detailed, excellent overview of open source versus Microsoft security was written by Nicholas Petreley in October 2004. Even though it's not explicitly about Firefox or IE, the methodology and explanations Petreley provides are outstanding and definitely relate to those web browsers.

Microsoft on ActiveX

http://www.microsoft.com/office/ork/2003/seven/ch23/SecA05.htm

http://www.microsoft.com/windowsxp/using/web/sp2_infobar.mspx

ActiveX defined at Google

http://www.google.com/search?q=define:ActiveX

CNET on ActiveX

http://news.com.com/A+question+of+safety/2009-1001_3-208208.html

David Hopwood's "A Comparison between Java and ActiveX Security"

http://www.users.zetnet.co.uk/hopwood/papers/compsec97.html

Vic Laurie's web site

http://www.vlaurie.com/computers2/Articles/activex.htm

http://www.vlaurie.com/computers2/Articles/ieseczone.htm

http://www.vlaurie.com/computers2/Articles/ieseczone3.htm

US-CERT's "Vulnerability Note VU#713878"

http://www.kb.cert.org/vuls/id/713878

The Register's series on Download.Ject

http://www.theregister.co.uk/2004/06/25/virus_hits_websites/

http://www.theregister.co.uk/2004/06/28/ie_is_complex/

http://www.theregister.co.uk/2004/07/02/ie_vuln_workaround/

http://www.theregister.co.uk/2004/07/05/ie_vuln/

http://www.theregister.co.uk/2004/08/02/ms_ie_mega_patch/

Paul Thurrott on Download.Ject

http://www.win2000mag.com/Article/ArticleID/43222/43222.html

Netcraft web server survey

http://news.netcraft.com/archives/2004/11/01/november_2004_web_server_survey.html

Nicholas Petreley on Linux and Windows security

http://www.theregister.co.uk/security/security_report_windows_vs_linux/

Mozilla

If you want to learn more about Mozilla, the best place to start is the official Mozilla site (or you can check out Wikipedia's superlative overview of the browser). For some crucial details, I recommend looking at Neil

Deakin's classic piece titled "101 things that the Mozilla browser can do that IE cannot." Lots of sites offer help for Mozilla users on the Web; don't forget to check them out if you need aid.

As I mentioned earlier, reviews for Netscape 6.0 and 6.1 were not kind. Both *InfoWorld*'s review of 6.0, titled "Netscape strikes out with Navigator 6.0," and *eWeek*'s review of 6.1, titled "Netscape 6.1 Delivers—Kind Of," are still available online.

Mozilla 1.0 received much better reviews. Jim Rapoza wrote a positive assessment in the June 10, 2002 issue of *eWeek*, entitled "Mozilla Lacks Nothing Except Extra Baggage."

And finally, Firefox's success has been easy to measure. According to the "Spread Firefox" blog, when the browser was first released, ten million copies were downloaded in a little over a month. At the same time, IE's market share went down 5% and Firefox's went up the same amount. Nice job, Firefox!

The official Mozilla site
 http://www.mozilla.org

Mozilla at Wikipedia
 http://en.wikipedia.org/wiki/Mozilla

Neil Deakin's "101 things that the Mozilla browser can do that IE cannot"
 http://www.xulplanet.com/ndeakin/arts/reasons.html

Mozilla help sites
 http://mozilla.gunnars.net
 http://www.mozillatips.com
 http://gemal.dk/mozilla/
 http://www.granneman.com/webdev/browsers/mozillanetscape/

Reviews of Netscape 6.0 and 6.1
 http://infoworld.com/articles/tc/xml/00/11/29/001129tcnetscape6.html
 http://www.eweek.com/article2/0%2C1759%2C96681%2C00.asp

Jim Rapoza's "Mozilla Lacks Nothing Except Extra Baggage"
 http://www.eweek.com/article2/0,1759,1506652,00.asp

Firefox's success
 http://www.spreadfirefox.com/?q=node/view/7177
 http://www.mozillazine.org/talkback.html?article=5658

2

INSTALLING
AND
CONFIGURING
FIREFOX

etting Firefox is incredibly easy: just head over to the official Mozilla Organization web site, at *http://www.mozilla.org*. At the time of this writing, it's impossible to miss Firefox—the top half of the web page is a gigantic graphic encouraging you to download the browser. You can also go directly to the Firefox page at *http://www.mozilla.org/products/firefox/*, or use the easy-to-remember *http://www.getfirefox.com*.

The Mozilla web site will automatically detect the operating system you're using and will provide an appropriate Firefox download.

Where is it?

If you're looking for the Windows download, but you're not using a Windows machine to download the browser, click the link for "Other Systems and Languages," or go directly to *http://www.mozilla.org/products/firefox/all.html*.

Click the download link and save the installer to your hard drive (note that Mozilla, in order to spread the load and make downloads easier, has allowed official sites all over the world to offer copies of the installer, so you will probably not download it from mozilla.org directly). If you have a folder to which you always save downloads, use that; otherwise, make things easy on yourself and just save the Firefox installer on your desktop, where it will be easy to find.

Take your pick

If you do a lot of poking around on the web site, you may eventually notice that there are actually three different versions of Firefox available: stable, beta, and nightly. The nightly build will be as up to date as you can possibly get, but it will suffer from potentially serious bugs and other defects; the beta will be better but will still have issues. If stability and security are your goals, stick to the official releases, which occur a couple of times each year.

Installing Firefox

Firefox's installer is a pretty small download for a web browser—Version 1.0 weighed in at a mere 4.8 MB (compare that to IE's bloat, which requires you to download between 11 and 75 MB!)—so it shouldn't take that long to download it onto your hard drive. Got it? Then follow these steps to install Firefox:

1. Close any other open web browsers (Internet Explorer, Netscape, etc.), and then double-click on the installer you just downloaded. Firefox Setup will kick in, and you'll get the Welcome screen. As the cops say, "Nothing to see here... move along." So choose Next.

2. Now you get to the Software License Agreement, which you can see in Figure 2-1.

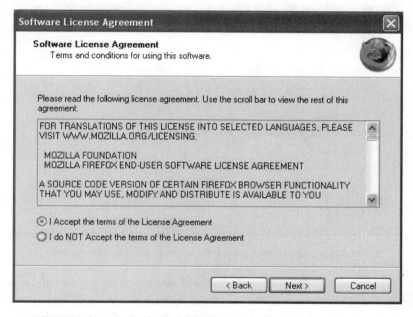

FIGURE 2-1. Agree to the Mozilla Public License—it's OK, since it's open source.

No one ever reads these things, since they're usually just legal mumbo-jumbo; however, you should read this one. The license for Internet Explorer is a typical proprietary, closed source license, warning you in the strictest, scariest terms that if you do anything at all that is not explicitly allowed in the license, you will be punished by having to count—by hand—Bill Gates's penny collection.

The Firefox license is different, though. It's an open source license (specifically, the Mozilla Firefox End-User Software License Agreement), and it actually sounds like it was written by a human being instead of a lawyer (I'm allowed to say that—my wife's a lawyer). It's also very generous. As one of my technology class students once said after I tortured the class by forcing them to read both the Windows XP and an open source license, "The Microsoft document is all about what you can't do, and the open source document is all about what you can do." That's about as simple as it gets.

So, read the license agreement, and when you're done, choose "I Accept the terms" and press Next.

3. Figure 2-2 shows you what you'll see next: the Setup Type window.

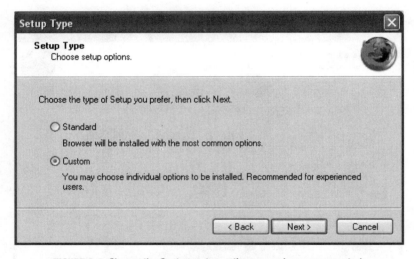

FIGURE 2-2. Choose the Custom setup option so you have more control.

If you choose Standard, Firefox will make its best guesses about the next several choices, and you won't get asked any more questions. If you choose Custom, you'll be asked a few questions about the installation. Here's my advice: always pick Custom, no matter what program you're installing. That way you'll know what's actually going onto your system. If you choose Standard (or Typical, as it's sometimes called), the installer can put files all over your computer, and it can sometimes be difficult to determine where the installer put everything. So, choose Custom and press Next.

4. The next screen asks you to choose the Install Folder. This is an easy one. The vast majority of users should accept the default location and just press Next. If you need a different location for some reason (if you're not performing the installation on a Windows 2000 or XP machine as an Administrator, for instance), go ahead and change it by pressing Browse, picking a new folder, and then pressing Next.

5. The next window allows you to select a few components, as shown in Figure 2-3.

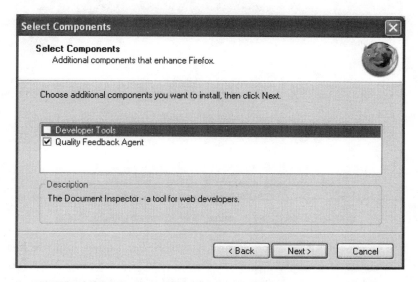

FIGURE 2-3. Unless you're a web developer, you don't need the Developer Tools.

At this time you have only two choices, although that may change in future versions of Firefox. Your two choices are for Developer Tools and the Quality Feedback Agent (QFA). Please leave the Quality Feedback Agent box checked. If Firefox crashes (though it's an excellent browser, like any program, it may crash at some point) and you have the QFA turned on, an anonymous report will go back to the Firefox developers so they can try to fix the problem that caused the crash. The QFA is a good thing that will only make Firefox better.

You need to check Developer Tools only if you're a web developer. If you're not a web developer, it doesn't hurt to select the Developer Tools, but you more than likely will never use them. Once you've made your choices, press Next.

6. The Set Up Shortcuts window, pictured in Figure 2-4, will appear next. Some people like to have icons for the programs they run on the desktop, some in the Start menu, and some on the Quick Launch bar. Firefox can accommodate all those preferences—just check the boxes for the locations in which you want icons to be created (I'd recommend leaving all three checked, and then later deleting the ones you don't want), and press Next.

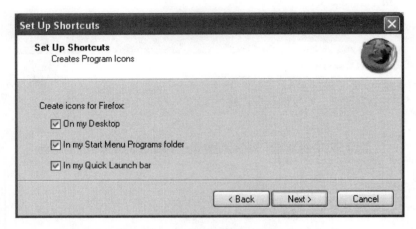

FIGURE 2-4. Make it easy on yourself later and create icons for Firefox.

7. The next window is the Summary screen. Do a quick look-see here to make sure that things are as they should be, and press Next. You should see a progress bar appear as Firefox installs itself on your PC. The process can take just a few seconds on a fast machine or a bit longer on a slow machine—it will never take too long, though, since Firefox is a pretty svelte application. Once everything has finished, you'll get the Install Complete window.

8. On the Install Complete screen, you need to make a quick choice: do you want the Firefox start page as your web browser's home page? Most people probably do not, and anyway, I'm going to tell you how to set your preferred home page soon, so I recommend unchecking the box next to "Use Firefox Start as my Home Page."

You're almost there! You've installed Firefox, but before you can actually start using it, there are a few post-installation hoops to jump through. Let's get those out of the way. Leave the checkmark next to Launch Mozilla Firefox now, and press Finish.

Running Firefox for the First Time

The first time you run Firefox, the browser will ask you to make two decisions. First, the Import Wizard will run and ask you if you'd like to copy over any of your settings from other web browsers to work in Firefox. You'll also have to decide whether you want Firefox as your default browser.

The Import Wizard

The Import Wizard makes it fantastically easy to switch to Firefox, or even just try it out. And no, don't worry—Firefox just copies over your settings; it doesn't move them or otherwise tamper with the originals, so you can still use your worn-out copy of IE all you want.

> **Repeat as necessary**
>
> If you want to import your settings from more than one browser, you can. However, at this time, the only way to do that is to use the Import Wizard when you first run Firefox and then, once the browser is running, go to File → Import and run the Import Wizard again. You can repeat the process for as many web browsers as you like.

Figure 2-5 shows the first screen of the Import Wizard. The options that this screen offers are based on the browsers that you currently have installed—these are the ones that were offered to me when I installed Firefox, but you may have slightly different options for importing your settings, depending on the browsers you already have on your PC.

If you don't want to import any settings into Firefox, just select "Don't import anything" and press Next. Jump ahead to "Default or Not?" later in this chapter for your next steps.

If you have IE set up just the way you like and you want to move those settings over to Firefox, select Microsoft Internet Explorer. If it's more important that you move over your Netscape or Mozilla stuff, then choose that option. If you've been using an earlier version of Firefox (good for you!), your previous settings will not automatically be carried

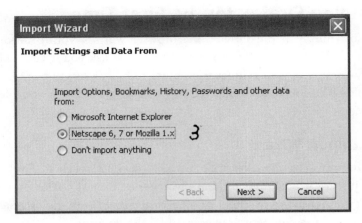

FIGURE 2-5. Choose the browser from which you wish to import.

over, so choose the earlier version of Firefox, Firebird, or Phoenix (if you're still using the antiquated Phoenix, I'm glad you're finally upgrading). Firefox does not currently support importing settings from browsers such as Safari, OmniWeb, or Konqueror, but this is due to be rectified in future releases.

Once you've chosen a browser to migrate your settings from, press Next. If you chose IE, you'll see a window that looks like Figure 2-6. You can choose what items you want to copy from IE to Firefox, but unless you know, for example, that you don't want to import all of your cookies, you can just go ahead and leave all the options checked. Once you've made your choices, press Next. A window will open showing you the progress of the import, and then you'll see a window reporting success. Close that window and jump ahead to the next section.

If you chose Netscape, Mozilla, or an earlier version of Firefox, you'll instead see a window that looks like Figure 2-7. For some reason, you have far fewer options if you're importing from Netscape, Mozilla, or Firefox, but the same rule that I specified for importing from IE holds here as well: unless you have a really good reason not to import certain items, go ahead and leave everything checked. Make your choices, press Next, wait for the import to finish, and then close the window that reports success.

Default or Not?

Once you've dealt with the Import Wizard, you'll be asked whether you want Firefox to be your default browser, as shown in Figure 2-8.

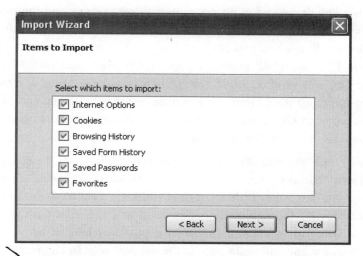

FIGURE 2-6. Choose what you want to import from Internet Explorer.

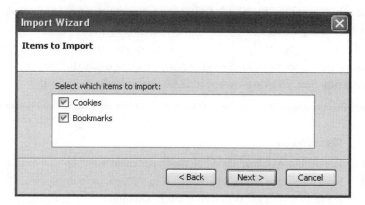

FIGURE 2-7. Choose what you want to import from Netscape, Mozilla, or Firefox.

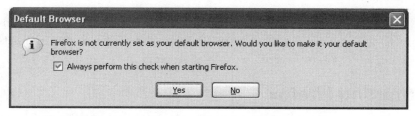

FIGURE 2-8. It's easy to make Firefox your default web browser.

This is a key decision, but it's not one that's set in stone and immutable. If you know for a fact that you want Firefox to be your default web browser (so that when you click on links in any application those links open in Firefox), by all means choose Yes. If you're not sure, if you're just trying out Firefox, or if you plan to continue using a different browser and just want Firefox as a backup or for testing, then choose No. No matter what your choice is, you can always change it later, easily and without fuss, if you decide differently.

If you choose Yes and make Firefox your default browser, I suggest that you leave "Always perform this check when starting Firefox" checked. That way, if any other browser should suddenly steal back the status of default browser through some nefarious means, the next time you run Firefox, it will detect that it has been deposed as king of browsers on your machine and will again pop up the window seen in Figure 2-8.

If, on the other hand, you choose No, uncheck "Always perform this check when starting Firefox." Otherwise, the next time you open Firefox it will ask you again if you want it to be the default...and again the next time...and again the next time. Unless you really like being asked the same question over and over again, just uncheck the box so Firefox understands that you don't want it to be the default on your PC.

Or not...

Remember, you can always change your mind later! To find out how, see the discussion of Firefox's General options in the upcoming section "Just the Way You Want It: Options."

Once you've made your choice about Firefox's destiny on your computer, it happens. The skies part, the light shines down, the trumpets sound, and...Firefox opens! See it in all its glory in Figure 2-9. Ta-da!

Starting Firefox

You'll have to close Firefox sometime after you start using it—maybe in just a few minutes, maybe after a few hours of satisfied browsing. But you will close it, and then you'll need to start it up again. You have a variety of options for doing so, which are described next.

FIGURE 2-9. Firefox is up and running!

Desktop

On your desktop there should be a Firefox icon, as seen in Figure 2-10. Double-click it, and Firefox will open.

FIGURE 2-10. You can start Firefox with its desktop icon.

Where did it go?

Of course, several of these options depend on your answer when Firefox asked during the installation process where you wanted to create shortcuts. For example, if you didn't let Firefox create a shortcut on the desktop, you won't have a desktop icon (although, of course, you can manually add one yourself later).

Quick Launch bar

If you allowed Firefox to create an icon on your Quick Launch bar, you can simply click that icon, and your favorite web browser will open, ready to do your bidding. (If you've disabled the Quick

Launch bar, right-click on the Windows taskbar and select Toolbars → Quick Launch to reactivate it.)

Start menu

The Start menu will contain a folder for Mozilla Firefox, and in that folder will be an icon for the browser. If your Start menu is a trifle cluttered, you may need to hunt about a bit before you find the Firefox folder.

Ye olde command line

You can start Firefox from the command line, which can come in handy in certain situations. Go to Start → Run and enter `"C:\Program Files\Mozilla Firefox\firefox.exe"` (you'll need to include the quotation marks). Press Enter, and shortly thereafter you should be able to access the Web.

Not there?

If you chose a different location in which to install Firefox (see Step 4 under "Installing Firefox," earlier in this chapter), you'll have to use that path on the command line instead.

It launched itself, I swear!

Finally, if you set Firefox to be your default web browser (as described earlier, in the "Default or Not?" section), clicking on a hyperlink in a program such as Outlook, Thunderbird, Word, or even Excel will cause Firefox to open and load that page.

It really doesn't matter how you start Firefox—just get that browser open, and start playing with it!

Just the Way You Want It: Options

Before you start exploring Firefox, you'll need to configure it. One of the aims of the Firefox project was to simplify the sometimes overwhelming number of options and preferences available in its parent, Mozilla. In this, it's succeeded—the configuration process is quite simple. To start configuring Firefox, go to Tools → Options (Firefox → Preferences for Mac users).

Information underload

While you can make many changes in Firefox's Options, in this chapter I'll focus only on those options that I think you really should change. If you want full details on all the options, check out Appendix B.

Firefox currently has five major option sets that you can change (General, Privacy, Web Features, Downloads, and Advanced), accessible through the icons on the left side of the Options window, which you can see in Figure 2-11. Let's work our way down, starting with General at the top.

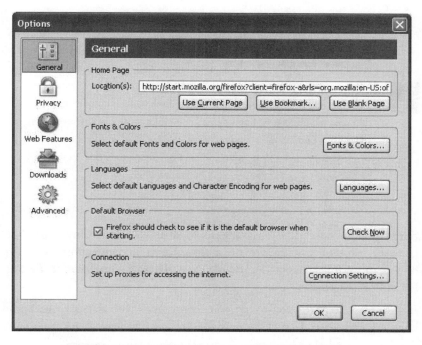

FIGURE 2-11. General preferences in the Firefox Options window.

General

Settings in this section are, well, general. They're about the browser as a whole—about its most basic behavior. Pretty much every web browser asks the same questions that Firefox asks here, so if you've ever configured IE or any other browser, these should be pretty familiar.

Home page

Your home page loads when you open the browser or when you click on the Home icon on the Firefox toolbar. You should change your home page to something you'll find useful. Personally, I like Google News (*http://news.google.com*), but this choice is entirely up to you. Some people like to use a favorite search engine, or a business's home page, or a preferred news site. If you've gone to the trouble to set up a portal page for yourself—at My Yahoo!, for example—that could be a good choice. You can always change your home page if you find something better: just enter a new URL in the box next to Location(s) and press OK.

If you're on a page that you want to be your home page, open your Options window, select General, and then press Use Current Page. If you want to use a bookmarked site, select Use Bookmark and make your choice.

Super bookmarks

You'll learn in Chapter 3 that you can bookmark a set of web pages so that they'll all open at the same time, with each page in a different tab. If you've bookmarked a set like that, you can even select that particular bookmark through Use Bookmark, so that when you open Firefox, your five favorite news sites (for example) all open simultaneously, each in its own tab!

Some people don't like anything to load at all when they start their browser, especially if they're on a slow Internet connection. If you're one of those folks, select Use Blank Page. There's something to be said for radical simplicity.

If your boss requires you to set your company's web site as your home page, by all means do that. I don't want to get you fired. But if you have the freedom to choose your own home page, here are some sites you might want to consider:

Google News (http://news.google.com)
> News gathered and sorted automatically from 4,500 news sources every 15 minutes.

My Yahoo! (http://my.yahoo.com)
> All the info you want, organized how you want it.

Google (http://www.google.com)

Ready, set, search! (If you're not a Google fan, feel free to change this to the search engine of your choice.)

Gmail (http://gmail.google.com)

If you're an email-aholic, this may be the site for you. (Of course, you can also select Yahoo! Mail, Hotmail, or whatever webmail site you use.)

CyberTimes Navigator (http://www.nytimes.com/ref/technology/cybertimes-navigator.html)

The home page for *New York Times* reporters—an excellent collection of links and resources.

The Internet Movie Database (http://www.imdb.com)

If you love movies, this is the site for you. Search by movie, actor/actress name, director, and more.

allmusic (http://www.allmusic.com)

If you love music, this is the place to go.

Random Wikipedia page (http://en.wikipedia.org/wiki/Special:Randompage)

Every time you go home, it's a new entry from Wikipedia, the open source encyclopedia!

Fonts & Colors

Next, let's get your fonts looking as nice and readable as possible. Select the Fonts & Colors button so that the window seen in Figure 2-12 opens.

Let's take a quick tour of your various font options and what they mean:

Serif

Serif fonts have serifs: the little "feet" that you see on letters like "t," "w," and "s" in this paragraph. Serif fonts look great in print—you're looking at one right now—but they don't look nearly as good on a computer screen.

Sans-serif

This paragraph uses a sans-serif font ("sans" is French for "without"), so the little feet don't appear. As opposed to serif fonts, which look best in print, sans-serif fonts make reading on-screen much easier.

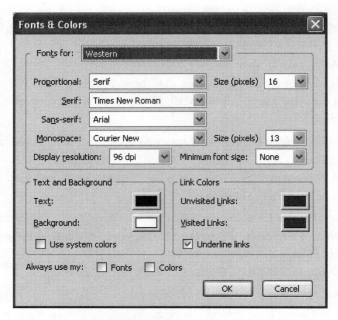

FIGURE 2-12. Setting fonts in Firefox.

Monospace

In a monospaced font, all the letters are the same width. Looks like a typewriter, doesn't it? If a web page wants to display computer code, monospaced fonts are usually used.

Proportional

If a font's not monospace, it's proportional: different letters are different widths. A "w" is wider than an "i," for instance, but an "x" isn't as wide as a "w." Both serif and sans-serif fonts are proportional.

For Proportional, I suggest changing the setting from Serif to Sans Serif, since sans-serif fonts are better for reading on your computer monitor. You can also change the default fonts. Times New Roman is the world's standard serif font, so you might as well leave it alone, and Courier New is OK as a monospace font (actually, I'd change Monospace to Andale Mono if you have it, but not every Windows machine does). However, I definitely recommend changing your sans-serif font to Verdana. Microsoft commissioned Verdana specifically as a sans-serif font for the Web, and it's far better for that purpose than, for example, Arial, which was developed as a sans-serif font for print.

If you sometimes have trouble reading the teeny-tiny fonts that some web designers think look cool, you can change the minimum font size to something you can live with, such as 10.

Here's another useful change: press the grey box next to Background, and a color-picker window will open up. Select the box for white and then press OK. You've just ensured that if you hit a web page that doesn't specify a background color, Firefox will use white, which makes text a heck of a lot easier to read than it is against grey.

And here's one final suggestion, for folks who have visual problems. If you have trouble seeing fonts or colors on a lot of web pages, set things up here the way you like (or need) them, and then check the boxes next to "Always use my Fonts and Colors". That way, it won't matter what a web designer specifies for a web page—your choices will win out every time. Most people don't need this, so they should leave those boxes unchecked.

Press OK to close the Fonts & Colors window, and you're back to the General settings.

Default browser

Remember in the "Default or Not?" section, when I said you could always change your mind about making Firefox your system's main web browser? Here's where you can exercise your choice. If you previously said that you wanted IE to remain your default browser, but you've now decided to make Firefox the default instead (a wise choice!), simply check the box next to "Firefox should check to see if it is the default browser when starting," press Check Now, and Bingo! Firefox is newly promoted to the head browser on your PC.

If you want to know about the other sections in the General area of Firefox's Options, take a look at Appendix B, where I cover everything that I don't discuss here.

Privacy

If you're finished with the General settings, let's move on to Privacy. Click the Privacy button on the left side of the Options window, and you'll see something like Figure 2-13.

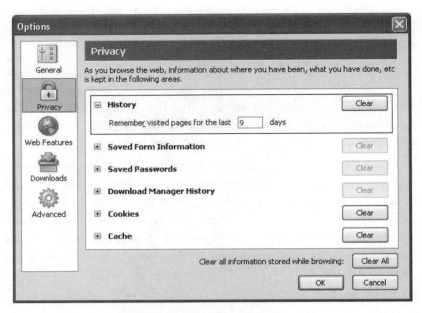

FIGURE 2-13. Privacy preferences in Firefox.

Here's a surprise: the default privacy settings that Firefox provides are all just fine. I'd make a few very small tweaks here and there, but nothing major. If you want to find out what those nips and tucks are, or you just want to learn more about the details of your privacy options, take a look at Appendix B, where it's all laid out for you.

Web Features

Next let's look at the Web Features options, displayed in Figure 2-14.

These options should be renamed from Web Features to Really Awesome Features That Make the Web Usable and Safe Again. However, as in the previous section, "Privacy," the default settings are all good enough to leave as they are. Again, I could suggest a few teeny tiny changes, but leaving them out doesn't really hurt much. For the full skinny on the Web Features section, take a look at Appendix B.

Downloads

Let's proceed to the Downloads options, viewable in Figure 2-15.

The most important item in this section is the download folder. Some people have a specific folder into which all their downloads go. If you're one of these people, choose "Save all files to this folder," and then select

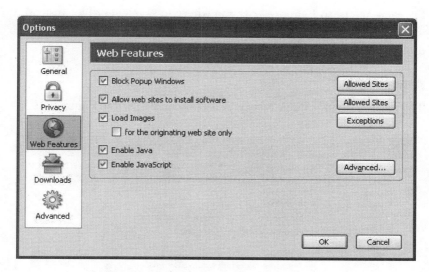

FIGURE 2-14. Change how Firefox interacts with the Web.

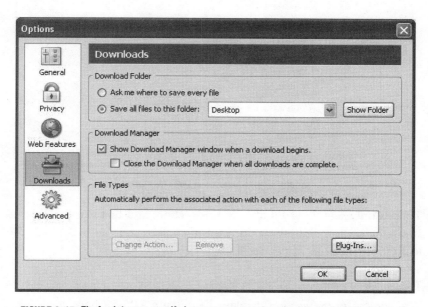

FIGURE 2-15. Firefox lets you specify how you want to download items from the Internet.

the folder. Notice that by default Firefox will use your desktop, which is just fine for a lot of folks, but watch out for clutter! I'm one of those people who download files into a variety of places, depending on the kind of file each one is, so I choose "Ask me where to save every file" instead. If you'd like more details about the options in the Downloads section, go to Appendix B.

Advanced

The Firefox options for Advanced settings can be seen in Figure 2-16.

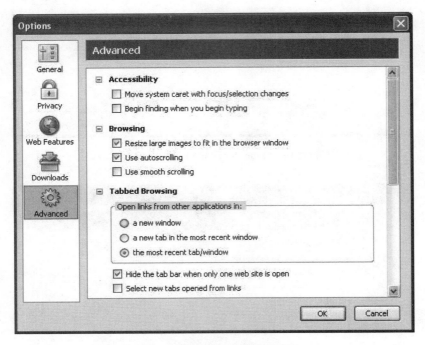

FIGURE 2-16. Advanced settings for Firefox.

There's only one thing I'd alter in this section, and that's in the Tabbed Browsing section. Still, there are a lot of choices you can make here. To learn more, head to Appendix B.

Tabbed Browsing

The choices in the section displayed in Figure 2-17 all have to do with tabs, one of the great features of Firefox.

I don't recommend leaving "Hide the tab bar when only one web site is open" checked, especially for new Firefox users. If you uncheck it, the tab bar is always visible, even if only one web site is open. For a recent convert from IE, which lacks tabbed browsing, that visual reminder will

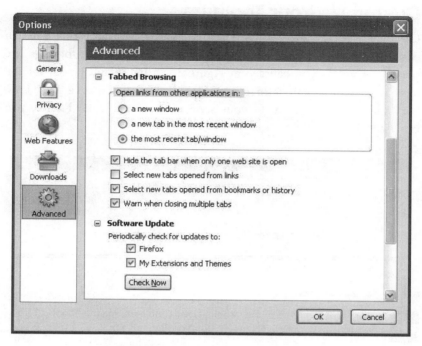

FIGURE 2-17. You're in control of your tabs.

Tab-tacular

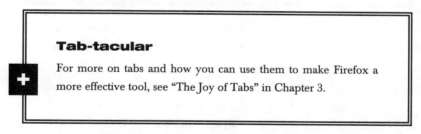

For more on tabs and how you can use them to make Firefox a more effective tool, see "The Joy of Tabs" in Chapter 3.

let you know that yes, tabs are available, and you should use them—tabs are great for keeping things tidy, and they make it much easier to switch between multiple open web sites. For more experienced Firefox users, you'll probably open several tabs pretty quickly anyway, once you get going in a browsing session, so why hide them to begin with?

That's it! You've now configured Firefox's options, so press OK to close the Options window, and let's move on to customizing your toolbars.

Customize Your Toolbars

One of the big advantages that Firefox has over Mozilla is that you can customize Firefox's toolbars. That's not to say that the toolbars are poorly set up; as you can see in Figure 2-18, the default layout for the toolbars is quite functional. However, you can easily improve those toolbars and change them to fit your style of working. Make Firefox *your* browser!

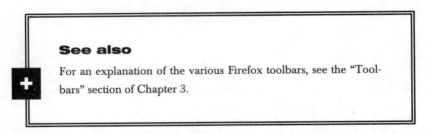

FIGURE 2-18. The Firefox toolbar before customization.

See also

For an explanation of the various Firefox toolbars, see the "Toolbars" section of Chapter 3.

To change your toolbars, go to View → Toolbars → Customize. The Customize Toolbar window will open up with various icons in it, as shown in Figure 2-19.

Once you're in customize mode, you can actually move—or remove—any of the icons that are already on the Firefox toolbar. Never use the Forward button? Drag it off the toolbar into the Customize Toolbar window, and it's gone (although you can move it back if you change your mind, of course). Want to move the Home button? Simply drag it where you want it. You can even move it to the menu bar if you want—for example, you can put Home to the right of Help—or you can move it to the far right of the main toolbar, next to the throbber (the circle of dots that is animated while a page is loading).

Three of the buttons in the Customize Toolbar window might be a little confusing: Separator, Flexible Space, and Space. Separator places a visible line on the toolbar, so that there's a clear division between certain buttons. Space is just that—a space that's the width of one of the icons. Flexible Space changes width; at first it will take up as much space as

FIGURE 2-19. Customize your Firefox toolbar.

there is around it, but if you place icons before or after it, it will adjust accordingly. All three can come in handy to create dividers on your toolbars, making it harder to accidentally click on the wrong button.

I would leave alone any existing buttons, such as Back and Forward, although you are welcome to rearrange them if you like. I've also placed a Print button to the right of Home and a New Tab button to the right of Print, resulting in the toolbar displayed in Figure 2-20.

FIGURE 2-20. The Firefox toolbar after customization.

As you learn about Firefox extensions in Chapter 4, you're going to want to modify your toolbars to make new features available to you. Make your initial changes now using the built-in buttons provided by Firefox, but be prepared for further changes ahead.

Help!

Of course, anything made by humans is going to be imperfect, and Firefox is no different. Problems will crop up with the browser, and it's important that you know how to resolve them.

Installation Gotchas

Installing Firefox shouldn't present any issues at all. If something with the installer doesn't work—like, for instance, you click on the installer and nothing happens, or the installer crashes while it's installing Firefox— you're probably dealing with a bad download. Throw the installer in the Recycle Bin and download a fresh copy. It should work.

If it doesn't, you have two choices: have a friend download the installer and burn it to a CD or drag it onto a storage device for you (these days, I prefer a USB flash drive), or order an installation CD from the Mozilla Organization. You can place your order at *http://www.mozillastore.com/ products/software/firefox*. It costs only $5.95 (cheap!), and it will benefit a good cause, so you might want to go this route anyway.

About the CD

In addition to Firefox, the CD also includes the complete Mozilla Suite (the Mozilla browser, email program, address book, and web page composer), as well as Thunderbird, a free, open source, email client developed by the Mozilla Organization to complement Firefox. Thunderbird is a great email program, and I highly recommend that you try it out.

If neither the installer from your friend nor the Mozilla Organization's CD works, you have bigger problems than just a Firefox issue—it's time to call in your local Windows expert for a gander at your machine.

Firefox Won't Start

If you install Firefox but it won't open when you double-click on any of the program's icons, try starting it from the command line, using the instructions I provided earlier in this chapter in the "Starting Firefox" section. If Firefox will start from the command line but not when you click on an icon, you need to right-click its icon, choose Properties, and change the installation path to the one you used on the command line. Hit OK and then click on the icon again, and you should see Firefox open before you.

If Firefox still won't start, uninstall it (go into the Control Panel, select Add/Remove Programs, then find and remove Firefox) and install it again. When that's finished, try opening the program again. If it still won't open, you need to follow the advice I gave in the previous section about a bad installer. If a fresh copy of the installer doesn't help, I'm afraid that you've got Windows problems, not Firefox problems, which means a visit from someone who can fix Windows.

Startup help

If Firefox used to open but won't any longer, you should take a look at the mozillaZine article, "Firefox : Issues : Firefox Won't Startup," found at *http://kb.mozillazine.org/index.phtml?title=Firefox_:_ Issues:_Firefox_Won%27t_Startup*.

A Little Help from Your Friends

Don't forget that there's a community of developers and fellow users out there who can help you. When you post a question or bug report, stay calm and provide as much information as you can when you ask for help. What operating system version are you using? What version of Firefox are you trying to install? Have you ever had Firefox installed on this computer? If so, what version? Did that version work, or was it problematic as well? Are you upgrading Firefox, or is this a clean install from scratch? What have you already tried as a fix?

To find these communities, see the section "Where to Learn More" at the end of this chapter.

Firefox Profiles

A key thing you need to understand about Firefox—in fact, about all Mozilla-based web browsers—is the concept of *profiles*. A profile (which is really just a folder on your hard drive) contains all the information you've customized about Firefox, including your bookmarks, settings, cookies, history, and more. When you run Firefox for the first time, it creates a profile for you (called, cleverly enough, "default"). Unless someone chooses to create an additional profile, all users of Firefox on your machine who share the same login name will use the same default profile. So yes, if you let your boyfriend log into your Windows machine using your login name, and he doesn't create his own profile, he *will* use your profile. Do you really want that? If not, either create a new Windows login for him (choose User Accounts from the Control Panel), or make him create his own Firefox profile!

Can't find it?

If you want to find your profile folder on your computer, it's best to read the mozillaZine article referenced in the "Where to Learn More" section at the end of this chapter, as different versions of Windows place the profile folders in different locations. If you want to find the profile so you can back it up, skip ahead to the section "Backing Up with MozBackup" for info on a great app that will take care of that for you.

To view your current profiles, or to create, delete, or rename a profile, first close Firefox. This is very important, as having Firefox open while you're working with profiles can cause bad things to happen to your web browser. Once Firefox is closed, open a command-line prompt (Start → Run) and type the following, which opens the Firefox Profile Manager, (seen in Figure 2-21):

```
"C:\Program Files\Mozilla Firefox\firefox.exe" -ProfileManager
```

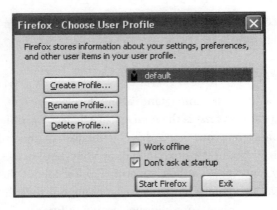

FIGURE 2-21. The Firefox Profile Manager.

To create a new profile, press Create Profile. The Create Profile Wizard will appear, and you'll be asked to enter a new profile name. Pick something short yet descriptive, like a person's name, or perhaps "work." If you don't want to store the profile in the default location, click on Choose Folder and pick a new place on your hard drive (normally, I'd use the default). Once you've made those two choices—name and location—press Finish.

The next question is which profile Firefox will use when it starts. If you have two or more profiles in place, every time you start Firefox the Profile Manager will open by default, allowing you to select a profile before pressing Start Firefox. If you don't want to get surveyed every time, select your desired profile and check the box next to "Don't ask at startup." The next time you open Firefox, it will run using the previously selected profile. To get back to the Profile Manager to change your selection, you'll need to open it using the method outlined above.

The other two buttons in the Profile Manager—Rename Profile and Delete Profile—are self-explanatory, with one caveat. If you choose Delete Profile, a window will open asking whether you want to delete the profile but leave behind the datafiles (bookmarks, cookies, and so on) or delete the profile and the datafiles along with it. Choose the latter only if you are positive that you want those datafiles gone forever! If you think you might someday want to use those bookmarks, cookies, and other information, just delete the profile and leave the files so you can recover them. Better yet, use MozBackup (detailed in the next section) first and then delete what you want, so you have a backup in case you ever realize you need something that's now gone.

Backing Up with MozBackup

Once you've set up your profile just the way you want it, it would really be a shame to lose all that work if your hard drive crashed or a virus or some kind of malware damaged your data. To protect yourself, you need to back up your Firefox profile so that you can restore it if necessary.

Backing up your data can sometimes be a real pain, but fortunately there's a great program available for Windows users that makes backing up and restoring your Firefox profile easy: MozBackup. It's not open source, but it is free, and it works well.

Multipurpose MozBackup

What's really cool is that MozBackup also backs up your Mozilla, Thunderbird, and Netscape profiles.

First, download MozBackup from *http://backup.jasnapaka.com*. Get the EXE installer, not the ZIP file, because it's easier to deal with the executable. Once it's on your hard drive, double-click on the installer and follow the steps, clicking Next, Next, Next. Once it's installed, open MozBackup, and you'll be presented with the screen you see in Figure 2-22.

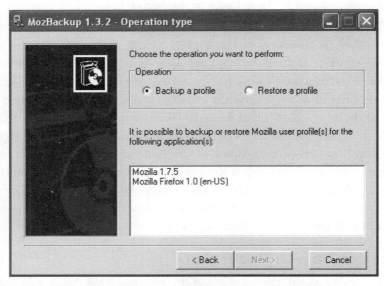

FIGURE 2-22. Choose the browser whose profile you want to back up.

Let's back up your Firefox profile. Highlight Mozilla Firefox and press Next. If Firefox is running, you'll be prompted to close it before Moz-Backup can continue. Once you've closed Firefox, you'll be asked to pick the profile you want to back up, as in Figure 2-23.

If you only have one profile, this is an easy decision: pick *default* (or whatever your profile is called), press Browse to choose the location for the backup file (by default, MozBackup uses *My Documents*, which is fine,

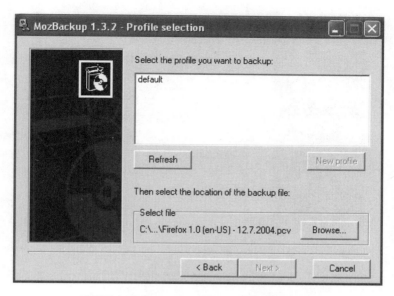

FIGURE 2-23. Choose the profile you wish to back up.

but you can change the location if you like), and then click Next. If you have more than one profile, choose the one you want to safeguard, select the location for the backup file, and press Next.

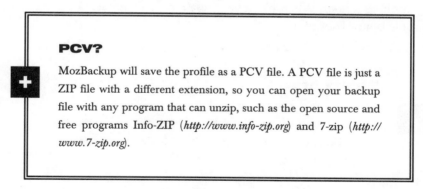

PCV?

MozBackup will save the profile as a PCV file. A PCV file is just a ZIP file with a different extension, so you can open your backup file with any program that can unzip, such as the open source and free programs Info-ZIP (*http://www.info-zip.org*) and 7-zip (*http:// www.7-zip.org*).

MozBackup will then ask you if you want to encrypt the backup file. If you're paranoid and choose Yes, you'll be prompted for a password. Go ahead and enter your password, press OK, and continue. You'll now be prompted to choose which files and data you want to back up, as you can see in Figure 2-24.

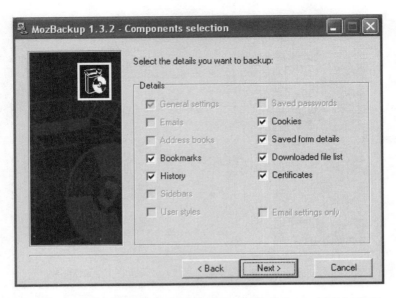

Select the details you want to backup:

Details
- ☑ General settings
- ☐ Emails
- ☐ Address books
- ☑ Bookmarks
- ☑ History
- ☐ Sidebars
- ☐ User styles

- ☐ Saved passwords
- ☑ Cookies
- ☑ Saved form details
- ☑ Downloaded file list
- ☑ Certificates

- ☐ Email settings only

[< Back] [**Next >**] [Cancel]

FIGURE 2-24. Select the components in the Firefox profile that you wish to back up.

There's no reason not to go ahead and leave everything checked, especially if you chose to encrypt the backup. Just back up the whole shebang and press Next. MozBackup will go to work, informing you of everything it does. When it's done, press Finish. Congrats! Your Firefox profile is now backed up.

Safety first

Of course, you should also back up the backup, just in case your computer crashes. Save the backup file generated by MozBackup onto a CD-R, a USB flash drive, or another computer's hard drive.

The nice thing about MozBackup is that it's easy to restore from your backup as well. Start MozBackup and choose "Restore a profile" instead of "Backup a profile." Again, you'll be asked which profile you want to work with; make your choice, press Browse to choose the backup file to use, and then click Next. You'll then be asked to choose which data you want to restore. Make your choices carefully, since you may not want to restore everything—just your bookmarks, for instance, or your saved form details. Make your choices, and then select Next. MozBackup will restore your files, and you're back to where you were.

MozBackup is a program that should be in every Firefox user's toolbox. Get it, use it, and be safe.

Where to Learn More

At the official site for Mozilla Firefox, you can download the browser, read the release notes, or even buy stuff from the Mozilla Store (a good idea, by the way, as it helps out the Mozilla Organization). Firefox Help also contains a wealth of vital information, including FAQs, tips 'n tricks, keyboard and mouse shortcuts, and much, much more.

Mozilla Firefox
> *http://www.mozilla.org/products/firefox/*

Firefox Help
> *http://www.mozilla.org/support/firefox/*

Companion Sites

Several good companion sites to the official site exist, providing different services to the Firefox community. Spread Firefox works aggressively to get the word out about your favorite web browser. The excellent mozillaZine provides a Knowledge Base and also hosts discussions about everything Firefox-related.

Spread Firefox
> *http://www.spreadfirefox.com*

mozillaZine
> *http://kb.mozillazine.org*
> *http://forums.mozillazine.org*

Troubleshooting

Firefox should import your bookmarks from IE without a problem; however, if the Import Wizard doesn't work, check out mozillaZine's "Firefox : FAQs : Import IE Bookmarks." If you instead want to import bookmarks from the Opera web browser (you can read more about Opera in Appendix A), follow the advice given in "Firefox : FAQs : Importing Opera Bookmarks."

If you set Firefox as your default web browser using the procedure in the "Default or Not?" section of this chapter, but for some reason it's not working, read mozillaZine's article "Setting Your Default Browser."

mozillaZine's "Firefox : FAQs : Import IE Bookmarks"
http://kb.mozillazine.org/index.phtml?title=Firefox_:_FAQs_:_Import_IE_ Bookmarks

mozillaZine's "Firefox : FAQs : Importing Opera Bookmarks"
http://kb.mozillazine.org/index.phtml?title=Firefox_:_FAQs_:_Importing_ Opera_Bookmarks

mozillaZine's "Setting Your Default Browser"
http://kb.mozillazine.org/index.phtml?title=Setting_Your_Default_Browser

Profiles

A lot has been written about Mozilla's profile system. mozillaZine's "Profile Folder" is a great overview of the contents of the Firefox profile and how to access and use it. The piece is well worth a read. If you want more information about the files in your profile, read Gemal's "Files in your Mozilla profile directory" or Mozilla's release notes (yes, these are both about Mozilla, not Firefox, but the two programs are close enough that a lot of the files are exactly the same).

mozillaZine's "Profile Folder"
http://kb.mozillazine.org/index.phtml?title=Profile_Folder

Gemal's "Files in your Mozilla profile directory"
http://gemal.dk/mozilla/files.html

Mozilla's release notes
http://www.mozilla.org/releases/mozilla1.7/installation.html#files

MozBackup

MozBackup has a pretty bare-bones site, but I'd check back every month or so to see how the application is progressing.

MozBackup home page
http://backup.jasnapaka.com

3

FIREFOX FEATURES

A s everyone knows, in relationships, it's the little things that matter. In the world of web browsers, a common set of features has emerged over the past decade and a half. Firefox has all those features, but it also goes beyond them to offer nice variations and additions—and it's that combination of the big, expected features coupled with the special little things that makes Firefox such a great browser.

Getting Started with Firefox

You've installed and configured Firefox; now it's time to start using it and learning about the various components. First, you should learn about toolbars, menus, and printing, three of the basic parts of every web browser. As you're about to find out, Firefox puts its own special touch on each of these vital browser tools.

Toolbars

Toolbars contain buttons that perform the same tasks and commands you can find in the menus; the difference is that toolbars put those commands right in front of you, so it's easy to access the ones you use most often. One of the complaints about Mozilla was the inflexibility of its toolbars. Firefox remedies that problem, in spades.

Navigation Toolbar

The Firefox *Navigation Toolbar*, shown in Figure 3-1, is a pretty standard affair, with one big difference that separates it from Internet Explorer. Let's move from left to right across the toolbar and quickly look at its features.

FIGURE 3-1. The default Firefox toolbar.

First are the traditional *Back* and *Forward* buttons (you can also use the Go → Back or Go → Forward menu commands, or press Alt+Left Arrow or Alt+Right Arrow on the keyboard). Back takes you to the previously visited page, while Forward takes you forward again. Pretty simple, really. However, just clicking the Back button isn't always very helpful. For example, sometimes web sites code things so that a page loads and then immediately propels you forward to another page. When this happens, the Back button is effectively broken, since pressing Back appears to do nothing. In actuality, Back does take you to the last page, but it immediately rockets you back to the page from which you're trying to retreat. Bad web developer, bad!

Another situation in which just clicking Back is inadequate is when you don't want to go back just one page—instead, you want to jump back 8 pages, or 14, or 35. Back back back back back back...ugh. Too tedious. In cases like that, Back doesn't meet your needs. Fortunately, Firefox (like most other web browsers) has a solution for this problem. Notice the little triangles to the right of the Back and Forward buttons? If you click and hold on those, a menu appears listing the titles of the last 10 web pages you've visited. Select the page you want to jump to, and back you go. If you want to go back more than 10 pages, press the last choice at the bottom of the list. Click and hold the down arrow again, and you'll see the previous 10 pages. Repeat as necessary, jumping back up to 10 pages at a go. The same technique works with the Forward button, but most people don't use it as much.

The *Reload* button reloads the page you're on. Maybe you think it's been updated and you want to see the changes, or maybe you're having problems viewing the web page and want to try it again: in either case, press the Reload button and the page will refresh itself.

Many ways to reload

If you don't want to use the toolbar, you can instead use View → Reload or press Ctrl+R, or F5, on your keyboard. If you want to force a reload, which bypasses the cache and makes sure that you get the latest version of the web page, press Ctrl+Shift+R or Ctrl+F5; on the toolbar, press Shift while you click the Reload button.

The *Stop* button stops any activity for the current page you're on. If the page is loading, Stop causes the browser to cease that process and display whatever has been downloaded. This can be especially useful if you suddenly realize that a web page is trying to display ridiculously enormous images, and you just don't want to wait. Likewise, if a sound is playing on the page, or a movie is running, Stop should end its activity. (Note that this doesn't always work—some multimedia isn't tied to the Stop button, so pressing it will do nothing; in those cases, try the Esc button.) You can also go to View → Stop or press the Esc key on your keyboard.

The famous *Home* button (or Go → Home or Alt+Home), which has been around for years, takes you to your home page. 'Nuff said.

Choose your home

Remember, you don't have to accept the default Firefox home page (although it's pretty darn useful: a customized search page at Google). If you want to change the home page, take a look back at the "Home page" section in Chapter 2.

After the default buttons, but still part of the Navigation Toolbar, comes the Location Bar, a close-up of which is shown in Figure 3-2.

FIGURE 3-2. The Location Bar in the Navigation Toolbar.

The Location Bar serves two purposes. It shows you the URL, or web address, of the page you're on, and it also allows you to jump to a new web page by typing or pasting in the page's address and pressing Enter or clicking on the Go button to the right of the Location Bar. On the right side of the Location Bar (just before the Go button) is a drop-down menu; if you click on the down arrow, a menu appears listing the URLs of pages that you've typed in before. If you don't want to retype the address of a page you went to a week ago, there's a good chance that it's sitting there in the Location Bar drop-down, waiting to be chosen.

On the lefthand side of the Location Bar pictured in Figure 3-2, you'll notice a small Google icon (the reason it's a Google icon rather than a Firefox icon is that the Mozilla Firefox Start Page is hosted at google.com). If you go to a web page and you see a little icon to the left of the page's address, that page has created a *favicon* (I know it's spelled funny, but it's pronounced "fave icon"). A favicon is an image file that a web site creates to identify the site visually. They're not required; they're just a fun way to distinguish a web site. If a site doesn't have a favicon, Firefox uses a generic "page" icon instead.

Cover your tracks

If you want to clear the list of addresses that you've typed into the Location Bar, select Tools → Options → Privacy. Select History on the Privacy screen and then press the Clear button. Keep in mind that this action will delete not only the history saved in the Location Bar, but also the history of all the web pages you've visited that appears in the History Sidebar.

Beyond being cute, these little icons do have a use, whether they're specific favicons or generic. They're used in Bookmarks, and they appear on tabs. Even better, if you click on a site's icon and drag it to your desktop, a shortcut is created to that web page. Go ahead and try it. Use Google all the time? Go to Google, then drag its favicon onto your desktop. Boom! A shortcut appears. Double-click on that shortcut, and Google opens in your preferred web browser (which I'm hoping is Firefox).

Tab trickery

If you have multiple tabs open and you want to open a copy of the web page you're viewing in another, already open tab, just grab the icon and drag it onto the other tab. Pretty slick, eh?

On the far right of the Navigation Toolbar is its most interesting feature: the Search Bar, shown in Figure 3-3. This is one of many ways Firefox differs from competitors like IE.

By default, Firefox comes with six search engines already installed and ready to use in the Search Bar: Google, Yahoo!, Amazon.com, Creative Commons (for more information about this important project, see *http:// creativecommons.org*), Dictionary.com, and eBay. Google is the default, but you can use any of them. Just type your search words into the text box, select your desired search engine, and press Enter on your keyboard. You're immediately taken to that search engine's site, with the results of your search displayed before your eyes.

FIGURE 3-3. The Firefox Search Bar ships ready to go with six search engines.

Many ways to search

You can use your mouse to click in the Search Bar, or you can use Tools → Web Search or press Ctrl+K on your keyboard.

What's really cool about the Search Bar is that you can add more search engines to it if you like. Just choose Add Engines at the bottom of the Search Bar menu, and Firefox will take you to the Mycroft Project's home page, at *http://mycroft.mozdev.org.* You can search for new search engines, or you can browse by categories such as Reference, Shopping, Computer, Arts, and the all-purpose General. Mycroft also keeps a list of the most popular engines, which is a good place to look for ideas.

Elementary

"Sherlock" is Apple's search technology that's integrated into all Mac OS X computers. However, Mycroft Holmes was smarter than his brother, Sherlock (at least, that's what Arthur Conan Doyle said in his stories).

Once you find a search engine that you want to add, select it. A small window will open, asking if you want to add the search engine to the Search Bar. If you really do, select OK; if you made a mistake, select Cancel. When you click OK, the search engine will install, and you'll be able to start using it in the Search Bar right away.

Back it up

Now that you know where your search engine files are stored, you can also back up that directory so that reinstalling your operating system won't mean that you have to reinstall all your search engines as well. Remember, laziness is *good* when it comes to computers (as long as you're not being lazy about making backups!).

If you want to remove a search engine once you've added it, open Windows Explorer and look in *C:\Program Files\Mozilla Firefox\searchplugins*. For each search engine, you'll find two files: a source file containing the code that makes the search engine work, and an icon file containing the icon that appears next to the search engine in the Search Bar drop-down. For instance, Amazon's A9 search engine has these two files in the *searchplugins* directory: *a9.png* and *a9.src*. If you delete both of those files and restart Firefox, A9 will no longer appear as an option in the Search Bar.

Bookmarks Toolbar

Under the Navigation Toolbar is the *Bookmarks Toolbar*, a place where you have quick access to your most visited, most useful sites. I'll cover the Bookmarks Toolbar later in this chapter, in the "The Bookmarks Manager" section. Be sure to read it—the Bookmarks Toolbar is incredibly useful once you change it to fit your specific needs.

Menus

In the same way that web browser toolbars have become somewhat standardized over the years, so have web browser menus. By and large, all browser menus look pretty similar to the basic Firefox menu, seen in Figure 3-4.

Search Engines to Add

The following are some search engines that I immediately add to a new install of Firefox. The name in parentheses is the category on *http://mycroft.mozdev.org* in which you'll find the search engine.

Google Images (Arts)
> Find pictures of just about anything. Warning: don't assume they're available to copy and use for free!

Google Glossary (Reference)
> Look up a word with Google.

Froogle (Shopping)
> Shopping for an item? Let Froogle show you the cheapest price.

A9 (General)
> Amazon takes Google's search results in surprising new directions.

AllTheWeb (General)
> A large, fast competitor to Google.

Teoma (General)
> An interesting new search engine that's worth trying out.

Wikipedia (Reference)
> An open source encyclopedia that contains the world's knowledge.

IMDB (Arts)
> Love movies? You'll love the Internet Movie Database!

All Music Guide (Music)
> Love music? This site's for you.

UPS Tracking (Business and Economy)
> Find out when that package is going to arrive.

Microsoft (Computer)
> Resistance is futile. You will be assimilated.

I'll go through these menus quickly, stopping only to look at interesting or unique features that Firefox brings to the web-browsing experience. Two of the menus—Edit and Go—are so routine that I'm going to skip

FIGURE 3-4. Firefox's menu bar.

them altogether so we can focus on the others, which have more to offer. I'll also leave a discussion of the Bookmarks menu until later in this chapter, in the "The Bookmarks Manager" section, as bookmarks are such a large and important topic.

The File menu

Moving from left to right, the first menu is File (shown in Figure 3-5).

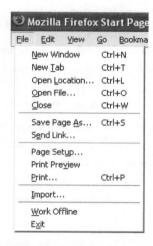

FIGURE 3-5. The Firefox File menu.

Much of the File menu is boilerplate stuff that every Windows program has, but I do want to draw your attention to the Save Page As option. If you find a page that looks particularly interesting, and you wish to save it, go ahead and select Save Page As from the File menu (or press Ctrl+S). You'll be given a choice, as you can see in Figure 3-6.

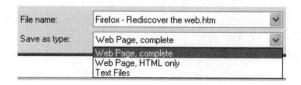

FIGURE 3-6. Choose how you want to save a page.

You can choose a format to suit your needs:

Web Page, complete

> Everything is saved—that is, the web page's text, pictures, and any other code needed to display the page later. If that's your choice, you'll end up with a file (shown in the "File name" box in Figure 3-6) and a folder containing any images or code needed to display the contents of the file. This is the best option if you want to see everything just the way it was on the Web.

Web Page, HTML only

> Just the HTML that Firefox uses to display text is saved. Pictures are not saved, and if you later view the page, gaps will appear in place of any pictures or other multimedia items.

Text Files

> The textual contents of the web page are saved in a file ending in .TXT (in other words, a plain text file). The resulting text file may look quite a bit different from the web page, but if all you're after is the actual words, this could be just the ticket.

There are two other options on the File menu that also bear mention. Found a link that you want others to check out? Select Send Link, and your default email program will open up a message window with the web address of your current page already in the body of the email, ready to go. If you're a compulsive web-page forwarder like I am, you'll love this feature.

Finally, the Import menu item pulls in settings and bookmarks from your old browsers. If you didn't go through the Import Wizard that I discussed in "The Import Wizard" in Chapter 2, you can start the process now with File → Import. For more details, see the Chapter 2.

Paper, pages, and preview

The Page Setup, Print Preview, and Print File menu options are vitally important—so important that they merit discussion in their own section, "Printing."

The View menu

You want some things, like certain toolbars, to show up in Firefox because you use them. However, there are other things that you don't use that you don't want in front of you. Likewise, you may want the option to change the way a web page looks in Firefox. For any of those needs, take a look at the View menu (Figure 3-7).

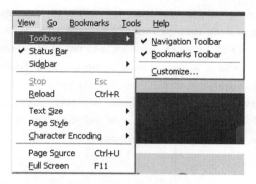

FIGURE 3-7. The Firefox View menu.

If for some bizarre reason you don't want to see the Navigation Toolbar discussed previously in this chapter, you can hide it by selecting View → Toolbars → Navigation Toolbar. The same thing goes for turning off the Bookmarks Toolbar (which I can more easily understand, since some people just don't have a use for it).

The *Status Bar*, located at the very bottom of the Firefox window, displays information about the web page, including a progress bar that shows you how far a page has loaded while you're waiting for it to finish. Several of the extensions discussed in Chapter 4 also use the Status Bar to show you valuable information. Since the Status Bar is important, I recommend leaving it alone. Don't hide it—it's simply too valuable.

Sidebars are a pretty cool feature of Firefox; they're discussed later in this chapter in the section "Sidebars." The Text Size submenu, displayed in Figure 3-8, enables you to adjust the size of text on web pages.

Ever found a web page that looks interesting, but the designer used a font so tiny that you can't read it? Just choose View → Text Size → Increase (or press Ctrl++, which mean Ctrl and the + key at the same time), and the font increases by one step. Increase it again to jump up another level. If you go too far and the fonts look silly, choose Decrease instead (Ctrl+-).

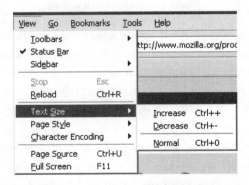

FIGURE 3-8. Change the size of text on a page.

Keep in mind that if you leave the page and continue on to another, your font settings will still be in place, and that may play havoc with the next web page. If you find this to be true, select View → Text Size → Normal (or press Ctrl+0–that's a zero, not the letter O) and you'll return to the font size the web page wants to use.

The Page Style options, shown in Figure 3-9, are a bit confusing if you're not a web developer, and frankly, most folks will never use this submenu. We'll take a quick look at it, though, so you know what it's all about.

Firefox 1, IE 0

One of the lamest things about IE is that while it has a similar feature, it doesn't work with all web pages. Firefox's implementation, however, works no matter how the web developer coded his page. Take that, IE!

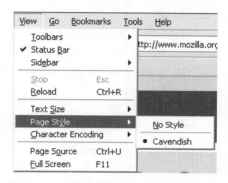

FIGURE 3-9. Choose different stylesheets offered by a web site.

Web developers can create different *stylesheets* for web sites, which allow them to change the way the site looks by simply updating the stylesheet. To see an example, head over to *http://www.mozilla.org/start/1.0/*. Scroll all the way to the bottom of that page, and you'll see three links: Orange Style (the default), Blue Style, and Plain Style. Select Blue Style, and the look of the page changes instantly. Now try Plain Style to see a third presentation. Pretty cool, huh?

Now go to View → Page Style. You should see three options there as well (actually, you'll see four options—I will cover No Style shortly): Orange, Very Simple, and Light Blue, which correspond to the styles listed at the bottom of the page. Choose one of these, and the web page changes.

There are two problems with Page Style. First, there's no way to know that a web page offers more than one style unless it happens to list them on the page itself. Otherwise, you'll have no idea, unless you start checking out Page Style for every single web site you go to—and unless you're extremely bored, I know that's not going to happen.

Second, because the vast majority of web sites have only one stylesheet (or none at all, which isn't good–stylesheets are a great thing, and virtually all web sites should use them!), Page Style is useless...unless you want to apply the No Style option, which can come in handy when a web designer has gone so over the top that it's difficult to read the text on the page. Choose No Style, and that overly busy web page turns into plain vanilla, ultra-boringly presented–but now readable–text.

Firefox 2, IE 0

Even with these problems, at least Firefox makes something like Page Style available. That's more than can be said for Internet Explorer, which fails to offer the ability to view a list of available stylesheets and switch between them.

Next up is the Character Encoding submenu of the View menu, shown in Figure 3-10. It looks a bit overwhelming, but fortunately, you'll probably never have to go into that forest of languages and letters.

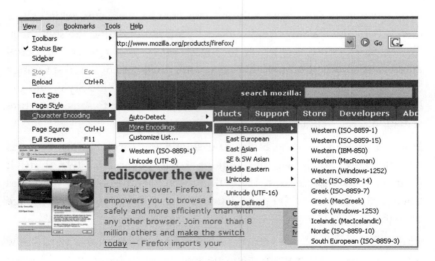

FIGURE 3-10. Which language set do you want to use?

On to View Source. Back in the old days (and by "old days," I mean the mid-1990s!), if you wanted to make a web page, you had to learn HTML, the language in which web pages are coded. There weren't a lot

All About Character Encoding

When a web developer creates a web page, she's supposed to put some hidden code in it that tells Firefox what character set to use when it displays the web page. In other words, should it use Western letters that are used in English, French, and Spanish, or should it use Cyrillic letters that are used in Russian? Perhaps it should use Hebrew characters, or Arabic, or Korean, or Greek? If she really wants to be safe, she can use a character set called Unicode, which is designed to encompass every character, in every language, that can be displayed on a computer (in fact, it currently contains over 100,000 characters!). She should use Unicode—every web developer should—although most developers in the U.S. use Western letters or, far worse, nothing because they don't know any better.

(I say "hidden" because you can't see this code by just viewing the web page in Firefox. Instead, you have to view the HTML source code to see it. I discuss how to do this later in this section.)

If you hit a web page on which the text looks funny—you see boxes or little black diamonds instead of letters, say—then you may have a case in which the developer did a poor job telling your browser what character set to use. In cases like that, you need to set the character encoding yourself. It shouldn't be that way, but sometimes you have do someone else's work. Your best choice is usually View → Character Encoding → Unicode (UTF-8), but sometimes you have to use something else. As to what that something else is, well, you'll have to make your best guess and then experiment. Perhaps you should also send an email to the maintainers of the web site and ask them to set their character encoding. It might help.

of books on the subject, so most of us learned by opening up our trusty copies of Netscape and selecting View → Page Source (or whatever it was back then). The results of that action are shown in Figure 3-11.

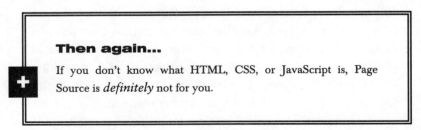

FIGURE 3-11. HTML: the results of View → Page Source.

Frankly, unless you know HTML, CSS, or JavaScript, looking at source code isn't going to help you much. But if you are interested in learning more about the web pages you're looking at, viewing the Page Source is how you do it.

Then again...

If you don't know what HTML, CSS, or JavaScript is, Page Source is *definitely* not for you.

The Tools menu

The Tools menu, as seen in Figure 3-12, offers many powerful options.

Several of these items are covered in other areas of the book. Web Search was discussed earlier in this chapter in the section "Navigation Toolbar," while Downloads is discussed later in the "Download Manager" section. Extensions and Themes are examined in great depth in Chapter 4 (and when I say "great," I mean it!). Finally, the Options

FIGURE 3-12. The Firefox Tools menu.

menu choice was the subject of much of Chapter 2 and is covered extensively in Appendix B. With those out of the way, let's look at the remaining items in the Tools menu.

Read Mail and New Message have to do with email, of course, and I think they're pretty obvious. Both of these commands work with the default email program on your PC.

The JavaScript Console is for webheads only. If you're a web developer programming JavaScript, you'll use this feature; if not, you won't. It's that simple.

Page Info provides access to a goldmine of information about the web page you're on. You can see some of it in Figure 3-13.

A lot of the stuff in Page Info is for advanced users or web developers, but there's something here for everyone. On the General tab, for instance, Size shows you how big the page is, which might explain why it takes so long to download. Referring URL tells you the page you came from to get to where you are now. Modified and Expires have to do with when the page was last changed and when any cached copies of the web page should try to update themselves.

The other tabs contain useful data as well:

Forms

If there are forms on the page you're viewing, this tab gives you details about what they do. If you're not a web developer, this tab will probably not be of much use.

Links

This tab gives you a list of every link on the page you're viewing. Warning: this list can be long!

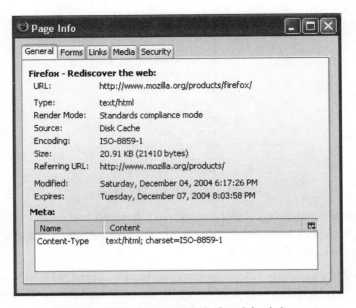

FIGURE 3-13. The General tab in the Page Info window.

What's a cache?

A *cache* is a location on your hard drive where web pages are stored to save time loading them if you visit the same sites repeatedly. For example, the Google home page changes only rarely, so there's no need to download the page from *http://www.google.com* every time you start a search. Instead, your computer stores a copy of the home page on your computer, in the browser's disk cache. The next time you go to Google, your browser asks Google if anything's changed. If not, it uses the cached copy. Otherwise, it gets the latest copy from Google.

Media

This is a very useful tab (see Figure 3-14), since it lists every image on the current web page. If you choose an image, you can learn its file size, dimensions, and location, among other information. In addition, from this tab you can easily save an image—even a normally hard-to-save background image—to your hard drive.

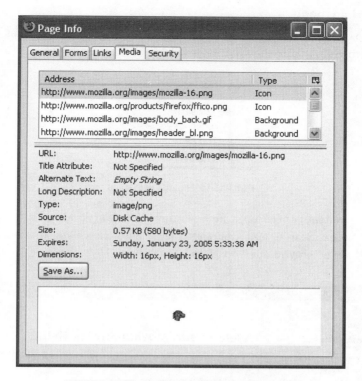

FIGURE 3-14. The Media tab in the Page Info window.

Security

If the web site uses encryption (SSL, indicated by an *https://* at the beginning of the URL), this tab displays information about that encryption, including how strong the encryption is and who is backing it. If you're concerned about security on a strange web site, this is a good tab to check out.

Page info

You can access the same wealth of data by right-clicking in a blank area of the web page and choosing Page Info from the menu that appears.

The Help menu

Firefox is easy to use, but sometimes you're going to need to refer to its built-in Help menu, shown in Figure 3-15.

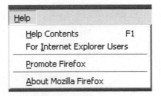

FIGURE 3-15. Firefox's Help menu.

Help Contents opens up a new window with four kinds of help: Glossary, Index, Search, and Contents. Figure 3-16 shows you the first page you'll see when you open up Help.

FIGURE 3-16. Firefox offers pretty comprehensive help for users.

Everything is covered, but not necessarily in depth (leaving the door open for this book and various Firefox web sites and other resources). Think of Firefox's Help as the first place to look, but probably not the last.

One particularly nice aspect of Firefox's Help is the For Internet Explorer Users feature, which opens to the screen shown in Figure 3-17.

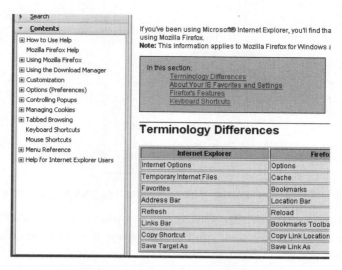

If you've been using Microsoft® Internet Explorer, you'll find tha
using Mozilla Firefox.
Note: This information applies to Mozilla Firefox for Windows a

In this section:
   Terminology Differences
   About Your IE Favorites and Settings
   Firefox's Features
   Keyboard Shortcuts

Terminology Differences

Internet Explorer	Firefo
Internet Options	Options
Temporary Internet Files	Cache
Favorites	Bookmarks
Address Bar	Location Bar
Refresh	Reload
Links Bar	Bookmarks Toolba
Copy Shortcut	Copy Link Location
Save Target As	Save Link As

FIGURE 3-17. Mozilla offers special help for former IE users.

In an effort to make things user-friendly for those leaving the dark side—uh, I mean the Blue E—Firefox offers special information comparing and contrasting the ways that IE and Firefox do things. Most are very similar, but there are a few differences, and this part of Firefox Help brings those to the fore.

Contextual (right-click) menus

Most computer users should know that right-clicking in almost every program brings up a special menu called a *contextual menu*, or *shortcut menu*. It's "contextual" because the menu's choices depend upon the context in which you click. The choices in the contextual menu can always be found in the program's normal menus, but these menus are handy because they gather together all the commands that you are most likely to need for the specific item on which you've clicked, so you don't need to go hunting for them.

For instance, right-clicking on an image in Firefox brings up a menu specific to images, with options such as View Image, Copy Image Location, Save Image As, and Set As Wallpaper. Right-clicking on the toolbars brings up choices for customization, while right-clicking on a blank area of a web page brings up the contextual menu seen in Figure 3-18.

I won't go through all the choices listed in Figure 3-19, since they're covered in various places throughout the book. I *do* want to encourage you to right-click everywhere in Firefox, though, and discover what options

FIGURE 3-18. The standard contextual menu in Firefox appears when you right-click on a page.

the contextual menus offer. Once you learn what's there, you'll find that contextual menus can save you time and make it easier to do the things you want to do with Firefox.

Printing

Firefox uses your computer's print system to do its work, so printing from Firefox is pretty straightforward. However, you should still take a look at the File → Page Setup screen, shown in Figure 3-19, so you can see what your printing options are.

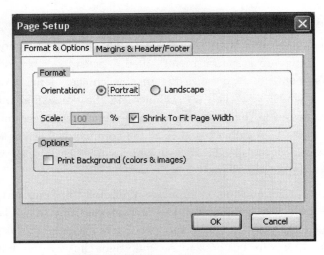

FIGURE 3-19. Set printing format and options.

I wouldn't change anything on the Format & Options tab, as these settings work for 99% of all printing needs, but you should know what they do. Portrait prints pages the way most people are used to. For American users, this puts the 8.5" side on the top and bottom, while Landscape puts the 11" side on the top. You should only need to choose Landscape if a web page is using graphics or tables that are so wide that printing in Portrait mode cuts something off.

When printing a page that is a bit wider than the page limits, Firefox will do its best to shrink the content to fit your paper. If for some reason you don't want this, uncheck the Shrink To Fit Page Width box.

Most of the time, you do not want to print a page's background, as it can use up ink or toner like mad. If you do need to print the background, check Print Background, but don't forget to come back to Page Setup and uncheck it once you're done with that page!

The other tab, Margins & Header/Footer, can be seen in Figure 3-20.

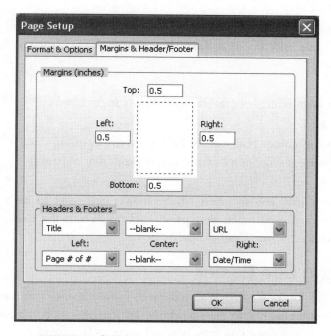

FIGURE 3-20. Set printing margins and header/footer text.

Again, the default settings on this tab are just fine for most folks, but you may occasionally need to make a few changes. The margins are usually fine, but you can adjust them as necessary. Headers and footers are more interesting.

When you print, Firefox by default inserts data in the header and footer of the page. The three drop-down menus in the top row are for the header, while the three drop-downs in the bottom row are for the footer. The choices that Firefox lists when you first open this tab are pretty good, but you can change them if necessary. Your options are as follows:

--blank--
> Nothing. Whitespace. Emptiness.

Title
> The title of the web page, such as "Firefox Central."

URL
> The address of the web page, such as "*http://www.mozilla.org/products/firefox/.*"

Date/Time
> The date and time that the web page was printed, such as "2/01/05 19:41."

Page #
> The page number of the current page being printed.

Page # of #
> A better choice than simply Page #, in my opinion, since it tells you the current page number and the total number of pages.

Custom
> This allows you to insert whatever text you want to be automatically displayed when you print, such as "From the desk of Scott Granneman" or "Confidential."

Making Life Easier

Firefox has lots of features that make web browsing easier, and even fun. If you're still attached to your old browser, the features described in this section may convince you to fully switch over to Firefox now.

The Joy of Tabs

Firefox was not the first browser to introduce tabs (that honor goes to Opera, discussed in Appendix A), but it has made excellent use of this now-essential feature. If you've never used tabs, you're in for a treat; if you're a confirmed tab user, you might learn a few new things in the following pages.

Never used tabs?

If you've stuck with IE for the past few years, you haven't used tabs, since IE doesn't support them. Microsoft says it has no interest in adding this truly awesome, browser-enhancing, can't-work-without-it feature. Thank you, Microsoft—you make it easier for people to switch to Firefox every day!

Let's make sure we understand what tabs are and why they rock. In a tabless browser—like, say, Internet Explorer—if you want to view another web page in addition to the one you're already viewing, you have to open it in another window. Suppose your home page is set to Google News (*http://news.google.com*), and when you open it, you see four or five stories you want to read. You could click a link, allow the new web page to open in the same window, read the story, click Back to return to the main Google site, click another link, allow the new web page to open in the same window, read the story, click the Back button again, and so on. Clearly, this is not the best way to process information. And what if you want to leave one or two of the stories open, so you can show them to someone else or easily come back to them later?

Another option is to right-click on the link for each story and choose "Open in New Window," but if you do that, you'll end up with multiple windows open on your desktop, and things will rapidly start to get messy. Each new window opens in front of the original window, and you have to click on the original window to return the focus to it. If you have three or four windows open, you may even need to hunt around a bit and click on them all just to find the original window. Not terribly convenient or tidy, is it?

Tabs make things much better. If I scan Google News using Firefox and see an article from Reuters that I want to read later, I right-click on the link and select "Open Link in New Tab" from the contextual menu that appears (or, since I use a mouse with a wheel, I press down on the wheel, which is a *middle-click*). Instead of opening in a new window, a new tab appears for the story. I do the same with other stories from *The New York Times, Forbes*, and *The Guardian*. Now my tab bar at the top of Firefox looks like the one in Figure 3-21. (You can also hold down Ctrl and left-click on the link to open it in a new tab.)

FIGURE 3-21. Tabs at work in Firefox.

Each tab opens without disturbing my reading of Google News—they open in the background, gathering the material I want to read without distracting me from the page I'm looking at. When I'm finished with Google News, I just click on the Reuters tab, and it becomes the active tab—the one that's now in front of the others. When Reuters no longer interests me, I move on to the next tab of interest. No mess, no clutter, and no hunting around for the window I want because the page title has been obscured by another window...or three. (As you'll see in Appendix B, this behavior is actually customizable. If you prefer newly opened tabs to grab focus rather than opening in the background, go to Tools → Options → Advanced button, click on Tabbed Browsing, and check the "Select new tabs opened from links" box.)

So, you can open a new tab by right-clicking on a link and telling the page to load in a new tab. But what if you just want a blank tab, so you can type an address in the Location Bar or click on a bookmark and go to a page that way? To create a blank tab, you have several options: you can press Ctrl+T on your keyboard; select File → New Tab; right-click anywhere in the tab bar and select New Tab; or, if you followed my instructions for adding a New Tab button to your toolbar in "Customize Your Toolbars" in Chapter 2, press that button.

Because tabs create so little clutter, I can leave a tab open when I've finished with it. If I want to reuse a tab, I can simply click on it, enter a new address in the Location Bar, press Go, and bam! That tab now displays a new web site.

Tab training

In "Customize Your Toolbars" in Chapter 2, I recommended that you change a default setting in Firefox's Advanced options so that, by default, tabs are *not* hidden until more than one is open. If you do not change the default option, when you first open Firefox, the tab bar does not appear until you have two tabs open. Because visual cues remind new users of features they're not used to, if this bar isn't displayed, many users will forget about tabs, since they won't see any. Change this setting, and the fact that Firefox supports tabs will always be obvious.

On the other hand, I can easily close the active (topmost) tab using one of several methods:

Keyboard

Press Ctrl+W.

Close Tab button

Look back at Figure 3-21. See that little orange X on the far right of the tab bar? Press that, and the active tab instantly closes.

File menu

Select File → Close Tab.

Contextual menu

Visible in Figure 3-22, this is the most powerful method, as it gives you the most options. You can close the tab you've clicked upon or instead close all the other tabs. You can even reload the current tab (or all of the tabs), and you can create a new tab from scratch.

FIGURE 3-22. When you right-click on a tab, a contextual menu appears.

To close an inactive tab without switching focus to it, simply right-click on that tab and choose Close Tab.

If you want a link to open in a new window instead of in a tab in the existing window, just choose Open Link in New Window when you right-click on the link. If you'd like to create a new, empty window, select File → New Window. Ah, sane options. They're nice to have, aren't they?

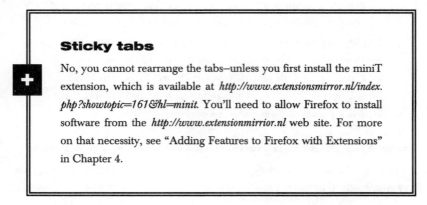

Sticky tabs

No, you cannot rearrange the tabs—unless you first install the miniT extension, which is available at *http://www.extensionsmirror.nl/index. php?showtopic=161&hl=minit.* You'll need to allow Firefox to install software from the *http://www.extensionmirror.nl* web site. For more on that necessity, see "Adding Features to Firefox with Extensions" in Chapter 4.

No More Pop-Ups!

I'll be plain: unrequested pop-up and pop-under windows stink, and the people responsible for them should be hung by their thumbs. Pop-ups that open when you first enter or leave a page have really ruined the Web for a lot of people, showering them with a blizzard of windows containing ads for spy cameras, pornography, or worse...and then your boss walks by your computer. Fortunately, Firefox blocks that garbage by default (I discuss the settings concerning pop-ups in Chapter 2 and Appendix B). When you hit a site that's rudely trying to shove an unasked-for pop-up window onto your screen, Firefox displays an alert at the top of your browser window like that shown in Figure 3-23.

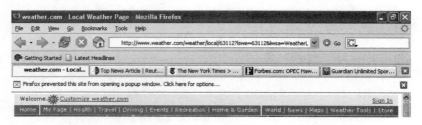

FIGURE 3-23. Firefox lets you know if it blocks a pop-up window.

Firefox's solution is really smart. Think about it: how annoying would it be for a web browser to generate a pop-up window telling you it has blocked a pop-up window? Aaaagh! Instead, Firefox lets you know that a pop-up window has been blocked in an obvious yet unobtrusive way. Nice! Even better, if you click on the alert, you'll get the options listed in Figure 3-24.

FIGURE 3-24. Firefox gives you choices about dealing with pop-ups.

Want to allow pop-ups for the site, for some reason? Easy. Interested in seeing the pop-ups that were blocked? No problem. Need to change the way Firefox handles pop-ups? You can do it.

I would *not* choose "Don't show this message when popups are blocked," however. You want Firefox to let you know when it blocks a pop-up, just in case you do want to view the pop-up or allow pop-ups from that particular site—after all, not all pop-ups are useless or malicious (some are used by webmail programs, for instance).

Since I started using the test versions of Firefox (and before that, when I was using Firefox's ancestor Mozilla, which also blocks pop-ups), I haven't seen a single pop-up window…unless I happen to open up Internet Explorer on a friend's computer. Ha!

The new blocker on the block

Yes, IE now blocks pop-up windows, but only if you're running Windows XP and you've installed Service Pack 2. Worse, people are already reporting problems with the new Microsoft pop-up blocker: it won't stay disabled, and it's not as easy to use as other solutions (like Firefox's).

Auto-complete

When it comes to computers, I'm lazy, and I'm willing to admit it. In fact, from my perspective, it makes sense: computers are good at all the boring, tedious stuff, so why not let them do what they're good at while I take it easy? One of the best ways that Firefox helps me embrace my laziness is with auto-complete, which you can see in action in Figure 3-25.

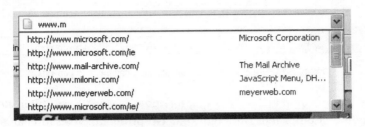

FIGURE 3-25. Auto-complete in action: www.m... what?

Auto-complete is pretty easy to understand, especially if you look at the example in Figure 3-25. I start typing in the Location Bar: "www.m". As I type each letter, Firefox helpfully brings up a list of web sites that I've visited whose addresses begin with the letters I'm typing. As I continue adding more letters, fewer and fewer web sites appear, until finally I get far enough into the URL that it's obvious which one I want. At any point, I can highlight the appropriate choice with the mouse or arrow keys and either press Enter on my keyboard or click on Go, and the site will load. Auto-complete makes it really easy to access sites you've visited, so you don't have to re-type the entire address.

In fairness, most web browsers, including IE, have some form of auto-complete function. However, many people don't notice it and don't use it, and one of my aims in writing this section was to bring it to more web users' attention. Now, go forth and be lazy!

Sidebars

Sidebars have been around in web browsers for some time, but most people don't know about them or how to use them. Firefox includes this feature, and it can definitely make your web browsing experience nicer. Let's look at the Bookmarks and History Sidebars.

Bookmarks Sidebar

Most people access their bookmarks by using the Bookmarks menu, and while that's not a bad way, it does have a few disadvantages. For example, the list of bookmarks disappears once you've made your choice, and if you have bookmarks inside folders inside folders inside folders, selecting the bookmark you actually want without clicking on the wrong thing can be tricky.

The Bookmarks Sidebar, shown in Figure 3-26, helps solve these problems.

FIGURE 3-26. Easily access all of your bookmarks with the Bookmarks Sidebar.

To open the Bookmarks Sidebar, go to View → Sidebar → Bookmarks, or press Ctrl+B on your keyboard. Your bookmarks will appear in a nice, easy-to-access, easy-to-manage list running down the side of your browser window. If you double-click on a bookmark, it will open in the active tab in the main browser window. If you right-click on a bookmark, the contextual menu will let you open it in a new tab or a new window, or delete it. If you choose Sort by Name, Firefox will put all the bookmarks in that folder into alphabetical order.

One of the nicest features is the Search box at the top of the Bookmarks Sidebar. If you know that a certain word is in a bookmark's name, but you can't remember where that bookmark is in your folder hierarchy, type that word in the Search box and press Enter on your keyboard. Only bookmarks matching your word will show up, making it easy to find exactly the bookmark you want.

Take that space back

After using the Bookmarks Sidebar, you'll probably want to close it, since it takes up room in your browser that could be used to display web pages. You can click the little "x" in the upper-right corner of the sidebar, but memorizing the keyboard command Ctrl+B will come in handy—press Ctrl+B to display the sidebar, and then Ctrl+B again to close it.

History Sidebar

The Bookmarks Sidebar is handy if you want to access a web site that you've saved because you thought you might find it useful later. On the other hand, the History Sidebar is handy if you want to access a web site that you've visited and want to return to, but didn't bookmark because you didn't realize until later that it might be useful. To display the History Sidebar, shown in Figure 3-27, go to View → Sidebar → History or press Ctrl+H on your keyboard.

FIGURE 3-27. View your browsing history with the History Sidebar.

The items in the History Sidebar function pretty much like those in the Bookmarks Sidebar: you click on a file representing a web page, and it loads in the main browser window. Right-click, and you can choose Bookmark This Link, or Copy Link Location if you'd like to paste a link to the web page into an email.

By default, your browsing history is sorted in folders by date, but you can change that. If you select the View drop-down menu in the upper-right corner of the sidebar, you can choose from the following sort options:

- By Date and Site
- By Site
- By Date (the default)
- By Most Visited
- By Last Visited

Personally, I find the By Date and Site option to be the most useful. The sites are still sorted chronologically, but a folder is created for each web site, with the web pages for that site listed in that folder. Try it—I think you'll find that it makes sense to you to organize your browsing history that way too.

Make the sidebar disappear

The History Sidebar takes up a lot of room, just like the Bookmarks Sidebar, so you'll probably want to close it when you're done using it. Use the "x" in the upper-right corner of the sidebar, or memorize the Ctrl+H command for super-fast opening and closing sidebar action!

Managers

Firefox includes several tools known as *Managers*, which allow you to oversee features and data that your browser uses. Firefox's Managers are incredibly useful, and in fact are required in order to work with things like Extensions and Themes. Let's take a look at two of the most important: the Bookmarks Manager and the Download Manager. If you're interested in finding out about the Extension Manager and the Theme Manager, skip ahead to Chapter 4.

The Bookmarks Manager

Need to manage your bookmarks? Of course you do! Say hello to the Bookmarks Manager.

Basic bookmarks

So, you're cruising through the Web when you find a page that you know you'll want to return to later. Time to bookmark it. Press Ctrl+D, go to Bookmarks → Bookmark This Page, or right-click in the page and select that option from the contextual menu. After doing so, you should see something like Figure 3-28.

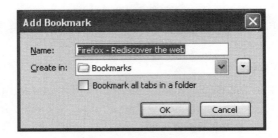

FIGURE 3-28. Add a bookmark to Firefox.

If you don't like the text in the "Name" field, feel free to change it. If you now press OK, your new bookmark will be added to the folder listed next to "Create in." But what if you don't want to put the bookmark in that folder? If you open the drop-down menu (by clicking on the down arrow at the righthand side of the field), Firefox shows you the last five folders into which you've placed bookmarks. But maybe those five folders don't include the one you want, or maybe you realize that the folder you need doesn't exist, so you need to make one. In either case, you need to press the little triangle button to the right of the "Create in" field. When you do, the Add Bookmark window gets a lot bigger, as shown in Figure 3-29.

Now you can drill down into your bookmark folder structure and place the new bookmark exactly where you want it. If a new folder is called for, first select the folder in which you wish to create the new folder and then press New Folder. Name the folder, and then choose OK to place the bookmark in the folder you just created.

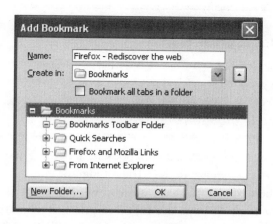

FIGURE 3-29. Precisely place a bookmark you're adding to Firefox.

Here's a really cool feature that IE can't touch, which combines tabs and bookmarks. Say you have three sites that you like to read every morning while you're drinking your coffee: NYTimes.com, WashingtonPost.com, and O'Reilly.com. Open those three sites in three tabs and then press Ctrl+D (or go to Bookmarks → Bookmark This Page). In the Add Bookmark window, check the box next to "Bookmark all tabs in a folder" (as in Figure 3-30) and change the name of the bookmark to something memorable, such as "Morning News."

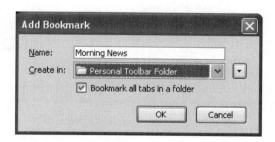

FIGURE 3-30. Bookmark a group of tabs.

Place the bookmark where you can easily get to it, like in your Bookmarks Toolbar Folder (discussed later), and press OK. Now when you choose that bookmark, press "Open in Tabs," and, lo and behold, three tabs will open, each loading one of your chosen sites. You have to admit, that's pretty slick.

Make it your home

And don't forget that you can make that special bookmark your home page, as I mentioned in Chapter 2, so that every time you open Firefox, all the tabs will load. Pretty neat!

While you're busy doing all this cool bookmarking, you may make a mistake and place a bookmark in the wrong folder, or you may wish to reorganize your bookmarks. In that case, you need to open the Bookmarks Manager by going to (I hope this isn't a surprise!) Bookmarks → Manage Bookmarks. The Bookmarks Manager is shown in Figure 3-31.

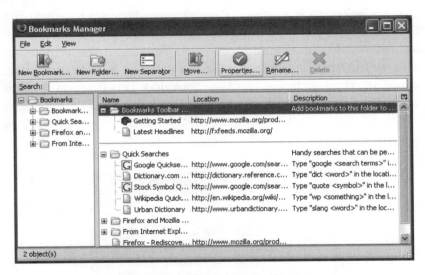

FIGURE 3-31. Firefox's Bookmarks Manager.

The Bookmarks Manager is one of the best ways to manage bookmarks in any web browser; in particular, it puts IE's anemic Organize Favorites to shame. Your folders are listed in the lefthand pane of the window, while folders and bookmarks are in the large righthand pane of the window, making it super easy to drag a bookmark into the appropriate folder (and somewhat replicating the well-known Windows Explorer interface).

Can't find a bookmark? Use the Search bar at the top of the window. Need to create a new bookmark or folder from scratch, or add a new separator line? Use the buttons on the toolbar. Need to change the URL, the name, or anything else about a bookmark? Use the Properties toolbar button. And don't forget that you can cut, copy, and paste bookmarks as well, using either the Edit menu or the standard keyboard commands of Ctrl+X, Ctrl+C, and Ctrl+V.

Some of the menu items bear discussion. You should be aware of File → Import and File → Export, as they can be tremendously useful. When you first install Firefox, the Import Wizard asks if you would like to import bookmarks and other settings from the other browsers on your computer; if you decline at that time, you can later use File → Import from the main Firefox menu (as I discussed earlier in this chapter) to import your settings. If you just want to import bookmarks, however, you can do that using the Bookmarks Manager.

You can import bookmarks from IE, or from Netscape or Mozilla, or from an HTML file. This last option is useful if you wish to import bookmarks from Opera or another browser that can export bookmarks in an HTML file. On the other side, Export enables you to save all your bookmarks as an HTML file, for importation by browsers that support that file type (and they all do).

The View menu, seen in Figure 3-32, enables you to re-sort your bookmarks in a way that makes sense to you.

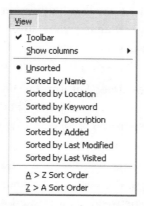

FIGURE 3-32. The View menu in the Bookmarks Manager.

By default, bookmarks are unsorted, with the order completely dependent on you. The other options are pretty obvious, but be careful: folders will be sorted in among bookmarks! In other words, let's say you previously had this:

History (folder)
Art (bookmark)
English (bookmark)
Science (bookmark)

When you choose Sorted by Name, you're going to have this:

Art (bookmark)
English (bookmark)
History (folder)
Science (bookmark)

This may be fine with you, but many people are used to having folders listed first, so it may be disconcerting. If you try out any of the sorting methods and decide that you don't like the results, you can just choose Unsorted again to go back to the way things were.

The Bookmarks Toolbar

You may have noticed a folder titled Bookmarks Toolbar Folder while you were in the Bookmarks Manager. The contents of this folder appear on the Bookmarks Toolbar in Firefox. And where is that, you may ask?

Right below the Navigation Toolbar, which was discussed earlier in this chapter, is the Bookmarks Toolbar (known in IE as the Links Bar). Think of this toolbar as containing your absolute favorite bookmarks—those you visit so regularly that clicking on the Bookmarks menu in order to find and choose them simply takes too much time and trouble.

Head over to eBay all the time? Put it in the Bookmarks Toolbar! Look up movies every Friday at your local newspaper's web site? Get there in one click from the Bookmarks Toolbar. Is My Yahoo! a constant destination? You know where to put it.

You can even create a folder on the Bookmarks Toolbar that contains links to several web pages. For instance, I maintain several web sites that I'm constantly jumping between, so I created a folder called "GranneStuff" that contains links to all of those sites. Now they're right there, available in just two clicks: one on the GranneStuff folder, and one on the bookmark for the site.

When you first install Firefox, the Bookmarks Toolbar appears as it does in Figure 3-33.

FIGURE 3-33. The default Bookmarks Toolbar.

Pretty plain, huh? You have a link to the Firefox Getting Started page, and a collection of Live Bookmarks (more on those in "Live Bookmarks" in Chapter 5) in the Latest Headlines folder. And that's it. Well, let's spiff this one up a bit, shall we?

I bookmarked the sites that I use all the time and opened the Bookmarks Manager. I then placed a selection of items into my Bookmarks Toolbar Folder, including the following:

Linux (folder)

Linux is my main operating system, and this folder contains links I use all the time to get help, find and download software, and keep up to date with Linux news.

Admin (folder)

To administer my home's router/firewall, I have to log into a web page. A link to that web page goes in this folder, as well as any other web sites that I use to administer hardware or software.

GranneStuff (folder)

As I mentioned earlier, this folder allows me to jump quickly to the various web sites of my own that I manage and use, including Granneman.com, The Open Source Weblog, and the web sites for the classes I teach.

My Yahoo! (bookmark)

A page I use all the time for news, weather, movies, and more.

URLinfo (bookmark)

A link to a web site that gives me a huge variety of information about any web page I'm visiting. Useful for security, research, or just plain nosiness.

Cybertimes Navigator (bookmark)

The home page used by *The New York Times* newsroom for research. Indispensable.

Usual (folder)

A collection of links to web pages that I load every time I start Firefox. I grew tired of manually opening Gmail, Bloglines, and my blog, so I created a quick link for those three sites so they open all at once.

Once I'd finished setting up my Bookmarks Toolbar Folder, I ended up with a Bookmarks Toolbar like that shown in Figure 3-34.

FIGURE 3-34. The Bookmarks Toolbar after some customization.

I'm certainly not expecting your Bookmarks Toolbar to look like mine, but I hope that I've given you some ideas. The Bookmarks Toolbar can be a great help for you in your daily web work, but you have to customize it to *your* specifications. Do so!

Download Manager

Most web users download files at various times, be they PDFs, software, MP3s, or video files. Internet Explorer opens a dialog box for every download, meaning that if you're downloading 10 files, you'll have 10 little windows open, tracking each separate download's progress. Talk about a busy working environment! Firefox's Download Manager helps alleviate this problem by consolidating information about all downloads in a single window, and giving you control over the downloads as they occur.

To try it out, I visited *http://www.opsound.org*, a record label that makes it easy to download all sorts of free, "open source" music from artists who want to release their work in a new and innovative way. I found some tunes by the Barefoot Brothers, a so-called "psychedelic rock trio" from Japan, and started downloading. A few seconds later, the Download Manager window opened, as shown in Figure 3-35.

The Download Manager is useful because it shows you at a glance what is happening with all of your downloads—you can see the progress each one is making, even to the point of knowing how fast each download is moving and how much longer it should take. If you want to temporarily Pause or Cancel a download, you can.

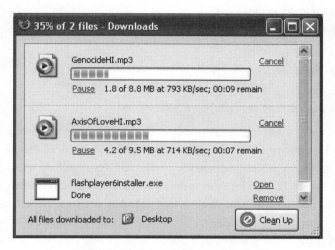

FIGURE 3-35. The Download Manager in action.

To change the location to which downloads will be saved, press the button to the right of "All files downloaded to" (the default is Desktop) and choose a new location. Once a download has completed, you can delete it from the list by pressing Remove. If you want to delete several completed downloads in one fell swoop, just press the Clean Up button.

When your downloads are finished and the files are safely stowed on your computer, an alert similar to that in Figure 3-36 will appear.

FIGURE 3-36. Firefox pops up an alert when your downloads are finished.

If you click that alert, it opens the Download Manager; otherwise, the alert will disappear after a few seconds. The Download Manager is both useful and unobtrusive, and that's a great combination.

Where to Learn More

Mozilla's support site for Firefox has a great collection of pages explaining keyboard and mouse shortcuts in Firefox, along with their equivalents in IE. In addition, the Firefox site has a brief reference for each menu entry.

Keyboard Shortcuts
> *http://www.mozilla.org/support/firefox/keyboard*

Mouse Shortcuts
> *http://www.mozilla.org/support/firefox/mouse*

Menu Reference
> *http://www.mozilla.org/support/firefox/menu*

For a complete explanation by Microsoft of the new Windows XP SP2 pop-up blocker, see the company's own rather technical discussion. As for the question of tabs appearing in IE, ZDNet reported the following on November 11, 2004: "Microsoft's [security and management product manager, Ben] English reiterated that features such as tabbed browsing were not important to IE users. 'I don't believe it is a true statement that IE doesn't have the features that our customers want'... said English."

Microsoft on the SP2 pop-up blocker
> *http://www.microsoft.com/technet/prodtechnol/winxppro/maintain/*
> *sp2brows.mspx#EEAA*

Microsoft on tabbed browsing
> *http://news.zdnet.co.uk/internet/security/0,39020375,39173345,00.htm*

Wikipedia has articles on both character encoding and Unicode that do a good job of explaining what they are and how they should be used. For Firefox-specific Unicode instructions, see Alan Wood's "Setting up Firefox Web Browsers for Multilingual and Unicode Support."

Wikipedia on character encoding
> *http://en.wikipedia.org/wiki/Character_encoding*
> *http://en.wikipedia.org/wiki/Unicode*

Alan Wood's "Setting up Firefox Web Browsers for Multilingual and Unicode Support"
> *http://www.alanwood.net/unicode/firefox.html*

4

KILLER
FIREFOX
ADD-ONS

The vision behind Firefox was to create a great browser that is just that: a great browser. Not a great browser that also includes an email program and a chat client and a million other widgets. Just a browser that, out of the box, delivers an easy-to-use, highly functional web experience that is second to none.

However, the programmers realized that different users have widely differing needs; consequently, they made sure that Firefox is extensible, so other developers can create add-ons that add new and interesting functionality to the browser. In this chapter, we'll look at three categories of add-ons: plug-ins, themes, and extensions.

Installing Plug-Ins for Multimedia and More

One of the coolest features of the Web is that it allows users to view and interact with multimedia such as pictures, sounds, and movies. Although browsers can display pictures in a couple of different formats by default, that's about it–they can't play sounds or display movies without the help of external applications.

For instance, suppose that you run across a web page that has an Apple QuickTime movie embedded in it. In order for the movie to play, you need Apple's QuickTime movie player installed on your computer. But that's not enough: your browser also needs a way to load QuickTime so that the movie appears inside the web page instead of in a separate QuickTime window on your desktop. That's where the QuickTime plug-in comes in. It enables your web browser to use QuickTime to display the movie directly inside the web page.

For plug-ins to work, you need to have the player software *and* a plug-in that knows how to get that software to run inside your browser. Fortunately, most player software includes the appropriate plug-in.

When you install Firefox on a PC, it doesn't come with any plug-ins, but don't worry. If you were previously using Netscape or Mozilla, Firefox looks in the *plugins* folder for those programs to see if there are any plug-in files it can use. Also, as you browse the Web, Firefox will alert you if you need certain plug-ins to view content on a page and will automatically download and install those plug-ins for you using the Firefox Plugin Finder Service. However, not all plug-ins work that way, so you'll have to install some of them manually. This process isn't difficult, and as most people don't need too many plug-ins, you shouldn't have to do it often.

If you can't find it

Flash and Shockwave are currently the only plug-ins discussed here that will install via the Plugin Finder Service. This will undoubtedly change after this book has gone to press, so feel free to try installing other plug-ins using the Plugin Finder Service. At worst, Firefox will report that it cannot install a plug-in using that method, and you'll have to use one of the techniques discussed later in this chapter.

Macromedia Flash and Shockwave

Macromedia's Flash is one of the most popular plug-ins in use on the Internet, and increasingly cool things are being done with it (although you probably won't think it's so cool when advertisements start talking to you through your PC's speakers—I'll discuss a great extension called FlashBlock in "Counteracting Web Annoyances" in Chapter 5, which you can use when Flash gets annoying). Shockwave is like Flash's big brother: it lets web designers create more complex multimedia than they can with Flash. The easiest way to get these plug-ins is to go directly to the source, to the "Test Macromedia Shockwave & Flash Players" page at *http://www.macromedia.com/shockwave/welcome/*. Once you're there, one of two things will happen: either you'll see animations and movements on the page, in which case you already have the plug-ins and can skip this section, or you'll get an alert message at the top of the web page, like the one displayed in Figure 4-1.

FIGURE 4-1. Firefox warns you that you don't have a plug-in…or maybe two.

If you get the alert, press Install Missing Plugins, and in a moment, a window titled Plugin Finder Service will open. Firefox will have figured out that you need the Flash and Shockwave plug-ins and will offer to download and install them for you. Press Next, and you'll be presented with the licenses for the software. Read them if you want, choose "I Agree," and press Next. The Flash and Shockwave plug-ins will download and install themselves on your computer; all you need to do is press Finish to close the Plugin Finder Service. If Macromedia's test page doesn't reload automatically, press the Reload button or hit Ctrl+R. This time some sort of animation should be visible—yes, it's that easy!

Apple QuickTime

Apple's QuickTime is one of the oldest and still one of the best formats for digital movies. In fact, virtually every Hollywood movie releases its trailers in QuickTime format, making it indispensable if you want to keep up with the latest releases.

Like Macromedia, Apple has an "Installation Check" page at *http:// www.apple.com/quicktime/troubleshooting/*. View the page in Firefox and read the instructions—if you see the animations, you're set. If you don't see the animations, follow Apple's links to download and install Quick-Time. Once it's installed, cruise over to *http://www.apple.com/trailers/* and enjoy a movie preview.

Windows Media Player

Not surprisingly, a lot of content is released on the Web in Windows Media format. If you're using Windows, you undoubtedly have some version of Windows Media Player (WMP) already installed. If so, Firefox will have seen it when you installed it and will make sure that the appropriate plug-in is used when you encounter WMP content on the Web. Easy peasy, as my British cousin says.

If you want to test WMP (did Microsoft have to give it a name whose acronym is pronounced "wimp"?), try the various demos at *http://www. microsoft.com/windows/windowsmedia/demos/demos.aspx*. To download WMP, go to *http://www.microsoft.com/windows/windowsmedia/mp10/default.aspx*.

Adobe Acrobat Reader

Adobe's Portable Document Format (PDF) has mushroomed in popularity in the past few years because it allows document producers to create files that look the same on virtually every major operating system. Chances are you already have the free Adobe Acrobat Reader on your computer. To verify its presence, try loading this link in Firefox: *http:// www.oreilly.com/catalog/bluee/chapter/index.html*. If you already have Acrobat

Reader installed, skip ahead to the next section; otherwise, download and install the software from Adobe's web site, at *http://www.adobe.com/products/ acrobat/readstep2.html.*

RealPlayer

After years of relying on closed source programming, RealNetworks decided a few years ago to open source the development of its flagship RealPlayer. Consequently, RealPlayer 10, the latest version available at the time of this writing, is a far less obnoxious and better-quality piece of software.

If you don't have the latest RealPlayer, you really should uninstall your old version and acquire Version 10 from *http://www.real.com,* as it is a major improvement over previous versions. During the installation, Real will install the necessary plug-in so Firefox will work with multimedia in the Real formats. If you already have RealPlayer 10 on your machine, Firefox should automatically use it. If it doesn't, just reinstall RealPlayer 10, and things should be copasetic.

Java™

Java is a programming language that allows web developers to create programs that run inside your web browser, such as games, animations, text editors, and more. For Java to work, you must have a Java Virtual Machine (JVM) installed on your machine. Microsoft includes a JVM with some versions of Windows, but it is better to install and use the actual JVM made by Sun, the creator of the Java language.

You can verify whether you have a JVM installed by visiting Sun's "Test Your Java™ Virtual Machine" page, at *http://www.java.com/en/download/ help/testvm.jsp.* If the page indicates that you have a JVM installed, keep reading; otherwise, follow Sun's instructions on installing a JVM.

Other Plug-Ins

If you find content on the Web that looks interesting to you and requires a plug-in that hasn't been mentioned here, it's probably OK to install it, but do a Google search first just to make sure it's legitimate software. (To see what people are saying about it in discussion forums, search *http:// groups.google.com* as well as using Google Search.) If it looks okay, install the plug-in and see if it makes your web experience better. If Firefox's

Plugin Finder Service can't find the plug-in, don't give up; look at some of the resources in the next section for help, and you'll probably be able to view the content. If the content requires a plug-in that isn't available to Firefox users, send the creators a polite email asking them to consider supporting Firefox. You'd be surprised what several nice emails can do.

There is one plug-in that I want to warn you against, because it could potentially cause security issues with Firefox (which would be a shame, because Firefox's tight security is one of the biggest reasons to start using it in the first place). As I mentioned in Chapter 1, one of Internet Explorer's biggest security holes is its support for a Microsoft technology called ActiveX, which doesn't work at all in Mozilla, Netscape, or Firefox—and that's good news for those browsers. However, there is a plug-in available on the Web that enables Firefox (and Mozilla and Netscape) to install and use ActiveX controls. Downloading this plug-in is not a good idea. Enabling ActiveX will introduce security hazards into Firefox that just aren't worth it. You may find some web sites out there that need ActiveX for playing movies or running games, but these are few and far between, because most web sites have started using Flash for active content. The ActiveX plug-in has also been linked to browser crashes and conflicts with other plug-ins. Consider yourself warned.

If you want to read about the ActiveX plug-in, go to *http://www.iol.ie/ ~locka/mozilla/plugin.htm.* Just promise me you'll read and not touch, OK? If you need ActiveX to use an application at work or school, you may be better off switching back to IE when you need to run those programs, so that you keep your copy of Firefox as secure as possible.

ActiveX-related program activity

Development on the ActiveX plug-in seems more oriented toward Mozilla than Firefox. It also seems that Netscape 7.1 (and presumably higher) ships with the ActiveX plug-in, but it's enabled to work only with Windows Media Player. The fact that it's so limited somewhat alleviates my queasiness, but I'm still not happy about it.

Troubleshooting Plug-Ins

If you have to download and run a plug-in's installer—Adobe Acrobat Reader, for instance—it's always a good idea to download the installer with Firefox, but then close Firefox before actually installing the plug-in. That way, any Firefox files that need to be overwritten or modified by the installer can be safely overwritten. After the install has finished, open Firefox and test the new plug-in to verify that it works.

If you're having trouble with plug-ins, or you're not sure which plug-ins you have installed, go to Tools → Options, and choose Downloads. On the Downloads settings screen, press the Plug-Ins button, and you'll see a list of all currently installed plug-ins (as shown in Figure 4-2).

FIGURE 4-2. Firefox's Options will show you a list of all your installed plug-ins.

If a particular file type is not opening with the correct plug-in, simply remove that file type's checkmark from the Enabled column, and Firefox will download files of that type rather than trying to open them with a plug-in. You can then open the downloaded files with the correct application.

Another way to get more information about all your plug-ins is to type *about:plugins* into Firefox's Location Bar (don't type *http://*, *.com*, or anything else). Firefox will list all your installed plug-ins, along with information about each plug-in. This page is read-only: you can't use it to change how plug-ins behave, but it can provide valuable diagnostic data in case you're having a problem.

Changing the Look and Feel with Themes

Firefox is a pretty nice-looking web browser, and you may be just fine with its icons, colors, and overall look. However, Firefox makes it easy for you to change how your browser looks by enabling the use of *themes*, or "skins." Pick a new theme, and Firefox completely changes its appearance, with new icons, new colors, and a whole new look. You don't have to use themes, but they're fun to play with, and they continue one of the main ideas of Firefox (and, indeed, all open source software): this is really *your* software, and therefore you can do with it what you wish.

Installing a Theme

Starting with Version 0.9, Firefox changed the default theme from Qute to one called Winstripe. While the current theme is fine, a lot of people, myself included, prefer the Qute theme, so I'll show you how to install it. If you hate Qute, you don't have to use it, and I'll also show you how to uninstall it.

Before we start, let's take a look at Figure 4-3, which shows the default theme as it appears on the toolbar.

FIGURE 4-3. Firefox's default theme—it works, but let's try something better!

So that's Winstripe—now let's try Qute. Select Tools → Themes to open the Themes window, shown in Figure 4-4.

You have one theme already installed (the default), but you know you want more. Select Get More Themes, and Firefox will open a new window at Mozilla Update's Themes page (*https://addons.update.mozilla.org/ themes/*). Look for the Qute theme; it's often listed in either the Most Popular or Top Rated sections, but if it's not, click on All, under Categories, and look for it there, or use the search box at the top of the page. Once

FIGURE 4-4. Firefox comes with only one theme preinstalled.

you're on the Qute page, select Install Now to download the theme. When it finishes downloading, the small Themes window will now show two themes: Firefox (default) and Qute. Select Qute, and then press Use Theme. Restart Firefox, and now things look very different, as Figure 4-5 demonstrates.

FIGURE 4-5. Qute is, well, cuter.

If you don't think Qute's for you, you can either go back to the default or try out some other themes. If you really don't like Qute, you can uninstall it by choosing Tools → Themes, selecting Qute, and then pressing Uninstall.

A Few of My Favorite Themes

As you can see from our experience with Qute, themes are easy to work with in Firefox, so there's no excuse not to try various themes until you find one or two you really like.

I've installed Doodle (Classic) and Doodle (Plastik)–they're big, garish, and fun. If you like bright colors and cartoonish icons, you'll like both of these themes. You can see Doodle (Plastik) in Figure 4-6.

FIGURE 4-6. The Doodle themes look like a kid drew them—and that's OK!

If you want Firefox to look like the default Mozilla install, try Firefox-Modern (Figure 4-7). I like the Modern theme for Mozilla, but I prefer to use a different theme for Firefox so I can keep them visually separate.

FIGURE 4-7. The FirefoxModern theme makes Firefox look like Mozilla.

If you're feeling retro and want your ultra-modern web browser to party like it's 1997, install Perennial; as you can see in Figure 4-8, it turns Firefox into the spitting image of Netscape 4. Eeek!

FIGURE 4-8. The Perennial theme is retro... in a bad way. Blecch!

Plastikfox Crystal SVG, visible in Figure 4-9, is a pleasant theme that borrows icons and ideas from the Linux operating system, as does Nautical, shown in Figure 4-10. The difference is that Plastikfox borrows from KDE, while Nautical uses GNOME. For non-Linux users, that means that Nautical is plainer and less colorful than Plastikfox. Both are worth trying out.

FIGURE 4-9. The Plastikfox Crystal SVG theme is bright and colorful.

FIGURE 4-10. The Nautical theme for Firefox is simple and more muted in color.

If you like cats—no, if you're *crazy* about cats—then you're in luck, because there's a superabundance of cat-related themes for Firefox, in just about every pastel color known to humankind. I'm a dog person, so I avoid these themes, but you may want to check out a few of them.

There are several themes that I like, but really, themes are all about aesthetic judgments, so what I consider cute or cool you may find hideous or dorky (and vice versa, of course!). Play around with Firefox's themes. Download a bunch. Change them whenever the mood strikes. Have fun—that's one of the main things Firefox is about, and themes are a big part of the experience.

Adding Features to Firefox with Extensions

As we've seen, plug-ins allow Firefox to use third-party software to display multimedia and other programs in the web browser, and themes change the appearance of Firefox—sometimes radically. Extensions, on the other hand, provide Firefox with new features, or take existing features and extend them in new ways. Consequently, Firefox developers can deliver a lean, mean browsing machine, and then individual users can add additional features to their hearts' content, customizing the browser to serve their specific needs. As of this writing, there are over two hundred extensions available for Firefox, with more coming every day. Many of them are absolutely brilliant must-haves.

There are several ways you can acquire Firefox extensions (don't worry, I'll tell you about several), but the official way is by selecting Tools → Extensions to bring up Firefox's Extension Manager. When the Extension Manager window opens, you will see a list of currently installed extensions (of course, when you first install Firefox you don't have any extensions installed, so this part of the window is blank). At the bottom of the window are three buttons—Uninstall, Update, and Options—and a Get More Extensions link, as seen in Figure 4-11.

If you select an already installed extension and press Uninstall, the extension will be fully removed once you restart Firefox. To see if an extension has an update available, select it and then press Update. Firefox will check, and if there is an update, you will be prompted to install it. Finally, if an extension has preferences available, the Options button will be available to press in order to access those preferences; otherwise, the button will be grayed out and will not work.

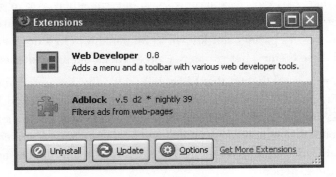

FIGURE 4-11. The Extension Manager gives you a lot of control over your extensions.

Check 'em all

Unfortunately, it is not possible at the time of this writing to click on Update in the Extension Manager and have all your extensions checked at once. Instead, you need to select and check each one individually. However, here's a workaround: open Tools → Options, and then select Advanced. Click the + next to Software Update, if it's not expanded already. Make sure that there are checks next to Firefox and My Extensions and Themes, and then press Check Now. Firefox will look for updates for the browser, extensions, and themes. One-stop shopping!

The Extension Manager actually allows you do more than just uninstall, update, or view options. Right-click on a selected extension, and a contextual menu opens with several other possibilities, as Figure 4-12 shows.

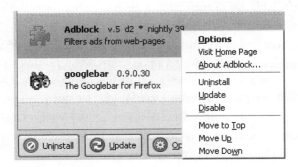

FIGURE 4-12. Right-clicking gives you a contextual menu for each extension.

Three of the choices on this menu duplicate the buttons at the bottom of the Extension Manager window: Options, Uninstall, and Update. Most of them, however, are new. Visit Home Page takes you to the home page of the extension, which can be really useful if you want to gather more information about it. The About choice opens a small window that lets you know who worked on the extension, what the current version number is, and what the extension is designed to do.

Disable is a nice addition to Uninstall and Update. What if you just want to turn off an extension temporarily? Maybe it's causing a problem on a web site, or maybe you think it might be causing a problem with Firefox. Disable the extension and see what happens.

The last three options help you position the extensions in the order you'd like. By default, extensions are listed in the order in which you added them, with the oldest at the top. To reorder your extensions, right-click on an extension and choose Move to Top, Move Up, or Move Down. If you have a lot of extensions, this can grow tedious, and most people probably won't care what order their extensions are in. For those of you who like to have everything just so, however, I'm sure you'll appreciate the ability to reorder your list of extensions.

Firefox gives you a lot of power with extensions, but thankfully, a couple of features greatly reduce the likelihood that an extension will cause a security or stability problem. First, Firefox comes with a built-in *whitelist* of sites that can install extensions, including *update.mozilla.org* by default. If you find a cool extension at a site that isn't on the whitelist (such as *http://cardgames.mozdev.org*, which we'll be looking at later in this chapter) and try to install it, Firefox shows an alert at the top of browser, as in Figure 4-13.

FIGURE 4-13. Firefox warns you if a site hasn't already been approved.

To install software from *cardgames.mozdev.org*, you need to press the Edit Options button to open the Allowed Sites window (shown in Figure 4-14) and add that site to the list of allowed sites.

FIGURE 4-14. You have to explicitly approve a site in order to install an extension from it.

Press Allow to add the web site's address to the list of allowed sites, and then press OK to close the window. You can now install the extension from *cardgames.mozdev.org*. Sure, this process adds a few seconds when you're trying to install an extension, but really, it's quick, it's easy, it only needs to be done once for each site, and it makes your computer safer, so stop complaining!

Caution!

Keep in mind that this whitelisting is in effect only for Firefox extensions. You can still download and install whatever dangerous Windows software you want, and Firefox won't get in your way.

In addition to implementing a whitelist, Firefox won't let you accidentally install an extension that won't work with your version of the browser, as you can see in Figure 4-15.

Firefox does everything it can to ensure that extensions don't damage your installation of the web browser. Still, if you want to install multiple extensions, I recommend installing them one at a time and restarting the

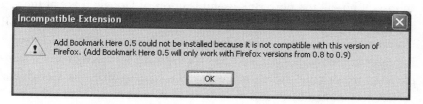

FIGURE 4-15. Firefox won't let you install incompatible extensions.

Dropping Sanctions

If you ever want to remove a site from the whitelist, go to Tools → Options → Web Features and press the second Allowed Sites button. That will bring up the Allowed Sites window seen in Figure 4-14.

browser and testing each extension as you go, and then repeating the process with the next extension. Yes, it's entirely possible to install 10 extensions at a time before restarting Firefox, and things may well work just fine, but if you do have a problem, it'll be far more difficult to diagnose the source. Better to take it slow and install them one at a time, immediately removing any that cause problems.

So, grab some extensions and see what sorts of cool things you can do to spiff up this already great web browser! The next sections cover quite a few extensions, but there are many more out there.

Better Searching

Firefox comes with a built-in Search Bar, which is already far more than Internet Explorer offers. Searching, however, is one of those features that most people just can't get enough of. Consequently, there are several excellent extensions that enable searching in a variety of new, innovative ways.

GoogleBar

Google is the king of search engines right now, and with good reason: it often seems to read your mind and show you exactly the web page you're looking for. When Google introduced the Google Toolbar, it was an instant hit—all the powerful, useful features of Google there at the top of your web browser, always available and ready to be used... how cool! Unfortunately, however, the Google Toolbar runs only in Internet Explorer (c'mon, Google!), and this was enough to dissuade some people from making the switch to Firefox. To remedy that, the GoogleBar project was inaugurated, and now there's one more reason to cross over from tired ol' IE to fresh Firefox.

Google and the GoogleBar

Google does not sponsor the GoogleBar project, but they don't frown on it either. Actually, Google is very supportive of open source (they have the largest installation of Linux servers in the world), so I'm not surprised that they don't mind the GoogleBar project for Firefox.

To get the GoogleBar, select Tools → Extensions → Get More Extensions, select Search Tools on the resulting page at Mozilla Update, and then find GoogleBar (or use the search box at the top of every page at Mozilla Update). Once you're on the GoogleBar page, select Install Now. At that point, a Software Installation window will open. When the window first opens, the Install Now button is inactive, in order to give you time to think about the software you're about to put on your computer and cancel the installation if necessary. After a few seconds, the Install Now button will activate so that you can press it, so go ahead. You will see the extension installing, and then the Extension Manager will report "This item will be installed after you restart Firefox." Close all open Firefox windows and restart the browser. There's your new GoogleBar, shown in Figure 4-16!

FIGURE 4-16. GoogleBar patiently awaits your command.

The list of GoogleBar features is long and complete; basically, if you can do it at Google, you can do it with the GoogleBar, just faster and more conveniently. If you want to change your GoogleBar in any way, just select the drop-down menu next to the "g" icon on the left, and you can change your Search preferences or GoogleBar options.

I'd like to draw your attention to two buttons on the GoogleBar that you may find particularly handy. First, the drop-down next to the blue "i" button (shown in Figure 4-17) reveals several useful ways to work with web pages you visit.

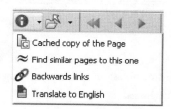

FIGURE 4-17. GoogleBar lets you work with web pages in a variety of useful ways.

Suppose you return to a web page but find that it has changed from the way you remembered it. Maybe some information is missing, a picture that used to be there has disappeared, or the design is completely different. Select "Cached copy of the Page" from the "i" drop-down menu, and you can see the page the way it looked when Google last visited it. Of course, that visit could also have been after the changes were made, but that's not always the case. You'd be surprised how many times you can "recover" information using Google's cache.

The next option, "Find similar pages to this one," does just that: it lists pages that bear some likeness to the content of the page you're currently visiting. Sometimes this works, and sometimes it doesn't, but it never hurts to try.

"Backwards links" can be tremendously helpful, but it's a little confusing at first. As Google crawls the Web, in addition to indexing the content of the web pages it finds, it also keeps track of the links that web pages make to each other. If you're on a web page that makes a convincing case that space aliens are poisoning the water supply, choose "Backwards links." You'll be presented with a page at Google that lists all the pages that provide links to the page you were just viewing. Take a look at those pages. If 20 pages link to the "Space Aliens are Poisoning Our

Water!" page, and 19 of those pages were written by people who are obviously crazy, then I think it's safe not to worry. If, though, 19 of the pages linking to the page in question are by the federal government and related health agencies, well, you might want to start drinking bottled water!

Finally, have you ever come across a page that's written in a language you don't read? "Translate to English" might help. Don't expect perfection, or even complete clarity, but often the results are good enough to give you the gist of a page's content.

Shortcut

The above features—and a couple of others—are also available if you select a word or phrase in a web page, right-click on it, and choose GoogleBar Items.

The second feature I'd like to point out is the icon of a folder with a diagonal arrow, located to the right of the blue "i" button. Pressing the drop-down next to that icon reveals a useful tool that allows you to easily jump up through the levels of a web site. For example, Figure 4-18 shows you what you would see if you had *http://www.mozilla.org/products/ firefox/* open in Firefox. If you want to jump up one level in the web site, just choose *http://www.mozilla.org/products/*; if you want to jump two levels to the home page of the site, select *http://www.mozilla.org/*.

FIGURE 4-18. Jump up several levels of a web site with the GoogleBar.

This feature is especially useful if you're lazy and don't want to have to type anything into the Location Bar or hunt around for a link on the page back to Home (and remember, lazy is good when it comes to computers!), or if you reach a page that is no longer there and you hope that going up one or more levels might expose it. Either way, it's nice to have this ability right there in your GoogleBar.

As cool as the GoogleBar is, you might not want it taking up your valuable screen real estate all the time. To hide the GoogleBar, either right-click on it and choose Hide Googlebar, select View → Googlebar, or press Ctrl+F8. To bring it back, repeat any of those steps.

GoogleBar with PageRank

The GoogleBar is an essential extension, but it's missing one feature that the official Google Toolbar has: PageRank. As Google crawls the Internet indexing web pages noting who links to whom, it is also busy calculating the "value" of each page, which Google calls its PageRank. Why is this important? The higher the PageRank of a page is, the more its links matter to Google. If a page with a low PageRank links to your site, it will not boost your PageRank nearly as much as a page with a higher Page-Rank would—and it's the PageRank in part that determines the order in which pages appear in a Google search.

If you're interested in knowing the PageRank values of the sites you visit (or even of your own web site!), you'll want to install the GoogleBar with PageRank extension. This replaces the GoogleBar with one that is exactly the same, with the addition of the PageRank feature.

Caution

If you have already installed the original GoogleBar, you should uninstall it first before installing GoogleBar with PageRank.

To get this extension, you'll need to go to its home page, at *http://www. prgooglebar.org*. Once there, click on the link to install the extension. After that process completes, close and reopen Firefox and enjoy the spectacle of your newly enhanced GoogleBar, shown in Figure 4-19.

FIGURE 4-19. Your GoogleBar now displays PageRank values.

Make an exception

Firefox will not let you download and install the software at first, since this site is not in Firefox's "OK to download from here" list. To download this extension, press the Edit Options button that appears in the alert box at the top of Firefox's window, add *www. prgooglebar.org* to the list of allowed sites, and retry the installation.

You don't really *do* anything with the PageRank feature, except view it as you cruise about the Web. But now it's there for your edification, so enjoy.

Yahoo! Companion

What if you're a diehard Yahoo! user instead of a Googlaholic? Don't feel left out—just as the Googlaholics can run their GoogleBar, you can run your Yahoo! Companion (shown in Figure 4-20). Just head over to Mozilla Update (Tools → Extensions → Get More Extensions) and select Search Tools, then Yahoo! Companion. Install it, restart Firefox, and there it is: your gateway to all things Yahoo!

FIGURE 4-20. Your new toolbar: the Yahoo! Companion.

Yahoo! Search is right there for you to use, but so are the personalized services that Yahoo! provides. Do you have a My Yahoo! page? It's there. Use Yahoo! Mail? It's available at the click of a button. Yahoo! News? Likewise. Yahoo! Finance? Natch. Weather? Sports? Games? Yup. All there, and all available at the click of a button. Just sign into your Yahoo! account, and the Companion instantly changes to match your saved settings.

Be sure to click on the drop-down next to the little pencil icon, so you can customize the Companion to your liking. Move buttons around, add the services you use, and remove the services you don't. After all, it's *your* Yahoo!

McSearchPreview

Google delivers exceptional search results, but you should never rely on just one search engine. Other sites–such as AllTheWeb, Yahoo! Search, and Amazon's A9, which repurposes Google's results in interesting new ways–can also help you in your search for information on the Net. Still, as great as these search sites are, they can always be improved–and that's where McSearchPreview comes in.

To install McSearchPreview, select Tools → Extensions and click on Get More Extensions. When Mozilla Update loads, go to Search Tools and find McSearchPreview. Choose Install Now, and then restart Firefox when the extension finishes installing. Now let's test it. Make sure Google is selected in the Search Bar, and search for "firefox." Now watch as the search results load. As you can see in Figure 4-21, your results now display a thumbnail of the web site next to each result.

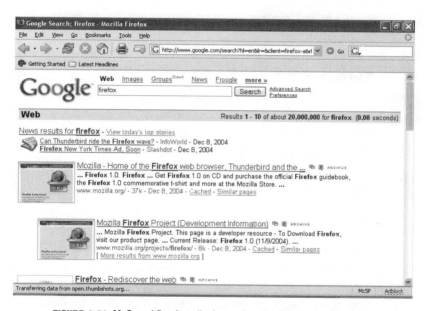

FIGURE 4-21. McSearchPreview displays a thumbnail next to each result.

This can be tremendously helpful, as it can prevent you from going to a site that obviously has nothing to do with your search, while helping you zero in on exactly the resource you need. Of course, if you're stuck on a dial-up connection, I wouldn't recommend this extension, as it will cause search result pages to take forever to load while Firefox acquires and displays every thumbnail image. On fast broadband connections, however, McSearchPreview is a super addition.

As you may have guessed, this extension works with more than just Google. McSearchPreview will also display thumbnails on the results pages of MSN Search (*http://search.msn.com*), Yahoo! Search (*http://search.yahoo.com*), AllTheWeb (*http://www.alltheweb.com*), Amazon's A9 (*http://www.a9.com*), and even my favorite online bookmark service, del.icio.us (*http://del.icio.us*). If the result of your search is a product sold on Amazon, a picture of the product will appear instead of a thumbnail of the web page.

Finally, McSearchPreview adds some new links in your search results, as seen in Figure 4-22.

 Mozilla - Home of the **Firefox** web browser, Thunderbird and the ...
... **Firefox** 1.0. **Firefox** ... Get **Firefox** 1.0 on CD and purchase the official **Firefox** guidebook, the **Firefox** 1.0 commemorative t-shirt and more at the Mozilla Store. ...
www.mozilla.org/ - 37k - Dec 8, 2004 - Cached - Similar pages

FIGURE 4-22. McSearchPreview adds two new links to your search results.

Turn it off

McSearchPreview is a useful extension, but you might not always want it changing your search engine results. After you install it, a new item will appear on the righthand side of your Status Bar: a little box that simply says "McSP." To toggle McSearchPreview off or on, simply click on that little box—a dialog will appear that lets you configure McSearchPreview.

To the right of the title of the web page are three small icons. The first will open the results in a new window if you click on it. The next one, Site Info, opens a new window and displays information about the web page collected by Alexa, a service purchased by Amazon.com a few years ago. Alexa tells you an astonishing amount about each web site that it tracks, including the length of time it has been online, contact info for the owner of the domain, and how it ranks compared to all other sites on the Web. If you want to determine whether a site is trustworthy, this is just what you need. Finally, the third link, labeled Archive, takes you to the Wayback Machine (*http://www.waybackmachine.org*), a web site that stores archived snapshots of web sites, some going back nearly a decade.

More Information

Firefox strikes a good balance between exposing obvious information about itself and the web pages you're visiting (the Location Bar turns gold if you're on a secure web page, for instance) and making further information available to those who want it (as an example, right-click on a web page and choose View Page Info). Some Firefox extensions, like those discussed here, make available even more information about web pages, or enable the browser itself to display other kinds of data. These extensions indicate progress toward a vision that's been 10 years in the making: turning the web browser into the hub of our computer experience, a focal point for all the data and information that we come into contact with every day.

TargetAlert

TargetAlert is a nice solution to a problem that's annoying, but not generally annoying enough to cause the people who create web browsers to do anything about it. What's the issue? Not knowing what's going to happen when you click on a link.

I know this has happened to you: you're looking at a web page, and a link looks interesting, so you click it. Suddenly a new window opens up, with the new web page in it. (Firefox won't block this because you specifically requested it, as opposed to an unsolicited pop-up or pop-under window.) But what if you wanted the site to open in a tab, not a new window? You have to close the window, right-click on the link, and choose Open Link in New Tab. If you'd known that it was going to open a new window, you would have opened the link in a new tab to start with, but since you didn't, you'll have to go through those steps to avoid cluttering up your screen with multiple windows.

Here's another one: you're looking at a web page, and you want to follow a link to another page, so you click it. Oh, too bad—it's not a link to a web page, it's a link to an enormous PDF file! Or a program! Or a Word document! And now you have to wait while Adobe Acrobat opens up and displays the PDF file, or while the program or document downloads.

The problem is that the folks who create web pages don't always identify what's going to happen when you click on a link. They should make it clear that a link is going to open in a new window, or is going to download and open a PDF file, but they don't. Fortunately, TargetAlert solves this problem.

If you want to see exactly what TargetAlert does, head over to this page on the program's web site: *http://www.bolinfest.com/targetalert/download.html*. When you get to the page, you'll see several links, appearing like they do in Figure 4-23. Notice that you have no idea what will happen when you click on any of those links. (Yes, I know he uses language that makes it clear, but the appearance of the links themselves tells you nothing.)

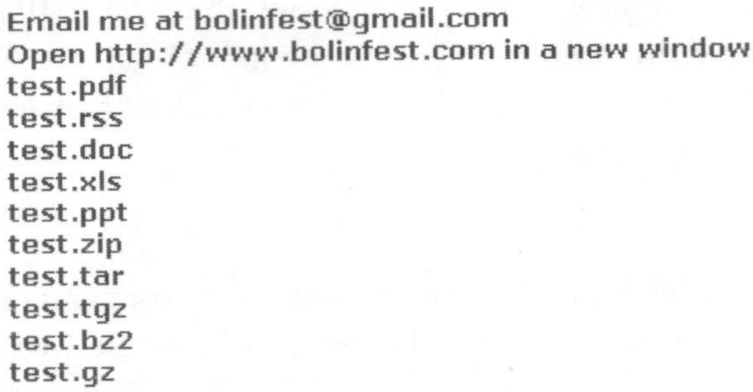

```
Email me at bolinfest@gmail.com
Open http://www.bolinfest.com in a new window
test.pdf
test.rss
test.doc
test.xls
test.ppt
test.zip
test.tar
test.tgz
test.bz2
test.gz
```

FIGURE 4-23. Before you install TargetAlert, it's impossible to tell what will happen when you click on one of these links.

To install TargetAlert, go back to *http://www.bolinfest.com/targetalert/download.html* and press Install. Firefox will ask you to give the OK that the site is safe, and then you can install the extension. Restart Firefox when the installation is complete. Now go back to the same URL again. This time a small icon is displayed next to each link, as shown in Figure 4-24, and it's clear what each link will do if you click on it.

I can't think why you'd want to disable any of TargetAlert's icons, but you can if you want to. To configure TargetAlert, go to Tools → Extensions, select TargetAlert, and press Options. You can toggle the indicators off and on, so that, for instance, PDF links don't advertise themselves as such.

TargetAlert has really helped me as I cruise about the Web, since now I know what I'm getting before I click on a link. Until all web developers realize that it's polite to make it clear to users what links are going to do, our only hope is an extension like TargetAlert.

Email me at bolinfest@gmail.com ▤

Open http://www.bolinfest.com in a new window ⧉

test.pdf 🄰

test.rss `XML`

test.doc 🅦

test.xls 🗷

test.ppt 🄲

test.zip 🗗

test.tar 🗗

test.tgz 🗗

test.bz2 🗗

test.gz 🗗

FIGURE 4-24. After you've installed TargetAlert, it's obvious what will happen when you click on a link.

ForecastFox

Most people like to keep an eye on the weather forecast, even if it's just to know how to dress for the day. Of course, there are many web pages that provide weather data, and there are programs that will display weather info on your Windows desktop or taskbar. There are problems with all three of these approaches, though: it can be a chore to have to load a web page just to check the weather, your desktop is usually covered up by programs you're running, and a cluttered taskbar is generally the last thing anyone wants. The ForecastFox extension is a great solution—it allows you to view the weather in Firefox's Status Bar, so the forecast is constantly (yet unobtrusively) available while you're using the Web.

To get ForecastFox on your PC, open Tools → Extensions, then go to the News Reading area of Mozilla Update (or search) and find ForecastFox. Install it and restart Firefox. After installing ForecastFox, you have to configure it so that it will show your local weather. Open ForecastFox's Options window (go to Tools → Extensions, select ForecastFox, and press Options), and you'll be asked for your location, as shown in Figure 4-25.

If you enter a Zip Code in the Forecast Location area, ForecastFox will probably work just fine. However, if you really want to be accurate, press the Find Code button. The ForecastFox Location Search window will open and ask you to type in a location (such as "Atlanta" or "Paris,

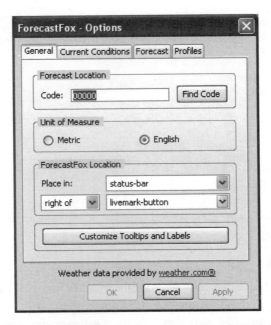

FIGURE 4-25. Tell ForecastFox where you live and where you want it to reside.

France"). In my case, I entered "St. Louis" and pressed Search. In a moment, ForecastFox reported back that it had found four locations with that name, in Canada, MI, MO, and OK. Since I live in St. Louis, MO, I chose that one and pressed OK. The window closed, and my Forecast Location code was automatically entered as USMO0787.

Change in the weather

There are more things you can customize in ForecastFox's options, but all you need to get going is a location. Feel free to play with the other settings and customize it to your liking. In particular, I recommend going to the Forecast tab and increasing the Forecasted Days from 2 to 3, as well as checking Show Labels so you can see the temperature.

ForecastFox sits in the righthand side of Firefox's Status Bar, by default. If you have the Firefox browser maximized, that will be just above the clock in your Windows taskbar. However, you can change where it sits in the ForecastFox Location portion of the Options dialog. You can also control what data it presents to you and the level of detail. Once you've finished customizing ForecastFox, press OK.

I told ForecastFox to display the weather information in my Status Bar, so Figure 4-26 shows what I see in the bottom-right corner of my Firefox window (my, it's yucky weather in St. Louis!).

FIGURE 4-26. ForecastFox sits in Firefox's Status Bar.

Every two times that ForecastFox refreshes its data, it also pops up a little alert window with the latest weather and an icon representing current conditions, as seen in Figure 4-27. You can click on the alert to make it disappear immediately, but if you leave it alone for a few seconds, it will close automatically.

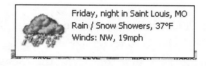

FIGURE 4-27. ForecastFox periodically pops up an alert with the latest weather.

Fun

Not everything has to be about work. Sometimes, as with themes, you just want to have fun with your web browser. Following are two extensions that certainly are not necessary, but are definitely pleasant additions to Firefox.

CuteMenus

By default, Firefox's menus—both those that appear when you click on the menu bar and the contextual menus that appear when you right-click anywhere in the browser—are pretty plain, text-only affairs. CuteMenus changes that, so you have icons next to many (but not all) of your menu choices.

To install CuteMenus, select Tools → Extensions and click Get More Extensions. On the Mozilla Update page, head to the Appearance section, find CuteMenus, and install it. Then restart Firefox and begin exploring your menus. Figure 4-28 illustrates the new icon explosion you should see.

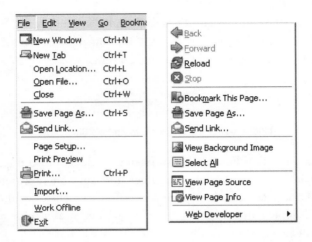

FIGURE 4-28. The File menu and the standard contextual menu...now with icons!

CuteMenus isn't a vital extension, by any means, but it can come in handy. After all, people learn to recognize pictures far sooner in life than they do words, so you may find that using the menus is faster for you now that you have pictures. Anyway, it never hurts to add a splash of color to your computing environment, so you might as well enjoy Cute-Menus.

CardGames

CardGames is not currently hosted at Mozilla Update (which is not to say that it won't be eventually—you may want to periodically check in the Entertainment section to see if it's been added). To get this fun extension, head over to *http://cardgames.mozdev.org* and click the Installation link to install the software.

After restarting Firefox, go to Tools → Cards, and a fresh game of Klondike Solitaire should open up in a new window. If you don't like Klondike, there are plenty of others to choose from, as Figure 4-29 shows (I like Spider Solitaire, myself).

Make an exception

Again, since this site isn't in the safe list, Firefox won't immediately let you download and install the software. You'll need to press the Edit Options button that appears in the alert box at the top of Firefox's window, add *cardgames.mozdev.org* to the list of allowed sites, and retry the installation.

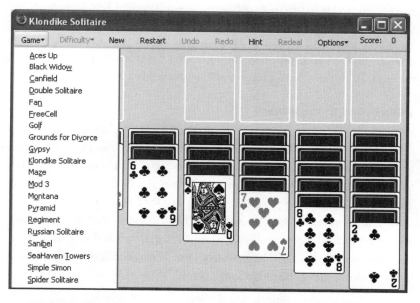

FIGURE 4-29. Enjoy any of 24 different card games with the CardGames extension.

This is actually a pretty sophisticated program, with undo and redo options, difficulty levels, animation, scoring, and hints. The customization options are pretty spartan: you can change the card size to small, and you can turn off animation. Still, how complicated can a solitaire game be?

Caveat Emptor

Most extensions are good things for your copy of Firefox: they'll add new features to it that you'll find useful and maybe even essential. But not every extension works well, or works in a way that benefits your web

Be careful

If you get fired for playing cards instead of working, I am not responsible.

browser. Always be careful when installing new extensions. Test an extension after you install it, to make sure that it works as advertised and doesn't cause problems. Read other users' comments at *http://addons. update.mozilla.org* before installing, to see if consistent problems are being reported. Also, install only one extension at a time—as I stated earlier, I know it's tempting to install 10 at a time and then restart Firefox just once instead of 10 times, but you're asking for trouble if you follow that method. In other words, practice safe extensioning.

Tabbrowser Extensions

With that said, there is one extension that I want to bring to your attention with a red flag: Tabbrowser Extensions (TBE), designed to provide almost-endless configuration options for tabs, and available at *http:// white.sakura.ne.jp/~piro/xul/_tabextensions.html.en.* Before I start getting angry emails from happy users, let me say that I have used this extension, and it worked for me...kind of. It did what it said it would, but I also experienced weirdness with some sites that, while I couldn't trace it back definitively to TBE, began only after I installed it. Once I removed the extension, things went back to normal.

Further, I have seen reports from users who had serious problems with their copies of Firefox after installing this extension—way too many reports to dismiss them. If you want to see some of these reports yourself, search Google for "tabbrowser extensions problems" or view the user comments for the extension at *http://extensionroom.mozdev.org/more-info/tbe/* or at *http://forums.mozillazine.org/viewtopic.php?t=47192.*

Finally, there is some justification to the statement that TBE is simply trying to do too much. There are over 100 settings in TBE, and it's not surprising that an extension of that magnitude sometimes causes problems for users, or even just confusion.

It can't be that bad

If you *still* don't believe me, go read this page on the author's web site: *http://piro.sakura.ne.jp/xul/_tabextensions.html.en#problems.*

I am not trying to denigrate the creator of TBE, and I'm certainly not invalidating the many positive experiences users have had with TBE. I'm just warning potential users that many others have found it to be problematic, so that you know to use it with caution and be on the lookout.

If TBE sounds like fun

If you want to get some of the features of TBE without having to install the extension, read mozillaZine's excellent "Extensions That Replace TBE." This is located at the URL *http://kb. mozillazine.org/index.phtml?title=Firefox_:_Tips_:_Extensions_That_ Replace_TBE.* (I use MiniT, because I like the ability to drag tabs to reorder them.)

Troubleshooting Extensions

If your browser starts acting funky after you install an extension, try to uninstall it. If you have any problems uninstalling an extension—if, in other words, choosing Uninstall in the Extension Manager doesn't work—read mozillaZine's detailed wiki page on "Uninstalling Extensions" at *http://kb. mozillazine.org/index.phtml?title=Firefox_:_FAQs_:_Uninstall_Extensions.*

If you're not sure which extension is causing the problem, go into the Extension Manager, then right-click on each extension in turn and select Disable from the contextual menu. Next, restart Firefox and re-enable the first extension. Restart Firefox again and test it. Repeat this process for each extension, and eventually you should be able to identify (and get rid of) the troublemaker.

If that doesn't work, you may need to take the more drastic measure of creating a new profile and starting from scratch (for a full explanation of profiles, see "Firefox Profiles" in Chapter 2, or go to *http://kb.mozillazine. org/index.phtml?title=Profile_Folder*). First close all running instances of

Firefox. Then back up your existing profile using MozBackup, as discussed in Chapter 2. Finally, open your command line (Start → Run) and type the following, which opens the Firefox Profile Manager:

```
"C:\Program Files\Mozilla Firefox\firefox.exe" -ProfileManager
```

Create a new profile and use it. Since this is a new profile, none of your bookmarks, settings, themes, plug-ins, or extensions will be available. Reinstall the extension that you suspect of causing trouble, restart Firefox, and test it. (Again, if you have no idea which extension is the culprit, you'll need to install and test them all, one by one.) Once you've identified the extension that's causing the problem, stop using it. Delete this testing profile and create yet another one. Do not install the troublesome extension! After creating the new profile, close Firefox and copy over these files from the original backed-up profile into the new profile's folder (if you don't know where to look, search your hard drive for these files):

- *bookmarks.html*
- *cookies.txt*
- *cookperm.txt*
- *userContent.css*
- *userChrome.css*

Open the Firefox Profile Manager again, using the instructions above. Select the newly created profile and check the box next to "Don't ask at startup" so the new profile will be chosen every time you start Firefox (i.e., so the Profile Manager won't bug you every time you open Firefox). Go ahead and press Start Firefox, and your browser should load. Again, you'll have to reinstall any plug-ins you've downloaded, your themes, and the extensions that work for you, but soon enough you'll be back up and running as good as new.

If you're *still* having problems, start Firefox in "Safe Mode," in which all extensions are disabled and do not load. To start in Safe Mode, click on Mozilla Firefox (Safe Mode) in the Mozilla Firefox folder on your Start menu, or open your command line (probably by going to Start → Run) and type the following (including the quotation marks):

```
"C:\Program Files\Mozilla Firefox\firefox.exe" -safe-mode
```

This will open Firefox without any extensions enabled. If you still have problems, you should uninstall Firefox, reboot, and reinstall.

Where to Learn More

I've given you a lot to chew on throughout this chapter, but there's always more to learn. If you want to investigate further anything I've discussed, the links in this section should help. Please keep in mind that the Web is an ever-changing environment, so links and sites may break or move. For such situations, you can fall back on Google (or your search engine of choice).

Plug-Ins

The single best place to go for information about Firefox (and Mozilla) plug-ins is the PluginDoc site, which contains a thorough discussion of the most popular plug-ins for Windows. If Firefox says it can't find a plug-in, head over to PluginDoc and look there. You'll probably find what you need.

PluginDoc also has a nice Frequently Asked Questions (FAQ) page for Firefox. It's not long, and it might be worth reading even if things are going swimmingly. It never hurts to learn as much as you can about your computing tools of choice.

Finally, some troubleshooting tips are contained in PluginDoc's "Before You Install" page. Some of it is a bit technical, but there are still a few helpful tips for beginners.

PluginDoc

> *http://plugindoc.mozdev.org/windows.html*
>
> *http://plugindoc.mozdev.org/faqs/firefox-windows.html*
>
> *http://plugindoc.mozdev.org/notes.html*

Themes

The official list of Firefox themes is at Mozilla Update. You can, of course, get there by choosing Tools → Themes and then clicking on Get More Themes. As of this writing there are 62 themes available, although more will undoubtedly show up over time.

Winstripe (the default) has received quite a bit of criticism; a piece written by "Jeff" is one of the most lucid and thoughtful critiques.

Themes at Mozilla Update

> *https://addons.update.mozilla.org/themes/*

Jeff's criticism of Winstripe

> *http://s95135199.onlinehome.us/2004/06/06/winstripe/*

Extensions

New extensions are becoming available for Firefox all the time, so in the following sections I'll point you to resources not just about the extensions I covered in this chapter, but also for those interested in searching out their own extensions to play with and use. For some more cool extensions, check out Chapter 5.

Collections of extensions

I have not tried all—or even most—of the extensions in these collections, so use them at your own risk. If you install one of these and your computer crashes, don't look in my direction. Use your head and install and test extensions one at a time, to make it easier to pinpoint the source of any problems.

Two articles on the Web discuss Firefox extensions in depth and contain within them a wealth of pointers to little-known (and many well-known) extensions. I highly recommend reading them and following any of the links that seem interesting to you. The first article, titled "A Guide to Firefox Extensions," was published on September 5, 2004, on the Flexbeta site. It's an excellent, quick overview. Slashdot, the online water cooler for nerds (and I count myself among that group!), picked up on the Flexbeta article and used it as a jumping-off point for a discussion on "Exploring Firefox Extensions."

As in your face as it gets

Be forewarned: the Slashdot discussion is long (currently nearly 500 comments!), detailed, and passionate, and many of the people involved in that discussion understand deeply the ins and outs of the unique Slashdot community. Consequently, things may be said that bewilder, anger, or offend you. You should still read the piece, but you might want to first read Wikipedia's discussion of the Slashdot community, at *http://en.wikipedia.org/wiki/Slashdot.*

Mozdev.org provides free hosting for projects based around Mozilla and related technologies, like Firefox. Currently, there are more than 150 projects there, and many of them have to do with Firefox extensions.

Mozdev is a pretty big site, but the designers have tried to make things as easy to find as possible. For instance, while it contains a full, 9-page list of all active projects (i.e., projects upon which someone has worked in the last 60 days), the list of the 50 most viewed projects might be more useful to you. In the spirit of generosity, Mozdev even features external projects that are not hosted at Mozdev but are considered worthy of mention.

And then there's the biggie at Mozdev: the Extension Room. Be prepared for an enormous list of 225 extensions just for Firefox. This list is kept up to date with what is apparently every known Firefox extension. All of them are placed into categories, such as "Blogging," "Bookmarks," "Configuration," "Navigation," and the always helpful "Miscellaneous." At the very top is a category called "Updated," for recently updated extensions; this might be the section to check first once you've started using this page. Keep in mind that this is not the official list at Mozilla Update, so it shouldn't be relied on 100%, especially since the extensions might not work with your version of Firefox. (Don't worry, though–Firefox won't actually let you install an extension that doesn't work with your particular version.) However, it's still an excellent resource.

Finally, if you'd like to keep up with the extensions I'm using, playing with, or just trying, check out "My List of Installed Firefox Extensions" on my web site. There are several that I just didn't have space in this book to discuss, which you might find interesting.

Flexbeta's "A Guide to Firefox Extensions"
> *http://www.flexbeta.com/main/printarticle.php?id=79*

Slashdot's "Exploring Firefox Extensions"
> *http://slashdot.org/article.pl?sid=04/09/06/1228202&threshold=3*

Mozdev.org
> *http://www.mozdev.org*
> *http://www.mozdev.org/projects/active.html*
> *http://www.mozdev.org/logs/top50.html*
> *http://www.mozdev.org/projects/external.html*

Mozdev Extension Room
> *http://extensionroom.mozdev.org*

My List of Installed Firefox Extensions
> *http://www.granneman.com/webdev/browsers/mozillafirefoxnetscape/*
> *extensions/installed.htm*

Individuals who have written several extensions

Jeremy Gillick creates useful, clever extensions with clear documentation, which is always appreciated. You can find the list of his work at "Jeremy's Mozilla Extensions." His work has been featured in many publications, as it should be.

Roachfiend's "Firefox extensions" page contains a good number of extensions for you to examine. Many of these are rather ingenious, like the Alt-Text for Links and Always Remember Password extensions. The same site also has a tutorial for those interested in learning how to make their own Firefox extensions, but be warned, you need to have a bit of web development or programming experience to do so.

Someone named Gorgias has also written a few good extensions, which he lists at "Gorgias's Firefox Extensions." There's not a lot here, and a couple of them have since been superceded by new features in Firefox, but his Add Bookmark Here extension is still very helpful. Take a look at it–you might find that it's exactly what you need.

In the "Caveat Emptor" section earlier in this chapter, I warned you about the problems that many people have reported with Tabbrowser Extensions, an extension that enhances tabs in Firefox in a zillion different ways. The creator of that particular extension has a page for his other work, titled "XUL Applications." There are lots of extensions there that may interest you, but be sure to read the author's warnings (click the Known Problems link on each application page) before you install them–many of these applications are bleeding-edge, and you could be the one who gets cut.

Jeremy's Mozilla Extensions
  http://jgillick.nettripper.com

Roachfiend's "Firefox extensions" and guide to creating extensions
  http://extensions.roachfiend.com
  http://extensions.roachfiend.com/howto.php

Gorgias's Firefox Extensions
  http://www.gorgias.de/mfe/

Piro Hiroshi's (the Tabbrowser Extension guy) "XUL Applications"
  http://white.sakura.ne.jp/~piro/xul/xul.html.en

Specific extensions

GoogleBar's home page contains good information about the project; in particular, the team has written a very good FAQ for its software. Since people can leave comments on this page and others, there is quite a long discussion under the FAQ that you may find helpful and informative. Note that the oldest entries are at the top, so bugs mentioned there undoubtedly have little relevance now.

What others have to say

If an extension is hosted at the Mozilla Update site (*https://addons. update.mozilla.org/extensions/*), there will be a link for Comments at the top of its page. Click that link to read and add comments about the extension.

GoogleBar with PageRank's home page points to forums and a mailing list, but at the time of this writing there's nothing there yet. Fortunately, the GoogleBar site should be able to cover most of your needs.

The Yahoo! Companion's home page provides lots of information about that extension.

McSearchPreview has a simple page up with a link to a message board where you can report bugs and ask for help, should you need it. If you want to bypass McSearchPreview for information about various sites, you can visit Alexa directly.

Michael Bolin's page about TargetAlert contains tests so you can make sure the extension is working.

ForecastFox's home page contains a good FAQ, along with a pretty long list of user feedback. If you're having problems, you can probably find your answer somewhere on the site.

There's not a tremendous amount at the CuteMenus home page, but then again, CuteMenus is a pretty simple extension. Still, if you feel like getting your hands dirty, there are a few advanced tricks listed there that you can try.

The CardGames home page doesn't really contain any vital information either, unless you want to track the changes that have been made to each iteration of the program. However, one thing it is missing is rules for the various games! The author explains that he copied many of the games from a Linux solitaire game named KPatience; the rules for several of the card games he includes can be found, therefore, at the home page for KPatience. A pretty complete collection of solitaire rules can also be found at Solitaire Central.

GoogleBar
> *http://googlebar.mozdev.org*
> *http://googlebar.mozdev.org/about.html*

GoogleBar with PageRank
> *http://www.prgooglebar.org*

Yahoo! Companion
> *http://companion.mozdev.org*

McSearchPreview
> *http://docs.g-spotting.net/code/mozilla_extensions/*

Alexa
> *http://www.alexa.com*

TargetAlert
> *http://www.bolinfest.com/targetalert/*

ForecastFox
> *http://forecastfox.mozdev.org*

CuteMenus
> *http://cute.mozdev.org*

CardGames
> *http://cardgames.mozdev.org*

Solitaire rules
> *http://docs.kde.org/en/3.3/kdegames/kpat/*
> *http://www.solitairecentral.com/rules/*

5

ADVANCED FIREFOX

've covered the basics now—how to install and configure Firefox, the browser's features and usage, and add-ons for Firefox that catapult it into the realm of truly great software—but in this chapter, I'd like to focus on some advanced topics. These things may not be necessary to your everyday use of Firefox, but if you learn and apply them, you'll find that you return to them often.

Searching

In the section "Navigation Toolbar" in Chapter 3, I discussed the Search Bar, which is a wonderfully useful feature in Firefox. However, the Search Bar is just the tip of the iceberg. Firefox actually offers users several search tools, making it truly, as one reviewer called it, the "Searcher's Browser."

Find in This Page and Find As You Type

What if you're trying to find a word or phrase in a web page you're viewing? In most browsers, you press Ctrl+F, which opens an annoying dialog box that you have to move out of the way of the text just so you can see what you've found. There has to be a better way, and Firefox has nailed it: the Find in This Page tool. To begin using this, press Ctrl+F or go to Edit → Find in This Page. At the bottom of your Firefox window, an alert bar will open, as shown in Figure 5-1.

FIGURE 5-1. Firefox makes it easy to find words in a page.

Even easier

The "Begin finding when you begin typing" option (Tools → Options → Advanced → Accessibility) lets you skip the Ctrl+F. If you enable this option, Firefox will automatically open the Find box and begin searching the page as soon as you type any letter.

No annoying dialog box for Firefox! Instead, the Find box appears at the bottom of the page, out of the way yet easily accessible. Now, you probably think you just type in the word or words you're looking for, and Firefox searches for them. You're right, but Firefox goes beyond that.

As you begin typing the first letters of the word you're searching for, Firefox immediately begins finding and highlighting those letters. For instance, say you're at an official Firefox web page, and you want to find the word "Firefox" on the page. Type an "f," and instantly Firefox jumps to and highlights the first "f" on the page. Type an "i" after the "f," and Firefox now jumps to and highlights the first instance of "fi" on the page. Add an "r" next, and then an "e," and now "fire" is the focus, which means you've probably found the word you were looking for: Firefox. Take a look at Figure 5-2 for a screenshot of what you might see.

FIGURE 5-2. Highlight each instance of a particular word on a page (the big orange "Firefox" is an image, not text).

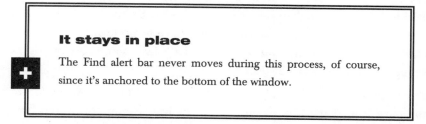

It stays in place

The Find alert bar never moves during this process, of course, since it's anchored to the bottom of the window.

This process of highlighting the letters, and eventually words, that you're looking for is called Find As You Type. Once you get used to it, you'll wonder how you ever searched without it.

But there's more! Find in This Page has a few more tricks up its sleeve. Take a look back at Figure 5-1. See the buttons for Find Next and Find Previous? Those allow you to move easily between instances of the word you're searching for, either down or up the page. Firefox highlights each instance of the word as it finds it, and they remain highlighted so you can see at a glance all the places where the word appears. You can use the Highlight button to toggle on and off the highlighting of your search words on the page, but I recommend leaving it on, as highlighting can really help you zero in on the terms you want to find.

Finally, the "Match case" checkbox does just that: if you check it, the word on the web page must match exactly with the word you typed. In other words, searching for "firefox" will not match "Firefox" if you have "Match case" checked.

If your search word isn't found, Firefox beeps and displays a note on the Find alert bar informing you that it's failed. The search text box that you were typing in also turns a dark pink, to further call attention to the fact that your search isn't working.

Firefox's in-page search tools are the best I've seen in any browser. It's amazing how simple, yet how effective, those tools can be, and the developers are to be commended. Excellent job!

Smart Keywords

Firefox (like its big brother Mozilla) also enables you to turn normal bookmarks into mini-search engines, through the use of Smart Keywords. So what are Smart Keywords and how do they work?

Let's say you constantly want to search my blog, The Open Source Weblog, but you don't want to have to go to the site every time you want to perform a search. Normally you have to go to *http://opensource. weblogsinc.com* to type in your query, but that's just too much work. Let's set up a Smart Keyword instead.

Point Firefox to the blog, at *http://opensource.weblogsinc.com*. At the top of the page is a search box. If this were a typical search, you would type "firefox" into the box and press Search, and then begin checking out the search results. Firefox, however, has a much more efficient method up its sleeve. Instead of typing in the search box, right-click in it and select "Add a Keyword for this Search," as pictured in Figure 5-3.

You will next see the dialog box shown in Figure 5-4, in which you need to set up your Smart Keyword.

theopensourceweblog

I'll show you mine if you show me yours

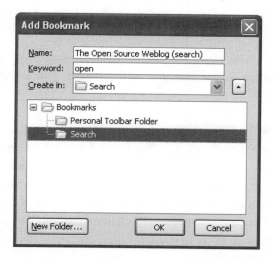

	Search
	Undo
Thursday, December 16, 20	Cut
	Copy
Dutch city of Haarlem switc	Paste
Posted Dec 16, 2004, 9:34 AM ET I	Delete
Read City of Haarlem and OpenOffic	Select All
switch:	Add a Keyword for this Search...
	Remove this object

Early in November it was announced that the municipal offices

FIGURE 5-3. Choose "Add a Keyword for this Search..." to simplify searching at this site.

FIGURE 5-4. Turn a normal bookmark into a super bookmark with Smart Keywords!

In the Name text box, enter the title of the site, but indicate that it's for search purposes by appending **(search)** at the end, like this: **The Open Source Weblog (search)**. Now you have to come up with a keyword, which will be used for all future searches of the bookmarked site. Enter your keyword in the Keyword text box. Since this is The Open Source Weblog, for the purposes of this example we'll use the word "open"; however, you can use any keyword meaningful to you. Finally, place the bookmark in a folder somewhere amongst your bookmarks, and press OK to close the Add Bookmark window. Now it's time to test your new Smart Keyword!

In Firefox's Location Bar (the place in which you normally see a web address, or URL), type the following and press the Go button or the Enter key on your keyboard:

```
open thunderbird
```

If everything has been entered correctly in the bookmark's properties, you should now be viewing the results page for your search of The Open Source Weblog, displaying a list of blog posts that mention Thunderbird, the open source email program that is Firefox's relative (they're both descended from Mozilla). Next, try some of the following searches by entering each one into the Location Bar and pressing Go or Enter:

```
open linux
open internet explorer
open mac os x
```

In each case, the search results page loads, ready to go with links to blog postings.

I use Smart Keywords as a way to perform fast searches of web sites that I use all the time. Once you get used to them, you'll start relying on them as well.

Smart keywords you'll love

Here are some Smart Keywords that I use. To add them manually, go to Bookmarks → Manage Bookmarks, then press New Bookmark and enter the following information.You can, of course, change the actual keywords to something you find easier to remember (the %s in each of the following is filled in with your search terms when you perform your search so make sure to leave it in):

Path	Location	Keyword
A9 (http://www.a9.com)	· http://a9.com/%s	a9
AllMusic Artist Search (http://www.allmusic.com)	http://www.allmusic.com/cg/amg.dll?p=amg&opt1=1&sql=%s	allm
AllTheWeb (http://www.alltheweb.com)	ttp://www.alltheweb.com/search?cat=web)=any&query=%s	all
Dictionary.com (http://www.dictionary.com)	http://www.dictionary.com/cgi-bin/dict.pl?term=%s	dict
IMDB (http://www.imdb.com)	http://us.imdb.com/Find?%s	imdb
Teoma (http://www.teoma.com)	http://s.teoma.com/search?submit=Search&q=%s	t

Path	Location	Keyword
Wikipedia (*http://www.wikipedia.com*)	*http://en.wikipedia.org/wiki/Special: Search?search=%s&go=Go*	wiki
Yahoo! Search (*http://search.yahoo.com*)	*http://search.yahoo.com/ search?ei=UTF-8&fr=sfp&p=%s*	y

Live Bookmarks

In the past few years, a technology named *RSS* (short for Really Simple Syndication) has taken the Internet by storm. RSS allows web sites to publish summaries of their content, so users can subscribe to a site's *RSS feed* (really, just a file that is periodically updated with the latest summaries) in order to be alerted if there is any new content on that site. If there is, a user can read the RSS feed and, if it looks interesting, click on a link that takes him to the web site, where he can read the entire post, article, or essay.

For instance, *The New York Times* makes its headlines available as RSS feeds, sorted by the various sections in the newspaper. I just checked the RSS feed for the Business section, and I see the following headlines:

- Credit Card Loyalty Put to the Switch Test
- Martha Stewart Gets an After-Prison Show
- I.B.M. Prepares Substitution for Pensions of New Hires
- "Retired" Rapper Finds a Job Atop Def Jam

Web logs are not made from trees

Web sites called *blogs*, short for web logs, are one of the principal drivers of RSS. Basically, a blog is a web site, usually written by one person, made up of short posts. The posts are arranged in reverse chronological order, so that the newest post is always at the top. Blogs tend to focus on a particular subject area, and they normally consist of lots of links and commentary. Think of blogs as self-published newspapers that anyone can write. (Of course, rules are meant to broken, so you can find blogs that break every one of the above prescriptions.)

Well, Martha sounds interesting ("Today we're going to learn how to make an attractive, functional shiv!"), so I click on the headline's link, and off I go to *The New York Times* article on Martha's future.

RSS is a fabulous technology—one that I use every day to gather news, opinions, search queries—and even cartoons. Firefox offers similar functionality via its Live Bookmarks feature. Live Bookmarks in Firefox are bookmarks to updated information—i.e., live content. Granted, web-based tools such as Bloglines offer far more features than Firefox's Live Bookmarks, but if you're an RSS newbie, I would recommend trying out Live Bookmarks to get your feet wet and then upgrading to a more powerful tool (such as Bloglines) once you get comfortable with RSS.

ATOMIC power

Another format has appeared in the past year or so that is complementary to RSS; it's called ATOM, and Google is its principal supporter. Firefox supports both RSS and ATOM, so you don't need to worry about which format a web site uses for its feeds.

To get started with Live Bookmarks, head over to The Open Source Weblog (*http://opensource.weblogsinc.com*), which is my blog dedicated to open source software for Linux, Mac OS X, and Windows (and yes, I talk a *lot* about Firefox). There's a link on the page to the site's RSS feed, but to be honest, it's kind of hidden amid all the other stuff on the page. Firefox knows that a lot of web sites are like mine, so it makes finding the feed super easy. Just look at the bottom-right corner of Firefox's window, and you should see a little orange box. Click on the orange box, and a short alert appears, as in Figure 5-5.

FIGURE 5-5. Live Bookmarks show up as a tiny RSS label on Firefox's Status Bar.

Select that alert, and you can bookmark The Open Source Weblog's RSS feed as though it were a bookmarked folder containing web pages. In fact, the Bookmark Manager's Add Bookmark window opens, allowing you to place the Live Bookmark anywhere you'd like. I recommend that you use your Personal Toolbar Folder, so that your Live Bookmarks are always available. In fact, you might like to create a special folder, called something like "Livemarks," for all your Live Bookmarks. Once you've placed the new Live Bookmark for The Open Source Weblog in the folder, wait a few seconds (perhaps more if you're on a slow network connection) for Firefox to download and process the site's RSS feed, and then click on the new Live Bookmark. Figure 5-6 shows what you should see.

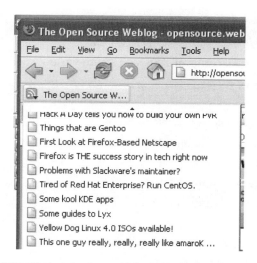

FIGURE 5-6. Live Bookmarks show each feed entry as a separate "bookmark."

Each of the menu items you see in Figure 5-7 takes you to a different post I made on The Open Source Weblog. The really cool thing is that Firefox will constantly update the Live Bookmark, so that new posts I make show up at the top of the list, while those on the bottom drop off over time. It's a bookmark, it's updated with live content—it's a Live Bookmark!

Some Great RSS Feeds

I subscribe to well over 200 RSS feeds, and these are some of my favorites. The first link is to the web site itself, while the second is for the RSS feed, should you wish to add it manually:

Slate (news, opinions, technology, arts, business, sports)
  http://slate.msn.com/id/2096678/
  http://slate.msn.com/rss/

Engadget (the latest in gizmos, gadgets, and toys for big kids)

> *http://www.engadget.com/*
>
> *http://www.engadget.com/rss.xml*

mozillaZine ("Your source for daily Mozilla news, advocacy, interviews, builds, and more!")

> *http://www.mozillazine.org*
>
> *http://www.mozillazine.org/contents.rdf*

Boing Boing (one of the best blogs on the Net, full of attitude, moxie, naughtiness, and chutzpah)

> *http://www.boingboing.net*
>
> *http://feeds.feedburner.com/boingboing/iBag/*

Here are a few collections of RSS feeds from various media outlets:

NYTimes.com RSS feeds (a collection of all RSS feeds, organized by paper section)

> *http://www.nytimes.com/services/xml/rss/*

NPR (links to audio of National Public Radio)

> *http://www.npr.org/rss/*

These are a bit different—use these search engines, and then subscribe to the results as a constantly updated RSS feed:

Daypop

> *http://www.daypop.com*

Feedster

> *http://www.feedster.com*

There are lots more where these came from. For a list of all the feeds I subscribe to, check out *http://www.bloglines.com/public/rsgranne*.

Counteracting Web Annoyances

The Web is a wonder of humanity, providing us with deep reservoirs of knowledge, fun sources of amusement, and amazing ways to communicate with folks all over the world. Unfortunately, it can also be the equivalent of walking down some streets during Spring Break in a party town: annoying, obnoxious, and even dangerous. In this section, let's look at some extensions that, my buddy, Ben Jones, once put it, "restore some sanity back to the Web."

IE View

Firefox is a fantastic browser, and I hope you use it the vast majority of the time you're on the Web. However, you may still have to use Internet Explorer every once in a while—maybe your bank requires it to do online banking, or perhaps some web developer has carelessly ignored common web standards and used proprietary code that needs IE to view it, or possibly your corporate intranet works only with IE. Things will hopefully get better over time, as Firefox and other standards-compliant web browsers gain market share and encourage developers to stick to the standards they should have been using all along, but for now, IE is still sometimes necessary. (Of course, Windows users can't get rid of IE anyway, since Microsoft has welded it into the operating system, but at least you can diminish its use.)

Oh, well

Not surprisingly, Microsoft requires Internet Explorer to access Windows Update. There's just no way around it.

IE View is an extension that helps alleviate the annoyance of hitting a web page in Firefox that requires Internet Explorer. To get IE View, go to Tools → Extensions and click on Get More Extensions. When the Mozilla Update web site opens, go to the Miscellaneous section (or search) and find IE View. Select IE View, and then click on the Install Now link.

Let's test IE View on a page that doesn't require Internet Explorer, but will still illustrate how the extension works: *http://www.mozilla.org*. Point Firefox to that web site. Once it loads, right-click on a blank area of the page. One of the choices you'll see in the contextual menu is View This Page in IE. Select it, and IE should open with the Mozilla home page loaded. Bingo! It's really that easy to use IE View.

FlashBlock

Whenever the subject of Macromedia Flash comes up on any of the various web developers' discussion lists I'm a part of, it seems that I end up in a flame war sooner rather than later. A lot of web developers have learned (I won't say "mastered," since that would be a false statement) Flash, and they want to use the shiny new tool in their tool belts as often as possible.

Oh, I'm sure you've seen the results on the various web pages you visit: overblown web site "intros" that people skip as fast as they can, confusing navigation schemes that are pretty to look at but impossible to actually use, and, of course, ads. Colorful, animated, annoying ads, calculated to distract you in every possible way as you're trying to actually read the content on a web page. Las Vegas in a web browser, here we come.

Now, just to stem the flood of angry emails I'm sure to get, let me make this clear: I'm not reflexively anti-Flash. Flash is a tool, and like all tools it has its place. Unfortunately, web designers too often misuse Flash ("too often" = 98% of the time), and it's that misuse that I'm protesting. For every great use of Flash, there are too many (for the meaning of "too many," see "too often" above) annoying uses of Flash that I just don't want to see or "experience."

The FlashBlock extension gives me the best of both worlds: it automatically blocks Flash animations (as well as animations in the Shockwave and Authorware formats, also owned by Macromedia), but it enables me to view a Flash animation that looks interesting with just one click. Install this extension, and you can bring some sanity back to your web-browsing experience.

To start the installation process, head over to *http://flashblock.mozdev.org* and click the Installation link. Select the version of FlashBlock for Firefox, add *flashblock.mozdev.org* to the list of sites that can install software, and finally press Install Now in the dialog box that asks if you really want to install this software.

After a few seconds, another dialog box will open, informing you that FlashBlock is installed and that you should restart Firefox. Press OK, and then close and reopen Firefox. Annoyingly (but it's only a one-time annoyance), you have to restart Firefox a second time to complete the installation of FlashBlock, so immediately close and reopen it again.

Now that Firefox is back up, you can test the FlashBlock extension by heading over to the mothership—Macromedia itself, at *http://www. macromedia.com*—as shown in Figure 5-7.

Cool Flash

Here are some great uses of Flash that you might want to check out. Keep in mind that the Web changes often, so some of these might not be there now:

http://www.angryalien.com

> "The Exorcist in 30 seconds, re-enacted by bunnies" and its many sequels, including "The Shining in 30 seconds, re-enacted by bunnies" and "Alien in 30 seconds, re-enacted by bunnies" (sensing a pattern here?).

http://www.trevorvanmeter.com/flyguy/

> The always wonderful FlyGuy is a surrealistic dream, a game, and a meditation on life. Do all you can to get to the end, and dance all night.

http://www.nba.com/history/timeline.html

> The perfect use for Flash: dynamic timelines. Follow the history of the National Basketball Association, from the 1940s to the present.

http://www.adgame-wonderland.de/type/bayeux.php

> Using images of a tapestry created in 1077 as its base, you can create your own medieval comic strip. Brilliant.

http://randomfoo.net/oscon/2002/lessig/

> Lawrence Lessig is the leading scholar and activist in the area of intellectual property reform in the U.S., and this is one of his best speeches. Flash enhances the speech in incredible ways. Do your duty and watch.

Nothing to block?

Of course, for FlashBlock to work, you need Flash installed on your computer. If you haven't installed Flash and don't intend to (or are a die-hard Flash fan and never want to turn it off), feel free to skip to the next section.

Preserve your customizations

FlashBlock will back up your current *userContent.css* file (discussed later in this chapter) in your Firefox *chrome* directory as *userContent-flashblock-backup.css* and create a new *userContent.css* file. If you have never edited *userContent.css*, don't worry about it; if you have, you will need to restore your changes in the new *userContent.css* file. If you have no idea what I'm talking about, you probably haven't edited it.

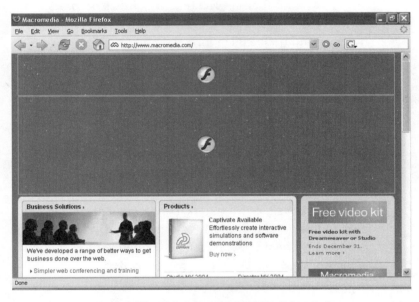

FIGURE 5-7. FlashBlock in action at Macromedia's web site.

If everything is working, you shouldn't see any Flash at all; instead, you should see boxes where the Flash animations would be, with the stylized "f" logo Macromedia uses for Flash. Move your mouse over that f, and the icon changes to the universal "Play" icon. Click anywhere in that box, and the Flash animation loads and starts working. Pretty cool, huh?

Click to play

FlashBlock doesn't remember which Flash animations you like and which you don't like, so every time you go to a web site that has a Flash animation that you want to view, you're going to have to click the Play icon. I don't find that limitation to be a big deal, but you should know about it.

Adblock

I find that the explosion of advertising on the Web in the past five years has really made it difficult to read the content on many web sites. The idea behind advertising is to grab your attention, but a lot of times my attention is so distracted by the ads that I can't focus properly on the site's content. The FlashBlock extension helps negate that problem, but only if the ads are using Flash for their display. What about graphical ads that don't use Flash? Adblock to the rescue.

To install Adblock, select Tools → Extensions and click on Get More Extensions. A new Firefox window will open, at the official Mozilla Update web site. Select the Miscellaneous category (or search), and on the resulting page, select Adblock. On the Adblock page, click Install Now. After installing, restart Firefox. If you want to go directly to Adblock's web page, head to *http://addons.update.mozilla.org/extensions/moreinfo.php?id=10*.

Adblock offers a couple of preferences that you'll probably want to set, since they'll improve your experience with this wonderful little tool. To configure Adblock, choose Tools → Adblock → Preferences, and then press the Options button. You should see something like Figure 5-8.

The one preference that I would immediately check is Keep List Sorted. Over time you're going to accumulate quite a long list—mine is over 200 lines and growing—and you may eventually want to find an entry, either to edit it or to remove it because you've made a mistake. Having the list sorted will make that task a lot easier.

Collapse Blocked Elements can be a handy setting, but you should be aware that it could change the display of web pages containing blocked ads. If the ad is contained in an HTML paragraph, for instance, Adblock

Not that there's anything wrong with that

It's not that I hate all ads. I'm fully aware that some sites get part or all of their revenue through the sale of ads, and I respect that. However, in the same way that I believe consumers have a right to use TiVo and other personal video recorders (PVRs) to skip the television ads that we find annoying or ineffective, I believe we have the right to block web site ads that we find annoying or ineffective. Notice the overwhelming success of Google's ad model: text-only ads that are relevant to your search keywords, or to the web sites you visit. Google's model makes sense, actually matches the users' interests, and isn't annoying, so I support it completely. For everything else, there's Adblock.

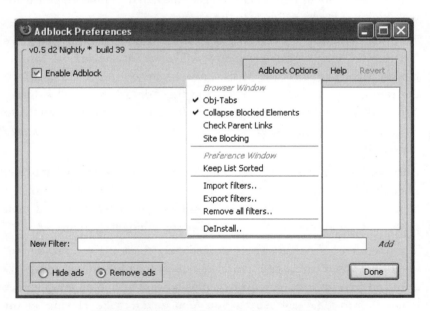

FIGURE 5-8. Configure Adblock to do its wonderful work.

will remove the entire element, and the text may reflow upward to fill in that space. It's not really a big deal, and I actually like how Adblock tightens up pages, but you should be aware of the potential.

If you have more than one machine, or you want to help friends who have just started using Adblock, you might be interested in "Import filters" and "Export filters." I use my laptop *Homer* most of the time, so my Adblock file on that machine is pretty extensive. However, my desktop *Dante*'s Adblock file is sadly anemic, since I don't use the machine as much. To help bring *Dante* to parity with *Homer*, I just choose "Export filters" on *Homer*, save the file as *adblock_filters.txt*, copy it from *Homer* to *Dante*, and choose "Import filters" on *Dante*. In just a few seconds, I have both machines blocking the same ads. Thank you, Adblock!

To see how Adblock works, check out my favorite web site for viewing and blocking gaudy, hideous banner ads: *http://www.gambling.com*. (No, dear readers, this isn't a site I frequent often—but if you're looking for a vast overabundance of flashing, beat-you-over-the-head banners, it's tough to beat!) Take a look at Figure 5-9—if you dare!

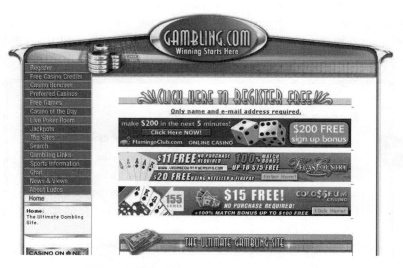

FIGURE 5-9. Gambling.com, before Adblock performs its magic.

Head to the site and gasp in amazement at the grotesque profusion of banner ads, the Web's equivalent of the mating of New York City's Times Square and the Las Vegas Strip. Aaaagh...I can't take it any longer—let's get those puppies blocked!

Right-click on the top banner ad on the page and choose Adblock Image. When you do, a dialog box will open displaying the URL for the banner image. At the time of this writing, that URL is *http://banners5. gambling.com/banner/files/468x60-2ACF1CDF.gif*. You could just hit OK at this point and block the ad served from this URL, but that wouldn't be very efficient, since you'd only be blocking that one ad. All the others would still show up, so you'd have to right-click on each one, choose Adblock Image, and then press OK. Too much work for us lazy web users, eh?

Fortunately Adblock supports wildcards, including the friend of every computer user, the asterisk (*). The * wildcard matches any character or characters, so it's both wonderful and dangerous. Be careful when you use it.

You can use the * wildcard to turn a long, overly specific URL such as *http://banners6.gambling.com/banner/files/468x60vcountry2ACF201F.gif* into more of a catch-all: *http://banners6.gambling.com/banner/*.* Now you're blocking all banners on the site. That's good, but you can do one better. Using the previous URL blocks banners from *banners6.gambling.com,* but *gambling.com* uses more than one server, so this is even better: *http:// banners*.gambling.com/banner/*.* No matter what server you hit on Gambling.com in the future, you won't see any banner ads, and that's very, very good news.

Express yourself

If you know regular expressions, you can use those as well. They're quite a bit more complicated to use than the * wildcard, but they're also a heck of a lot more powerful. If you want to learn more about regular expressions, check out *Mastering Regular Expressions,* by Jeffrey Friedl (O'Reilly).

Figure 5-10 shows that changes at Gambling.com are immediately apparent after just a few clicks with Adblock.

After you use Adblock for just a few weeks, you'll find that you see hardly any obnoxious ads on the Web. Peace and quiet will be restored, and you'll be able to actually read the content on the sites you visit without distractions and annoyances.

FIGURE 5-10. Ahhh... a quieter, less distracting web page after Adblock does its work. Now, where did I put my credit cards?

Not so loud

Sadly, Gambling.com has dumped the profusion of banner ads and is now a barebones, even boring, site. Ah well—the old, grotesquely, gaudy one lives on in this book.

NukeAnything

Most people are familiar with the idea of a "printer-friendly" link or button on a web page that opens up a new page or window containing a plain version of the web page, without ads or extraneous graphics. Unfortunately, however, many web sites don't contain printer-friendly links, and some web sites' so-called printer-friendly pages still contain ads or unnecessary images, which is tremendously irritating. NukeAnything helps you get around that issue, so you use less printer toner and end up with pages that are easier to read.

If you've been following along, you know what to do: go to Tools → Extensions, click Get More Extensions, go to the Miscellaneous section on Mozilla Update, find and install NukeAnything, and restart Firefox. Now let's nuke some annoyances!

Adblock Wildcard Examples

Here are some other examples using the * wildcard from my own Adblock file. Remember, my Adblock file may not be right for you, so just use these as guidelines:

http://*.doubleclick.net/*
http://*/RealMedia/ads/*
http://ads.vnuemedia.com/*
http://ar.atwola.com/*
http://content.ad-flow.com/ad-flow/*
http://graphics*.nytimes.com/ads/*
http://images.usatoday.com/sponsors/*
http://oz.valueclick.com/*
http://sp*.atdmt.com/*
http://ttarget.adbureau.net/*
http://us.a1.yimg.com/us.yimg.com/a/*

MIT's *Technology Review* is a great magazine with fascinating content, and I am grateful that many of the articles are available online. Recently it published an interview with Tim Berners-Lee, the inventor of the World Wide Web, at *http://www.technologyreview.com/articles/04/10/frauenfelder1004.asp*. That page is very busy, with sidebars, ads, pictures, and, of course, text. Fortunately, there's an icon at the top of the page labeled Print Version. Click it, and you get the page seen in Figure 5-11.

I'm sorry, but that is *not* a printer-friendly page. Three enormous ads (there's a third one further down, in the middle of the text)? And a large graphical logo? I should bill them for all the toner I'm using printing their so-called printer-friendly web page. Fortunately, I can use NukeAnything to get this page into the state it should have been in in the first place.

Right-click on the ad at the top of the page, and you should see a new entry in the contextual menu: "Remove this object." Choose it, and poof! The ad is gone. Do the same to get rid of the ad on the righthand side of the web page, then scroll down and nuke the ad in the middle of the text. Poof! Poof! Ahhhh. Now you have the page shown in Figure 5-12.

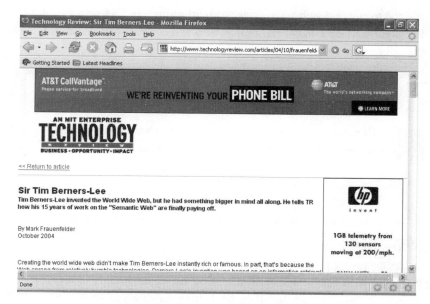

FIGURE 5-11. This is a printer-friendly web page?!

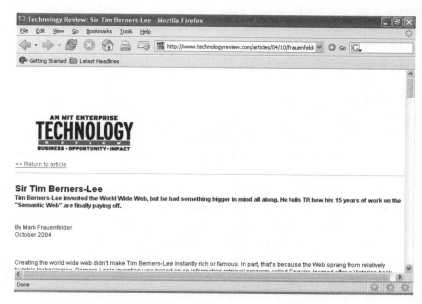

FIGURE 5-12. This IS a printer-friendly web page! Thank you, NukeAnything.

I'd probably also get rid of the graphical logo, but even with it in, this is a real printer-friendly web page. NukeAnything, however, is not just for printing. You can use the extension to get rid of any annoyance, even if it's just to make a web page easier to read online. In fact, you can drag to highlight part of a page, right-click, and select "Remove selection" from the context menu. Nice.

Your own private nuke

Of course, you're not actually affecting the web page on its server; you're just changing the local copy of the web page that's on your computer. So feel free to nuke anything you want—no one else is going to see your changes.

NukeAnything does a great job of getting rid of things, but you do need to be aware of one issue: you may nuke more than you planned. For example, you may think you're getting rid of an image, or even a column containing an ad, but then find that you've accidentally deleted all of the text on the page! This isn't a big deal—just reload the web page by pressing the Reload button, typing Ctrl+R on your keyboard, or choosing View → Reload, and then start nuking again (more carefully!). An undo feature for NukeAnything would be nice, but it's not essential since you can always reload the page.

TextZoom

As folks grow older, the eyes are often the first things to go, as I can attest. Consequently, the Web becomes impossible to use, due to the small size of many fonts on web pages. You can increase the font size temporarily in Firefox by going to View → Text Size → Increase, but when you restart the browser, the font settings will go back to the default. You can also change the default font size by choosing Tools → Options, selecting General, then clicking the Fonts & Colors button. In the Fonts & Colors window, change "Minimum font size" to a number you're comfortable with. However, the problem with this approach is that you can only select a font size in pixels (from 9 to 24), which is not always the best choice, since it's rigid.

TextZoom solves the problem of teeny fonts and also gives you greater flexibility than a hardcoded pixel size. To install it, select Tools → Extensions, click Get More Extensions, go to the Miscellaneous section of Mozilla Update, and then find and install TextZoom. Restart Firefox, and you can make your text readable.

Configuring TextZoom couldn't be easier. Choose Tools → Extensions, select TextZoom, then click Options. As you can see in Figure 5-13, you have two choices: use the default size of 100% or use a custom zoom based on a percentage you enter.

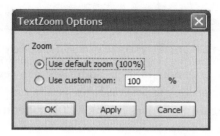

FIGURE 5-13. Make the default text on every web page a more reasonable size for you.

This is where TextZoom's flexibility comes in. Instead of a limited number of exact pixel sizes, you have the full range of percentage increments from which to choose. Select the radio button next to "Use custom zoom" and enter a percentage value that makes sense to you. Press OK and then cruise over to a couple of web pages that have been problematic. If they're readable, you're all set; if not, repeat the process and bump up the percentage until you're happy.

My eyes thank you, TextZoom!

Safety and Security

Perhaps the main reason folks are quitting IE in droves is that the browser is plagued with security issues. I'll make this short and simple: Firefox is more secure than IE out of the box, Firefox implements security features more intelligently than IE, and Firefox fixes security issues faster than IE. I'm not saying Firefox is perfect; I'm saying it's better. A lot better.

Hey! You're on a Secure Page!

Every web browser warns users if they are entering or leaving a secure, SSL-encrypted web page. Firefox is no different, as Figure 5-14 shows.

Similar alert dialogs open if you're leaving an encrypted page, if a page has a mix of encrypted and unencrypted content, if you're submitting form content over an unprotected connection, and so on. That's good. You want that in a web browser, especially if you're the kind of person

FIGURE 5-14. Firefox tells you if you've requested an encrypted page.

who doesn't pay attention to web addresses. However, Firefox goes beyond a simple alert box to let you know you're on a secure web page. Take a look at Figure 5-15—does it look a little different from your standard Location Bar?

FIGURE 5-15. Firefox makes it obvious that you're on a secure web site.

Most web users know that if they go to a secure site (such as Gmail or an online banking site) to enter or view sensitive information, the beginning of the URL changes from *http://* to *https://* and a little gold lock appears in the Status Bar at the bottom of the browser. These are nice indicators, but they're not exactly obvious to everyone—it's easy to overlook the little lock, and you may not always scrutinize the URLs in the Location Bar. Firefox fixes that problem. If you hit a secure site, you still get a changed URL and you still get a little gold lock, but now you get something extra: the entire address bar turns gold, and a little gold lock appears to the right of the URL. This is flat-out brilliant. Now it's easy to see, and hard to ignore, that you're on a secure web site.

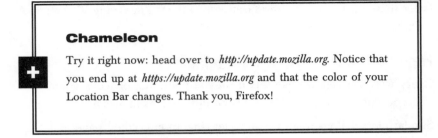

Chameleon

Try it right now: head over to *http://update.mozilla.org*. Notice that you end up at *https://update.mozilla.org* and that the color of your Location Bar changes. Thank you, Firefox!

Anti-Phishing Measures

"Phishing" is a growing problem on the Web. Basically, a bad guy sends you an email that appears to be from a bank, an ISP such as AOL, or an e-commerce site such as eBay or PayPal. The email informs you that there are problems with your account, that someone has been illegally accessing your funds, or that the company is performing a "security audit" (you get the drift). In any case, the email requests that you click on a URL and fill in the needed information on the company's web site.

You click on the URL, and the web page really does appear to be that of Citibank, or AOL, or Paypal. You fill in the asked-for information, including your username and password, your account number, and your credit card details, and then you hit Submit. Guess what? You just sent your most valuable information to a criminal in Russia.

Phishing works because the bad guys know how to obfuscate the URL of the web site you're on to make it appear that you're on Citibank's web site when in fact you're somewhere else. Here's a sample URL that illustrates the issue:

```
http://www.mozilla.org&item%20blah:4356abdc@evilhackerdude.com/
   gotcha.htm
```

Many users would see the *www.mozilla.org* part of the address and assume that they are on the Mozilla.org web site. The problem occurs because of the way browsers allow users to log into password-protected web sites. The usual method involves a URL of this form:

```
http://username:password@www.website.com
```

Take a look back at the phishing URL. See now how the username is *www.mozilla.org&item%20blah*, the password is *4356abdc*, and the real web site is *evilhackerdude.com*?

Phishing is a big problem, and it's getting worse. Fortunately, Firefox is smart enough to recognize if something fishy (phishy?) is going on. If you go to a site that has the *username:password* combination in the web address, Firefox opens up a dialog box similar to that seen in Figure 5-16.

That's smart—very smart. Firefox still allows you to use the *username: password* method for sites that are legitimate, but it warns you in a way that makes phishing sites obvious.

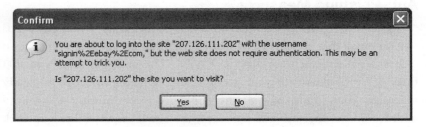

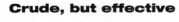

FIGURE 5-16. Firefox won't let web pages lie about who they are.

Crude, but effective

IE's solution? Just remove support for URLs in the form *username:password@www.address.com* completely. If you have a flat tire, abandoning the car will solve the problem.

Smart Update

I have to give credit where credit is due: Microsoft's Windows Update, introduced first in Windows 98, is a great thing. After all, if your operating system is that buggy and vulnerable to constant security problems, you should make it as easy as possible for your users to keep up to date with your never-ending stream of patches, fixes, and updates. To this day, Windows Update is a great first step to keeping your OS (relatively) safe and secure.

Other programs since then have realized the value of using the Internet to provide users with software updates, and Firefox is no exception. At any time, a user can go to Tools → Options → Advanced and press the Check Now button in the Software Update section to see if any Firefox updates are available. As nice as that is, though, most users will never remember to perform that action, so Firefox helps everyone out by automatically checking for updates, not only for the browser itself, but also for any browser extensions and themes that you have installed. If an update is available, Firefox displays a notifier in the upper-right corner of the browser, just like in Figure 5-17.

Different colors tell the user about the types of updates that are available:

FIGURE 5-17. Firefox lets you know if updates are available.

Green

Extension or theme updates are available, but they're not vitally important.

Blue

Extension or theme updates are available, and they're important.

Red

An update is available for Firefox itself.

If you hold your mouse over the notifier, a small tool tip appears stating that new software is available. Clicking on the notifier opens the Firefox Update window and immediately begins downloading information about any available updates. At that point, you can choose which updates, if any, you wish to download and install. What could be simpler?

Again, I have to give Microsoft credit for bringing the idea of simple online updates to a mass audience. And again, I have to give Firefox credit for, as it has in so many ways, taking Microsoft's ideas and improving them!

No More Killer Scripts

A programming language called JavaScript is widely used on the Web today, and it provides lots of useful functionality. Occasionally, however, a web developer will code his JavaScript poorly, or will only code it for IE and fail to test it in browsers like Firefox. This can be problematic. In the past, running these bad scripts might have caused browsers to crash, or to lock up and stop responding. Firefox takes care of that problem, as you can see in Figure 5-18.

FIGURE 5-18. If a script could potentially cause problems, Firefox will warn you.

If a killer script threatens Firefox, the warning dialog helps alleviate the problem. Feel like taking a chance? Press Cancel and see what happens. Things may be fine. I've tried Cancel before on certain sites, and after a moment, I was able to continue on my merry way. I've also seen Firefox crash, but that's not the browser's fault: after all, it warned me. If you want to preserve your browsing session, choose OK and drive a stake into that killer script. Follow that up with a polite email to the site's webmaster, asking him to test that page in Firefox. You may be helping a lot of fellow Firefoxers.

Advanced Configuration

In Chapter 2, I walked you through the essential configuration changes that you should make when you first start using Firefox, and in Appendix B, I cover the rest of your configuration choices in detail. In both cases, you use Tools → Options to access those choices. Firefox, however, contains within it a window to every possible configuration choice possible in the browser—I'm talking hundreds of possibilities now, far more than are visible in the Options window. Firefox even allows you to customize the browser's appearance and how it handles web pages, once you know where to look.

Or maybe wear gloves

I'm going to show you some files and settings in Firefox that are potentially dangerous, so be careful! Better still, back up your profile using MozBackup, which I covered in Chapter 2, before trying anything in this section. If something goes wrong, you can just revert to a good profile, and then try again.

The Secret Options

To access a wealth of options, simply type the following in Firefox's Location Bar and either press Enter on your keyboard or the Go button (make sure you include the colon):

```
about:config
```

Once you do so, your Firefox window should display an enormous list resembling that in Figure 5-19.

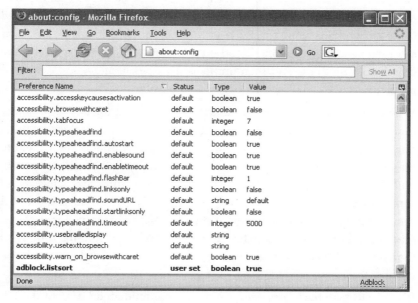

FIGURE 5-19. about:config exposes every possible Firefox option.

If you double-click on some lines, you instantly toggle the data listed in the Value column. For instance, double-clicking on *accessibility:browsewithcarat* changes it from "false" to "true." In other instances, as with *accessibility: typeaheadfind:timeout*, double-clicking opens up a small window in which you can enter new values. In every case, changing a value causes the line to become bold and the Status to change to "user set," so that when you open up *about:config*, it's obvious which settings are the defaults and which have been manually changed (whether through Tools → Options or through this list).

To find all preferences containing a certain name, enter the character or word you're looking for in the Filter box, and the page will instantly change to show only preferences matching your search. To see the full list again, empty the Filter text box or press the Show All button on the far right of the line.

I'm going to walk you though one change; if you're interested in finding out about additional changes you can make using *about:config*, consult the "Where to Learn More" section at the end of this chapter.

Animated GIF images can be a real annoyance on the Web. If you've ever been to a web site and seen a little animation that says "Email me!" and then metamorphoses into an envelope that zooms off to the left, over and over and over again, you've been the victim of an animated GIF. Or perhaps you've seen a little man running in place, or a cat swishing its tail, or dripping blood on a Halloween site—in each case, the object does its thing, and then immediately does it again, and again, ad infinitum.

When someone creates an animated GIF, she can specify how many times it is supposed to loop. The choices are never (so it does its thing once only and then stops), a number (5, for example, which literally means loop five times and then cease), or infinity (lather, rinse, repeat). Unfortunately, a lot of folks choose infinity, forgetting that what seems sort of cute once grows horrifically annoying the 43rd time you see it. I don't know about you, but I find it next to impossible to concentrate on reading text on a web page while an email icon keeps jumping around in the corner. Movement is distracting—why can't web developers remember that?

It's time to take back some control over these animated GIFs! In the Filter text box, enter the following:

```
image.animation_mode
```

That should filter out all the other options except the one you entered. Once it's visible, double-click on it so that the Enter String Value window opens. In the text box, enter **once** and press OK. You've just told Firefox to display the animations of any animated GIFs it runs across once and once only, so you get to "enjoy" the show and then get on with reading the page's text. If you want to see the animation again, reload the page.

Three choices

Your choices for this preference are *once, none,* and *normal.* The first two are obvious; the last one lets the animation play as many times as its creator intended.

To test your change, head over to *http://www.hampsterdance.com/hampsterdanceredux.html*, the location of the world-famous Hampsterdance web page (yes, I know it's misspelled) that swept the Internet in 1999. If the hamsters dance but once, you're good to go; if the hamsters dance the night away, try, try again. I'm sorry, but this tip won't help with the annoying music, which will keep on looping and looping and...

It didn't stop the madness?

The method outlined here works only for animated GIFs. If the web page is using Flash animations, you need to use FlashBlock, discussed earlier in this chapter.

Tweaking the Firefox Interface

And now for the most advanced technique of all, one that really requires that you know *CSS* (Cascading Style Sheets) to get the most out of it. If you don't know CSS, you can follow along, but things might be a bit confusing for you, as you won't understand why these methods work.

Firefox is a web browser, designed to process web technologies such as HTML, CSS, and JavaScript and display the results for users. The developers of Firefox decided to walk the walk as well as talk the talk, so they made it possible for users to change the interface of Firefox (the "chrome")—both the GUI interface itself and the ways in which Firefox displays web pages—using those same technologies. That's right: if you know some HTML and CSS, you can actually change the way your web browser looks and behaves.

Be careful

I'm going to say it again, and I'm not going to apologize for being annoying: be careful! Please back up your Firefox profile using MozBackup (discussed in Chapter 2) before you make any changes, so you can restore everything if there's a problem.

The easiest way to edit the Firefox files that govern the user interface (UI) is to first install the ChromEdit extension, which provides you with a way to edit those files without having to first locate them on your PC. To install ChromEdit, use Tools → Extensions → Get More Extensions. Once on the Mozilla Update site, click on the Developer Tools category (or search), find ChromEdit, and choose Install. Restart Firefox, and you'll find an Edit User Files option under the Tools menu. Choose it, and you'll see a window like Figure 5-20.

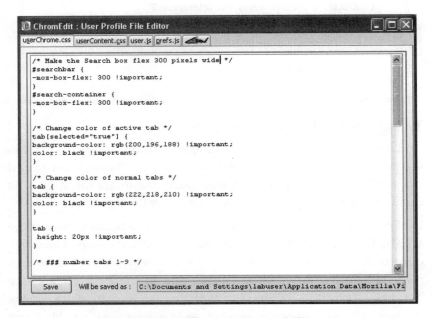

FIGURE 5-20. ChromEdit makes editing config files easy.

ChromEdit allows you to edit the following files:

userChrome.css

This file governs the user interface of Firefox itself. If you want to change how Firefox looks and behaves, this is the file to tweak.

userContent.css

This file controls how Firefox displays web pages. If you want to change how all web pages look and behave, edit *userContent.css*.

user.js

When you start Firefox, any settings in *user.js* are copied into *prefs.js*; thus, *user.js* settings are permanent, while Firefox may overwrite *prefs.js* at any time.

Make it stick

If you find that Firefox has undone a change you made using *about:config*, enter that change manually into *user.js* and it will become permanent. To make it easy, view *prefs.js* using Chrom-Edit, find the line that you altered using *about:config*, and then copy and paste it into *user.js*.

prefs.js

This file contains every preference used by Firefox; in other words, it is the file that you edit with *about:config*.

The possibilities for editing these files are almost endless, so once again I'm just going to show you one change you can make in *userChrome.css* and in *userContent.css* and provide further directions for your research in the "Where to Learn More" section at the end of this chapter.

Make a change in *userChome.css*, and you've changed how Firefox appears to you. Here's a simple change that many readers may find useful. If you find Firefox's menus (File, Edit, View, and so on) hard to read, you can change virtually any aspect of the fonts those menus use. Choose *userChrome.css* in ChromEdit and carefully enter the following lines at the top of the file:

```
/* Make menus more readable */
  menubutton, menulist, menu, menuitem {
  font-size: 125% !important;
}
```

Press Save at the bottom of ChromEdit, close it, and restart Firefox, and you'll see that the text used in Firefox's menus is now much larger, as shown in Figure 5-21.

Feel free to change 125% to any percentage that works for you. If you want to make the font even easier to see, change *userChrome.css* in ChromEdit as follows:

```
/* Make menus more readable */
  menubutton, menulist, menu, menuitem {
  font-size: 125% !important;
  font-weight: bold !important;
}
```

Once again, save your work in ChromEdit, close it, and restart Firefox. Figure 5-22 shows the results. Your menus will certainly show up now!

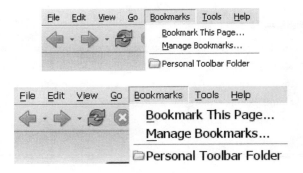

FIGURE 5-21. Menu fonts, before and after.

FIGURE 5-22. Menu fonts, now big and bold.

Now let's edit *userContent.css*, which will change how web pages look in Firefox. This next change is purely cosmetic, but it's also fun. I credit Jon Hicks, in his "Tweaking Firefox with CSS" post on his blog, with this idea. In ChromEdit, choose *userContent.css* and add the following code:

```
/* make form buttons prettier */
input[type="button"],
input[type="submit"] {
  font-size: 12px !important;
  font-family: 'Lucida Grande' !important;
  background: #eee !important;
  -moz-border-radius: 18px !important;
  padding: 1px 6px !important;
  border: 1px solid #ccc !important;
  border-bottom: 2px solid #999 !important;
}
```

Press Save in ChromEdit, close it, restart Firefox, and go to *http://www. google.com*. The Google Search and I'm Feeling Lucky buttons should look very different, as the before and after (top and bottom) pictures in Figure 5-23 show.

FIGURE 5-23. With a few tweaks to userContent.css, Google looks different.

The changes to *userContent.css* have changed the form buttons on every web page, so they're rounder, bigger, and easier to read (not to mention more fun). If you decide you don't like the new look, just delete the lines from *userContent.css* and restart Firefox, and things will be back to normal.

ChromEdit is an invaluable tool, as it gives you easy access to the advanced configuration files that Firefox uses. It's not an exaggeration to say that you can change virtually every aspect of Firefox using ChromEdit, some knowledge of HTML and CSS, and the contributions of thousands of smart, dedicated Firefox users all over the world. Go forth and tweak!

Contribute!

I've walked you through the ins and outs of Firefox, and I hope you've enjoyed learning about the fantastic browser that developers all over the world have worked on to bring to all of us. I'd like to close by asking *you* to consider giving back to the Firefox community. Here's what you can do:

Donate

The Mozilla Foundation is a nonprofit corporation, and they will certainly accept your donations. You can contribute money by check or electronically at *http://www.mozillastore.com/products/ donations/.*

Purchase

The Mozilla Store has t-shirts, CDs, books, mugs, and more for sale, at *http://www.mozillastore.com.*

Program

If you know how to program, working on Firefox is a great way to improve your skills and open up new job opportunities. Information for developers is located at *http://www.mozilla.org/developer/*.

Report bugs

Anyone can report bugs—even if you're not a programmer. It's not hard, and it is really appreciated. Best of all, you can watch as your bug gets addressed, and there's something really empowering about participating in that process. Let me emphasize again: anyone can report bugs. To do so, head over to *https://bugzilla.mozilla.org*, you'll see the web page pictured in Figure 5-24.

FIGURE 5-24. Use Bugzilla to report (and view!) bugs.

Spread Firefox

Tell your family, friends, coworkers, and others about Firefox. Help them install and configure it. Tell them to buy this book. Get the word out that there is a better browser available!

With your help, Firefox will keep improving. Let's work together to make what is already the best web browser in the world even better!

Where to Learn More

Advanced Firefox information can be found in a lot of places. Blogzilla, a blog about Mozilla, hasn't been very active lately, but the archives contain a wealth of good stuff.

If you want to keep up with new features as they are added to Firefox, make it a point to visit "Unofficial changelogs for Firefox releases," a volunteer effort to synthesize the lists of changes in new versions of the browser.

Blogzilla
> *http://www.deftone.com/blogzilla/*

"Unofficial changelogs for Firefox releases"
> *http://www.squarefree.com/burningedge/releases/*

Searching

The first place to go for more information about searching in Firefox is Mozilla Update, where you can find extensions that will take Firefox's already great searching abilities in new and interesting directions. I've also written several posts on The Open Source Weblog about various search tools and tricks for Firefox that you'll probably find useful.

If you're feeling ambitious, Mycroft's QuickStart page will tell you how to create your own search plug-in that you can contribute to the Firefox community. It's really not that hard. Finally, a Google query on "firefox search" produces a lot of hits pointing to interesting work in this area.

"Search Tools" at Mozilla Update
> *https://addons.update.mozilla.org/extensions/showlist.php?application=firefoxcategory=Search%20Tools*

Firefox and searching at The Open Source Weblog
> *http://opensource.weblogsinc.com/search/?q=firefox+search*

Mycroft's QuickStart
> *http://mycroft.mozdev.org/deepdocs/quickstart.html*

Google
> *http://www.google.com/search?hl=en&q=firefox+search*

Live Bookmarks

Mozilla has a nice informational page about Live Bookmarks that gives an overview of the technology and how to use it. Ben Goodger, the man behind Firefox, has posted his own thoughts on the feature on his blog.

Digging Bloglines

I mentioned Bloglines several times. It's a free, web-based RSS aggregator that works beautifully in Firefox. Check it out if you'd like something more sophisticated than Live Bookmarks.

Bloglines
  http://www.bloglines.com

Mozilla on Live Bookmarks
  http://www.mozilla.org/products/firefox/live-bookmarks.html

Ben Goodger on Live Bookmarks
  http://weblogs.mozillazine.org/ben/archives/006504.html

Extensions

For more on Firefox extensions, take a look at Chapter 4, where you'll find information on several great extensions as well as pointers on where to look for more.

IE View is developed at Mozdev.org. The site offers a very low-volume mailing list about the extension, but that's about it (which isn't surprising for such a simple extension).

FlashBlock's home page is also pretty bare, but that's OK—you install it, it blocks Flash. What more do you need?

Adblock's home page is intentionally grayed out to look like a blocked ad, which is cute but annoying. There's an FAQ page and a good forum that sees a lot of activity, which is no surprise—a lot of people hate ads, and Adblock does a good job of blocking them. Some people have exported their block lists and made them available on the Web, which can be helpful. There's even a collaborative effort under way by hundreds of folks to compile the ultimate Adblock list. Keep in mind that those lists may block things that you'd like to see, so be careful applying them.

NukeAnything was developed by Ted Mielczarek, but the only thing on his web site is an installer for the software. There are some useful comments that you may find helpful in the discussions about NukeAnything at Mozilla Update and the Mozdev.org Extension Room.

TextZoom is pretty simple, so its home page is pretty bare, but there are a few comments at Mozilla Update that are useful.

IE View
   http://ieview.mozdev.org

FlashBlock
   http://flashblock.mozdev.org

Adblock
   http://adblock.mozdev.org

Adblock block lists
   http://www.geocities.com/pierceive/adblock/ (once you are at this site, select *~instructions.txt*)
   http://aasted.org/adblock/viewtopic.
   php?t=284&sid=9bc3827a7354805b639dd8588ac1a563

Adblock collaborative block list
   http://aasted.org/adblock/viewtopic.
   php?t=45&sid=9bc3827a7354805b639dd8588ac1a563

NukeAnything
   http://ted.mielczarek.org/code/mozilla/
   https://addons.update.mozilla.org/extensions/moreinfo.
   php?id=79&vid=771&page=comments
   http://extensionroom.mozdev.org/more-info/nukeanything/

TextZoom
   http://www.cosmicat.com/extensions/textzoom/
   https://addons.update.mozilla.org/extensions/moreinfo.
   php?id=55&vid=809&page=comments

Other extensions

There are several other extensions that I would have liked to cover in this chapter, but either I didn't have room for them or I thought they were a bit too specialized. I'll mention them here as ideas for further investigation.

If you're a web developer, you should check out an extension named (surprise) Web Developer. It has everything you need to do your job, in one small package. Once you have that extension, you should also look at three further ones: Html Validator (with Tidy), EditCSS, and Color-Zilla. All are available in the Developer Tools area of Mozilla Update. If you can't tell what these extensions do from their names, you probably don't need them.

I'm generally paranoid when it comes to the Net, and an extension named SwitchProxy can come in handy if you want to hide your trail online. It's a bit advanced, but careful reading of the documentation at the extension's home page should allow anyone to use it effectively. You can find SwitchProxy in the Privacy and Security section of Mozilla Update.

Finally, if you'd like to keep up with the extensions I'm using, playing with, or just trying, check out "My List of Installed Firefox Extensions" on my web site. There are several that you might find interesting that I just didn't have space in this book to discuss.

Web Developer

> *https://addons.update.mozilla.org/extensions/moreinfo.php?application=firefox&id=60&vid=645*

Html Validator (with Tidy)

> *https://addons.update.mozilla.org/extensions/moreinfo.php?application=firefox&id=249&vid=1154*

EditCSS

> *https://addons.update.mozilla.org/extensions/moreinfo.php?application=firefox&id=179&vid=1258*

ColorZilla

> *https://addons.update.mozilla.org/extensions/moreinfo.php?application=firefox&id=271&vid=1032*

SwitchProxy

> *https://addons.update.mozilla.org/extensions/moreinfo.php?application=firefox&id=125&vid=1144*
>
> *http://jgillick.nettripper.com/switchproxy/*

My List of Installed Firefox Extensions

> *http://www.granneman.com/webdev/browsers/mozillafirefoxnetscape/extensions/installed.htm*

Security

The best place to go for information about Mozilla and Firefox security is, not surprisingly, the Security Center at Mozilla.org. There you'll find alerts, announcements, tips, and more.

One of my other writing gigs is as a columnist for SecurityFocus, the leading web site for professional security information. I wrote a column in June of 2004 that is still accurate today: "Time to Dump Internet Explorer." Check it out if you want to read a bit more about security in IE and in Firefox.

Noted columnist Nicholas Petreley has written an excellent analysis of the security differences between Windows and Linux; although not explicitly about Firefox, many of his conclusions about the open source operating system Linux apply equally to the open source web browser Firefox. It's long, but it's worth the read.

David A. Wheeler performed a similarly broad analysis in "Why Open Source Software / Free Software (OSS/FS)? Look at the Numbers!" Again, while not specifically about Firefox, his conclusions and his impressing marshalling of evidence make his paper required reading—especially the section about security.

Mozilla Security Center
>   *http://www.mozilla.org/security/*

"Time to Dump Internet Explorer"
>   *http://www.securityfocus.com/columnists/249*

Nicholas Petreley: "Security Report: Windows vs Linux"
>   *http://www.theregister.co.uk/security/security_report_windows_vs_linux/*

David A. Wheeler's "Why Open Source Software / Free Software (OSS/FS)? Look at the Numbers!"
>   *http://www.dwheeler.com/oss_fs_why.html*
>   *http://www.dwheeler.com/oss_fs_why.html#security*

Advanced Configuration

An older Mozilla extension (which appears to be no longer under active development) compiled what was then a complete list (53 printed pages!) of Mozilla preferences at "Documented Preferences." The list hasn't been updated since late 2003, but many of the preferences listed on that page apply to Firefox, and the explanations of the options are often excellent. mozillaZine's "About:config entries" provides a long list of preferences and their meanings, while its "User.js file" has a page or so of entries you can make to *prefs.js* or *user.js*.

For an enormous discussion of various "about:" entries that you can use, their advantages and disadvantages, and the best methods for using them, see the 24-page discussion at mozillaZine on "Firefox Tuning." TweakFactor has also published a great article—the "Firefox Tweak Guide"—with settings that you can change if you want to speed up your web browsing with Firefox.

"Customizing Mozilla" on the Mozilla web site contains suggestions for customizing the Firefox UI and web pages. In spite of the fact that the URL has "unix" in it, the tips work on virtually every operating system. For more from the Mozilla web site, see "Tips & Tricks."

Jon Hicks's "Tweaking Firefox with CSS" is an excellent blog posting that covers some clever, advanced tricks that users can perform with *userChrome.css* and *userContent.css*, and Daniel Cazzulino provides more tips on his blog in "Extreme browser customization." Pratik Solanki also provides some useful information in "Hidden Mozilla/Firefox/Thunderbird Prefs," but it's hosted on the ultra-annoying Geocities web site, so grit your teeth.

"Daihard's userChrome.css" focuses on changes you can make to Firefox's user interface. mozillaZine's "UserChrome.css Element Names/IDs" is a brief page listing key element names in Firefox that can be used as CSS selectors; if you have no idea what that means, don't bother going to that page!

Another good way to find examples you can use for your own tweaks is to search Google (or your favorite search engine) for *userChrome.css* or *userContent.css*, although I can tell you that many of the results you'll get for *userContent.css* have to do with blocking ads. Personally, I think Adblock is far easier to use, so I'd stick with that.

The ChromEdit extension's home page doesn't have much on it, but you can view a list of known bugs and enter any new ones that you encounter.

Finally, here's something fun. Enter *about:mozilla* into Firefox's Location Bar and press Enter. Want to know what that means? Read about it at mozillaZine's "New Chapter in The Book of Mozilla."

Finally, if you want to learn more about the notorious Hampsterdance, Wikipedia has a great short piece on it.

"Documented Preferences" at Mozdev.org
    http://preferential.mozdev.org/preferences.html

mozillaZine's "About:config entries"
    http://kb.mozillazine.org/index.phtml?title=About:config_Entries

mozillaZine's "User.js file"
    http://kb.mozillazine.org/index.phtml?title=User.js_file

mozillaZine on "Firefox Tuning"
    http://forums.mozillazine.org/viewtopic.php?t=53650

TweakFactor's "Firefox Tweak Guide"
    http://www.tweakfactor.com/articles/tweaks/firefoxtweak/4.html

"Customizing Mozilla" at Mozilla.org
    http://www.mozilla.org/unix/customizing.html

"Tips & Tricks" at Mozilla.org
    http://www.mozilla.org/support/firefox/tips

Jon Hicks's "Tweaking Firefox with CSS"
    http://www.hicksdesign.co.uk/journal/545/tweaking-firefox-with-css

Daniel Cazzulino's "Extreme browser customization"
    http://weblogs.asp.net/cazzu/archive/0001/01/01/FireFoxCustomization.aspx

Pratik Solanki's "Hidden Mozilla/Firefox/Thunderbird Prefs"
    http://www.geocities.com/pratiksolanki/

"Daihard's userChrome.css"
    http://daihard.home.comcast.net/firefox/tips/user_chr.html

mozillaZine's "UserChrome.css Element Names/IDs"
    http://kb.mozillazine.org/index.phtml?title=UserChrome.css_Element_Names/IDs

ChromEdit
    http://cdn.mozdev.org/chromedit/

mozillaZine's "New Chapter in The Book of Mozilla"
    http://www.mozillazine.org/talkback.html?article=3607

Wikipedia on Hampsterdance
    http://en.wikipedia.org/wiki/Hampsterdance

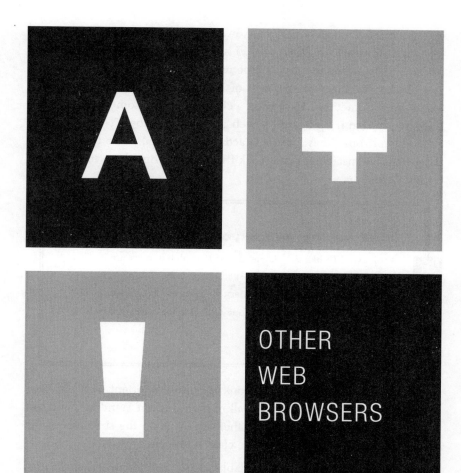

A + ! OTHER WEB BROWSERS

I love Firefox, and I hope I've shown you enough reasons in this book that you now love Firefox too. I also love my dog Libby, but I still have to occasionally spend time away from her; in the same way, I use Firefox for the vast majority of my web-browsing needs, but not exclusively. Sometimes I just want a change of pace, sometimes (increasingly rarely) I run up against a web site that just doesn't work right in Firefox, and sometimes Firefox is acting kinda wonky due to some new extension I've installed or new trick I've tried. During those times, I look to other browsers.

Just say no (when you can)

I still avoid IE like the plague, unless I absolutely must use it. This almost always means just one site: Microsoft's Windows Update, which forces victims to use Internet Explorer—the most insecure major web browser available today—to install security updates on their computers!

In the rest of this appendix, I'll look at some important web browsers that you should know about. Not all of them run on Windows, and this is often a good thing, as it allows them to focus on the strengths of the operating systems on which they've chosen to focus.

I can't cover every browser available today, as that would make this appendix the same length as the rest of the book. The following are some browsers I'm *not* going to cover. Feel free to check them out if you're interested:

Amaya (http://www.w3.org/Amaya/)

An open source browser sponsored by the World Wide Web Consortium (W3C), this is both a web page viewer and a web-authoring tool. It tends to incorporate new web technologies before most other browsers, which is not surprising, since the W3C is the source of the specifications for most of those technologies. Unfortunately, Amaya is an incredibly ugly browser that renders most web pages a bit strangely. As a demonstration tool, it's great; as a daily web browser, forget it.

AOL (http://www.aol.com)

The web browser built into the painfully ubiquitous AOL client software is really just Internet Explorer—a dumbed-down, reduced-functionality Internet Explorer, but IE nonetheless. Yes, even though AOL has owned Netscape for over half a decade, its software still depends on its biggest rival for its web-browsing engine. Amazing…but then, AOL never ceases to amaze.

Avant (http://www.avantbrowser.com)

This browser is just a fancy GUI on top of IE. You get all the underlying problems of IE—lousy security and anemic support for standards, principally—with a pretty shell. Not a big enough improvement to warrant its use, in my opinion.

Epiphany (http://www.gnome.org/projects/epiphany/)

In the same way that Avant is just IE with a pretty interface, Epiphany is Gecko, the rendering engine that drives Firefox and Mozilla, with an interface designed for Linux users who use the GNOME GUI. Translation for Windows, Mac OS, and Linux KDE users: if you'd like a totally bare-bones browser with no interesting features, or if you like browsing like it's 1996, you'll love Epiphany.

Galeon (http://galeon.sourceforge.net)

See Epiphany—the GNOME team has deprecated development of Galeon in favor of the above browser. Galeon is still under development, but its future is a bit uncertain.

iCab (http://www.icab.de)

Although this German-created browser for Mac OS has some interesting features, especially error reporting for incorrectly coded web pages, it's in use by only a tiny fraction of users.

K-Meleon (http://kmeleon.sourceforge.net)

K-Meleon is Epiphany for Windows users: a bare-bones shell around Gecko. If you want utter simplicity and few features, try out K-Meleon.

Mozilla (http://www.mozilla.org)

I discussed Mozilla at length in Chapter 1. It's not bad, but it's a big program, with a web browser, email program, address book, web page editor, and more. If you want a complete suite of programs, Mozilla may be perfect for you; if you want a lean, mean, extensible web browser, Firefox is a better choice.

MyIE2, now Maxthon (http://www.maxthon.com)
> Another IE frontend shell. See Avant.

Netscape Navigator 4 (http://channels.netscape.com/ns/browsers/archive47x.jsp)
> An ancient and awful browser—buggy, unstable, and with very poor support for basic web standards. No one should be using Netscape 4 in this day and age.

Netscape 6 (http://channels.netscape.com/ns/browsers/archive60x.jsp)
> Based on beta versions of Mozilla, this one should be avoided. Besides its bugginess, it's also heavily AOL-ized, with built-in links to AOL, AOL bookmarks, AOL Instant Messenger, and more.

Netscape 7 (http://channels.netscape.com/ns/browsers/)
> Netscape 7 isn't bad, if you have to use it—AOL has removed a lot of the junk that was in the way in previous versions, and also improved the interface. Interestingly, at the time of this writing AOL is working on a new version of Netscape...to be based on Firefox! (See *http://www.mozillazine.org/articles/article5691.html* for details.)

Now that those are out of the way, let's look at some web browsers that are worth your attention. There's a big, beautiful world of web browsers out there, and these are some of the shining lights!

Opera

If you're looking for a web browser that is fast, powerful, infinitely customizable, and supports just about every major operating system out there (Windows, Linux, Mac OS, FreeBSD, Solaris, OS/2, and even mobile phones!), Opera might be the web browser for you. As you can see in Figure A-1, Opera is not your grandpappy's web browser.

If you'd like to download Opera, just head over to *http://www.opera.com* and click on the Download button. (If you don't already have Java installed, check the box next to Include Java, but be forewarned that this adds another 13 MB to your download.) Opera's installation is an easy process, and you should be up and running in minutes.

Background

Opera was developed in 1994 by two engineers who worked at Telenor, the Norwegian phone company, for use on the corporate intranet. In 1995, the two left Telenor to start a software company that, with their

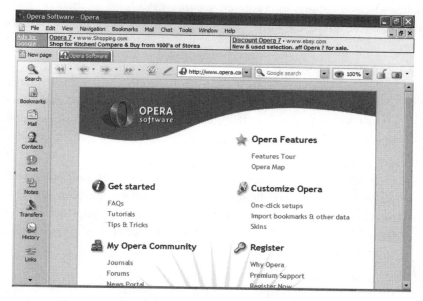

FIGURE A-1. One of the most innovative web browsers available: Opera.

former employer's blessing, focused on the web browser they had created. Since it was coded from scratch, it's always been a unique alternative to the IE and Netscape branches of the web browser family tree.

The first release that saw widespread use was 2.1, which came out in late 1996. Releases have been steady since then, and the current version is 7.5.

Opera has always cost a small fee to own—around $40 (upgrades are $15)—but starting with Version 5.0, released in 2000, users could instead download a free, ad-supported version of the browser. Over time, the included advertisements have changed from sometimes-obnoxious banner ads to pretty innocuous text ads served by Google. Some might say the inclusion of ads is a negative of the browser, but I think an ad-supported version is a reasonable compromise for users who can't or won't purchase the software.

What's Cool About Opera?

In addition to pioneering many of the features that most modern browsers now possess—such as searching directly in the Address Bar, pop-up blocking, skins (equivalent to Firefox's themes), and password management—its security record is excellent, to the point that several acknowledged experts in computer security use Opera as their primary web browser. Here are some of the other features that Opera offers its users:

Excellent standards support

Opera has always been focused on strong support for web standards such as HTML, XML, XHTML, the DOM, JavaScript, and especially CSS; in fact, one of the major contributors to the original CSS specification was an Opera employee.

Speed

One of Opera's big selling points is its speed at rendering web pages. Its proponents claim it is faster than other web browsers; I've never timed it, but I can say that the browser is quite fast. Faster than Firefox? I'm not sure about that, but it does display web pages at a nice clip.

Tabs

One of the many features that Opera pioneered was tabs. Yes, Opera was the first web browser to provide tabs for different web pages inside the same window. Those tabs can also be saved as a session, or group of tabs, that you can open later (Firefox offers similar functionality, no doubt modeled on Opera).

Zooming

Opera was also one of the first browsers to allow zooming, so users can change the size of text on a web page on the fly. Opera went one better than the others, though: zooming also changes the sizes of any images on the page.

Mouse gestures

The ability to control the browser simply by moving the mouse in a predefined motion is another pioneering feature introduced by Opera. (Firefox has extensions that support this feature.)

Others

Other special features include a built-in email client and a separate chat client. Also, if you want to use web pages for presentations instead of PowerPoint, it's easy to turn Opera into a presentation tool with just a few clicks. Another unique feature, which is obviously due to Opera's presence in the portable device market, is that a user can press Shift+F11 to see what the web page she's viewing will look like on a cell phone or other device with a small screen.

What Needs Work?

Opera is really one of the best web browsers out there. I think Firefox is better, overall, but I must credit Opera's excellence. That said, it has a few problems that you should be aware of before you start using it.

Opera has a very different interface from either IE's or Firefox's. Take a look back at Figure A-1 for a moment. The menus are different, with Mail and Chat prominent. There is a large set of text ads running across the top of the window (these go away if you purchase Opera). There are also several buttons whose functions are not clear. What is the camera icon on the right side of the toolbar? What is the wand to the left of the Address Bar? What are those icons doing running down the lefthand side of the window? And why does that bar on the lefthand side take up so much space?

None of this is really bad—it's just different. After using Opera for a short time, you'll find yourself used to all these things. Further, things like the panel down the left side of the window can be hidden if you desire, as you have control over the interface. Still, former IE and even Firefox users will undoubtedly experience some disorientation when they begin using Opera.

If its interface is busy, Opera's configuration options are positively over-whelming. There are over 20 different screens of options available to the user, and each screen contains lots of choices. Almost every widget in the browser can be right-clicked upon and customized further, as well. On the one hand, this profusion of options is perfect for power users, as they can customize Opera's behavior to the nth degree, but for normal folks, bewilderment might occur. Again, Opera will take some getting used to for many users.

Another slight drawback of Opera is that many plug-ins for viewing mul-timedia online need to be installed manually (Flash and Shockwave are designed to work with Opera directly, so no manual intervention is required). To install the QuickTime plug-in, for instance, Opera's web site instructs you to "Copy the npqtplugin.dll file from the Plugins direc-tory under the QuickTime installation directory to your Opera plugins directory." This isn't onerous, by any means, but some people are going to be lost with that simple statement. Let's hope that in the future Opera can negotiate more with the organizations making the major plug-ins, so they work more smoothly with Opera.

Camino

Mozilla and Firefox are great browsers for Mac OS X, but they suffer from a similar problem: neither is a native Mac OS X application from the ground up, so neither is built using the native Cocoa user interface. For Mac users, Cocoa apps tend to be slicker and more polished, and they act more like standard Mac OS programs. With this lack in mind, the Mozilla Project hosts Camino (formerly Chimera), a web browser that is essentially the Gecko rendering engine found in Mozilla and Firefox, but with an interface built using Cocoa. The idea is to have all the power, standards compliance, and compatibility of Firefox, but with the elegance that Mac users expect from their programs. You can see the results in Figure A-2.

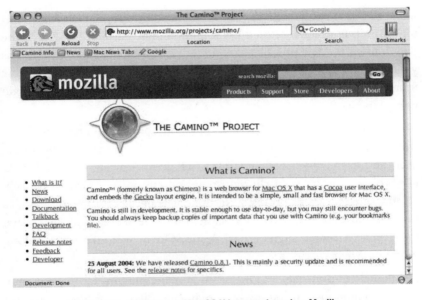

FIGURE A-2. Camino, a Mac OS X browser based on Mozilla.

To get Camino on your Mac OS X system, head over to *http://www. mozilla.org/projects/camino/*, download the disk image, install it, and go.

Background

Camino began life as Chimera in early 2002, but it was forced to change its name in March 2003 because a Unix-based browser named Chimera already existed. Camino is still being developed and shows no sign of slowing down.

What's Cool About Camino?

If you love the Mac OS X interface, you'll like Camino. In addition, Camino does a great job of supporting core Mac OS X features:

Rendezvous

> Apple has developed a new technology, named Rendezvous, that automatically detects networked devices and configures a computer to use them (it's currently being ported to Windows and Linux). Camino automatically detects any FTP or web servers on a network, as well as printers, webcams, and other networked devices.

Keychain

> The Mac OS X Keychain securely stores passwords for logging into web sites; Camino uses the Keychain to store and retrieve passwords, for more secure, simple web browsing.

Address Book

> Apple's Address Book integrates your contacts into one program that is available system-wide to any other program that wishes to use that data. Camino uses the Address Book when you're sending web pages to other people.

What Needs Work?

Camino is very much a project still under heavy development, so expect bugs, instability, and other problems. In addition, documentation is still somewhat lacking. Both situations will undoubtedly improve.

The bigger issue for Camino is its continued viability as both Firefox and Safari (discussed later) continue their development. It's always nice to have a choice among browsers, but Camino may get lost in the shuffle around these two well-known and well-marketed Mac OS X browsers.

Konqueror

You might have heard about Linux, an open source operating system that's been growing in popularity over the past few years (to the point that even Microsoft is starting to get worried). Since open source developers all over the world build Linux, and since one of the key principles of open source is giving the user choice, it should be no surprise that Linux users have many options when it comes to web browsers.

Firefox runs on Linux—beautifully, I might add—and so do Mozilla and Netscape. Browsers based around Mozilla abound as well, with names such as Epiphany and Galeon. There are also several text browsers, including Lynx and a similar browser called Links. One of the most important Linux web browsers—and it's available only for Linux and other Unix-based operating systems—is Konqueror, which you can see in Figure A-3.

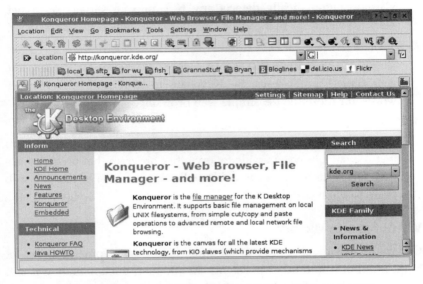

FIGURE A-3. Konqueror, one of the major web browsers that run on Linux.

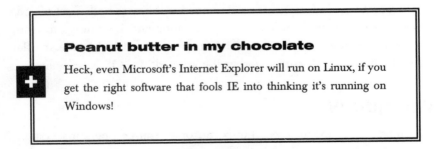

Peanut butter in my chocolate

Heck, even Microsoft's Internet Explorer will run on Linux, if you get the right software that fools IE into thinking it's running on Windows!

If you're running Linux and the basic KDE core system on your computer, you most likely already have Konqueror, even if you're using GNOME as your desktop environment.

Background

KDE–a GUI for Linux–saw its 1.0 release on July 12, 1998, but Konqueror was not part of it. It took two years, until KDE 2.0 was released on October 23, 2000, for Konqueror to see widespread distribution. Now up to Version 3.3, Konqueror continues to be an important part of KDE, serving as a web browser, file manager, FTP program, and viewer for a wide variety of file types, including images, text files, PDFs, and more.

What's Cool About Konqueror?

Konqueror does a good job of supporting basic web standards, such as HTML 4, JavaScript (mostly–90% of JavaScript-powered sites work with Konqueror, according to developers' estimates), CSS, the DOM, and SSL. Most plug-ins, including Java, Flash, and RealPlayer, work just fine in Konqueror; in fact, if it works in Netscape or Mozilla, it will probably work in Konqueror.

Konqueror's interface is modern, with support for a Google search bar, powerful bookmarking, pop-up blocking, and, of course, tabs. Tabs in Konquerer are themselves advanced, even without installing any add-ons: you can easily duplicate a tab, or detach a tab so that it opens as a separate window.

Several features that are add-ons for other browsers come built-in with Konqueror, and in fact are easily available on its Extra Toolbar:

Recovered Crashes

If Konqueror crashes, just use this drop-down menu to select which tabs you wish to reopen.

HTML Settings

Want to temporarily disable JavaScript? Java? Cookies? Plug-ins? Images? Change how Konqueror uses its cache? You can do all that and more with this drop-down menu. Select an item, and it's on; select it again, and it's off.

Translate Web Page

Chinese, Dutch, English, French, German, Italian, Japanese, Korean, Portuguese, Russian, Spanish. Convert web pages back and forth between those languages and never wonder what a web page says again.

Validate Web Page

Do you develop web pages? Do you want to validate your HTML, CSS, or links to make sure they're correct (you'd better say yes!)? Here's your tool, built into the web browser.

Change Browser Identification

Some web sites think that you need to use IE, or Netscape, to access their content. A lot of these sites don't know what they're talking about. Use this button to disguise Konqueror as another browser and Linux as a Windows or Mac machine.

Konqueror has several unique built-in features, including spellchecking of forms and the ability to split the window into multiple panes, both horizontal and vertical. You can view two pages (or more!) in the same window, or even view two places in the same page simultaneously. This can be quite useful at times, and Konqueror really makes it incredibly simple: just go to Window → Split View Left/Right or Window → Split View Top/Bottom.

What Needs Work?

Konqueror is a great browser for Linux users. There are a few little niggling issues that annoy me, however—for example, setting the home page is far more complicated than it should be. I realize that it's not hard, but it's also not obvious, especially to a newbie; in fact, I would argue that if you have to search Help to find out how to set your browser's home page, there's a problem.

Konqueror contains no support for bookmarklets (little bits of JavaScript code that are saved as bookmarks), because one of the developers has the strange idea that they are inherently a security hazard. In their stead, Konqueror provides a feature called Minitools—but finding documentation for it is worse than looking for the proverbial needle in a haystack. It *is* possible to run a bookmarklet if you copy its code and manually insert it as a Minitool, but how to do so is not at all obvious. Even if you finally get the bookmarklet's code installed as a Minitool, it's not nearly as convenient: a bookmarklet sits on the Bookmark Toolbar, where it is just a click away, but Minitools are by design at least two clicks away. Once again, we have major hoops that users must jump through in order to get functionality from their web browser. (Contrast that to Firefox, which makes things as easy as possible for the end user, while still preserving security.)

The Konqueror developers are to be commended for their work, but they should take a page from Firefox's book and make their browser a little easier to use. Doing so would catapult it into the vanguard of web browsers—on any platform.

Safari

In August 1997, a momentous deal was struck: Microsoft would invest $150 million in Apple, and in return, Apple would make Internet Explorer the default web browser for its Mac OS operating system for the next five years. Less than six months later, IE 4.0 for the Mac was released.

When IE 5.0 was released for the Mac in March of 2000, it was a break-through web browser, with excellent support for web standards—support, actually, that was way ahead of the Windows version of IE at the time—and innovative features that, again, the Windows version lacked (and still does!). Over the next few years, though, real work on the Mac IE browser pretty much stalled, as Microsoft contented itself with bug fixes and maintenance releases, culminating in the 5.2.1 release of July 2002. After that, nothing.

Meanwhile, Apple was hard at work on a browser of its own, to be based on the open source web browser Konqueror and named Safari. Steve Jobs announced Safari at the January 2003 Macworld Expo, explaining that the new browser was several times faster than the browser it was replacing, Internet Explorer.

June 2003 became a watershed month. On June 13, Microsoft announced that it was ceasing all further development on standalone versions of IE for the Mac, although it would continue to support the software for the foreseeable future and would still provide IE as part of its MSN subscription service for Mac users. The reason? According to Microsoft, it was Safari.

Today, Safari, pictured in Figure A-4, is the most widely used browser on Mac OS X.

You have to be running at least Mac OS X 10.2 (Jaguar) to get Safari. If you're running 10.3 (Panther) or later, Safari comes preinstalled with the OS.

FIGURE A-4. Apple's own web browser: Safari.

Background

Safari actually uses KHTML, the rendering engine created and used by Konqueror: Apple successfully broke past the "not invented here" syndrome and realized that it could make good use of open source technologies for its new browser, thus saving itself a lot of time and money. Furthermore, Apple has been very good about living up to its responsibilities under Konqueror's open source license and has been releasing its updates and fixes back to the Konqueror developers, so that everyone benefits.

Safari left beta in June 2003, when Version 1.0 was released. Version 1.1 came out in October of that year, for OS X 10.3 only. The current release is 1.2, available for OS X 10.3 only and sporting a number of new features and performance enhancements.

Apple has announced that the new version of Safari, due along with the next release of Mac OS X (codenamed Tiger) sometime in 2005, will include several new features, including a built-in RSS reader (for more on RSS, see "Live Bookmarks" in Chapter 5), private browsing (which doesn't record any information about the web sites you visit), the ability to easily archive and e-mail web pages, and searchable bookmarks.

What's Cool About Safari?

If you use Mac OS X, you can use other browsers, but you'll probably use Safari at least some of the time, if for no other reason than that it is the default on your operating system. Fortunately, Safari is a very good browser and is constantly getting better.

Safari includes all the usual features of good current browsers, including great support for web standards (including HTML, XML, XHTML, the DOM, and JavaScript), the almost-ubiquitous Google search box (almost ubiquitous except for IE, that is), tabs, a sophisticated bookmarking interface, automatic form completion, and pop-up blocking. In addition, Safari offers several unique features, including the following:

SnapBack

If you've ever sat down intending to look at just one web page, or search for just one item, and then looked up an hour later to realize that you've actually read far more web pages than you intended, SnapBack might come in handy. Click on the SnapBack button, and Safari jumps back to the last web page that you either typed into the Address Bar or chose from among your bookmarks. Pretty smart, actually.

Automatic detection of web addresses on a local network

Apple uses its innovative Rendezvous technology within Safari so that the browser automatically looks for and detects any web addresses broadcast by any web-enabled devices—such as printers, routers, webcams, and music servers—on your local network.

Automatic installation of downloads

If you download an installer for Mac OS X using Safari, the browser not only grabs it off the Net, but also unpacks it, installs it, and then cleans up any superfluous files...and it does all that in the background, without ever disturbing your web browsing. Slick.

Privacy Reset

Select one option (Safari → Reset Safari), and Safari erases your browser history, cache, download list, Google searches, cookies, saved names and passwords, and more. One click, and your secrets are safe.

As everyone who uses computers knows, love 'em or hate 'em, Apple is known for stylish, elegant, user-friendly software and hardware, and Safari continues that tradition.

What Needs Work?

Safari is good, but it's not perfect. It's a young browser, and KHTML still needs a bit of work so that it renders web pages perfectly. It's almost there, but some problems still exist. There are also some minor stability issues still to be ironed out—Safari crashes too often at this stage, but its crash reporting tool will help ensure that the number of crashes decreases as the browser matures. And of course, being open source software, it's constantly improving.

Frankly, the biggest problem with Safari is that it runs only on Mac OS X! It would be great if Apple ported it to run on Windows, but that will never happen. Ah, well—I can dream.

OmniWeb

OmniWeb is a Mac OS X–based browser that has changed in several significant ways since it was unveiled in 1995, and all for the better. In fact, it's now one of the most interesting browsers on any platform. The image shown in Figure A-5 doesn't really do it justice, as its simple exterior hides a plethora of really interesting, thoughtful, cool features.

FIGURE A-5. OmniWeb, an innovative web browser for Mac OS X.

OmniWeb runs only on Mac OS X, and it's available for download from *http://www.omnigroup.com.* You can try it for free, but it costs $30 to own, or $10 to upgrade. At those prices, it's a bargain.

Background

When OmniWeb came out in 1995, it wasn't that great. Oh, it had some interesting features, but reviewers and users criticized it as slow when rendering and displaying web pages. With Version 4.5 (released in the summer of 2003), however, that changed. OmniWeb dropped its proprietary rendering engine (the part of the browser that looks at a web developer's HTML and converts it into what you see in the web browser's window) and instead began using Apple's open source WebCore rendering engine, provided by Safari (which was itself based on Konqueror's KHTML). From then on, OmniWeb was able to offer both interesting features and an excellent, standards-based rendering engine. Its market share is still tiny, but more and more Mac OS X users are discovering this innovative browser.

What's Cool About OmniWeb?

As a fully integrated Mac OS X application, OmniWeb shares some cool features with Safari, such as synchronizing bookmarks and password management with the Mac OS X Keychain. However, OmniWeb is really a power user's browser. It will work fine for a web novice, but for someone experienced, OmniWeb offers many brilliantly thought-out features.

Tabs

OmniWeb's tabs are different from those in almost every other tab-enabled web browser. Instead of appearing in a horizontal row across the top of the window, OmniWeb's tabs run vertically down the left or right side of the browser window.

In addition, each tab displays a small thumbnail image of the web page currently displayed on the tab. This is a great way to facilitate quickly jumping to the tab you need (although users with smaller monitors set to an 800×600 resolution might complain, since things will be crowded). If you're going to use OmniWeb, you really need to have your resolution set to at least 1024×768 (virtually all Macs ship with at least this resolution today, so this shouldn't be a problem unless for some reason you need to work at a lower resolution).

Workspaces

Similar to Firefox's concept of bookmarking groups of tabs, Omni-Web allows you to save groups of web pages, tabs, and history in what it calls "workspaces." Interestingly, OmniWeb allows you to combine two or more workspaces into one, and even email a work-space to another OmniWeb user—a pretty smart innovation that Firefox should steal, uh, I mean, add.

Auto-saving of browsing sessions

Checking the box for "Auto-save while browsing" means that if you close your web browser, or if it crashes, your web browsing session is saved, including current open web pages, tabs, and browsing his-tory. Think of it as automatic workspaces, designed to save the day if bad things should happen.

Customized settings for each domain

Firefox allows you to set preferences for the browser, but Omni-Web allows you to set preferences for each web site. In other words, you can tell OmniWeb that *www.tinyfonts.com* should display with bigger fonts, *www.stuffidownload.com* should put all downloads in a special folder different from all other sites, and *www.popupsilike.com* should be allowed to display pop-up windows.

On-the-fly spellchecking

Safari has spellchecking, but it checks spelling only when you ask it to—and you have to ask it for every single form field on a web page! This is tedious, and OmniWeb knows it, so it offers automatic spell-checking for every form field on a page.

Zoomed Text Editor

This is a wonderful feature, which I would love to see in Firefox. Have you ever tried to type inside a text box on a web page, only to find that the small area made it difficult to see what you had written just a few sentences previously? OmniWeb allows you to click inside a text box and zoom the box into a normal-sized text editor, so that you can see everything you're writing. You have to see it to fully understand it; once you do, you'll want it!

What Needs Work?

OmniWeb's biggest problem, as with Safari, is that it runs only on Mac OS X. I want OmniWeb for Windows and Linux; barring that, I'd love it if the Firefox developers incorporated some of OmniWeb's more inno-vative and useful features into Firefox.

That said, OmniWeb does have some issues. The speed at which it renders web pages is a bit slow, especially compared to Safari. It's not terrible, but it is noticeable. Furthermore, since Safari and OmniWeb share the same KHTML rendering engine, they also have the same problems rendering some web pages—especially those that are resolutely IE-only (boo! hiss!).

Finally, stability is a problem, more so than with Safari. OmniWeb sometimes crashes suddenly, especially when you're working with lots of open tabs and lots of pages. That's where "Auto-save while browsing," discussed previously, comes in handy.

Lynx

First released in July 1993, Lynx (see Figure A-6) was originally designed for Unix-based computers, but it will now run on Windows if you install the version found at *http://csant.info/lynx/*.

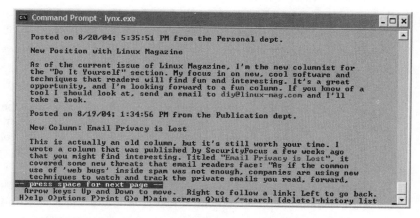

FIGURE A-6. Lynx, the text-only web browser, on my web site's home page.

Oh my gosh! Where are the pictures? Where's the styled text? Where are the colors? Is something broken?

Nope, nothing is broken. Lynx is a text-only browser: it doesn't display pictures, or fancy fonts, or anything other than plain text. You can't even use a mouse with it; to move around, you use arrow keys; to follow a link, you press Enter. It's not too difficult once you get used to it. Really!

Background

Lynx was developed at The University of Kansas in the early 1990s. Although it began life on Unix, it's been ported to other operating systems, including DOS, VMS, Mac OS, and, of course, Windows. In 1995, Lynx was released under the GPL, a free software license, and it is now maintained by a group of volunteers working in collaboration.

Its primary competitors in the text-only browser space are Links, ELinks, and w3m. All are free, so it's not a problem to try out all of them and pick the one you like.

What's Cool About Lynx?

I'm sure many of you are wondering why anyone would use such a browser when Firefox and other browsers with beautiful GUIs are available. Actually, there are a number of good reasons:

Speed
> Since Lynx doesn't render images, Java applets, movies, or anything, really, except text, pages load *really* fast. If you want to cruise around the Web on a rocket instead of in a sports car, try out Lynx. The Web ain't pretty that way, but you'll get what most web sites offer—text—and quickly!

Slow Internet connections
> Bogged down by a super-slow Internet connection? Lynx may be your best choice. It'll sure be a heck of a lot faster than any GUI-based web browser.

Accessibility
> For a time, Lynx was used by a lot of folks with visual disabilities, since they could couple Lynx with a text reader and still access and use the Web. There are specialized tools that provide this service now, but Lynx can still be used to satisfy those needs.

> If you design web pages and want to know how people with disabilities see your site, fire up a copy of Lynx. You may be horrified to discover how antithetical your site is to good accessibility practices.

What Needs Work?

Lynx is actually very advanced for what it is. If you accept Lynx as a text-only browser, it will do a great job; if you absolutely must have a graphical browser, Lynx is unacceptable.

Where to Learn More

Wikipedia has a good list of web browsers, with links to further articles about most of them, and a fascinating table that compares browsers and may help you in deciding which ones to use in various situations. An excellent historical overview of several browsers, including IE, Netscape, and Opera, can also be found on the Blooberry site.

An amazingly complete collection of web browser software, some dating back over a decade, is available for download at Evolt.org. If you can't find that web browser from 1995 that you miss, Evolt.org undoubtedly has it.

If you want to see the Web through the eyes of an ancient browser without having to install one, head over to Deja Vu and prepare for an astounding experience as you browse the Web as though you were using NCSA Mosaic, Mosaic Netscape, and others. Truly amazing—and it will make you appreciate what we have now all the more!

Finally, several good links to other historical browser sites can be found at the Google Directory page for Computers → Software → Internet → Clients → WWW → Browsers → History.

Wikipedia on web browsers
> *http://en.wikipedia.org/wiki/List_of_web_browsers*
> *http://en.wikipedia.org/wiki/Comparison_of_web_browsers*

Blooberry's historical overview
> *http://www.blooberry.com/indexdot/history/browsers.htm*

Evolt.org—download virtually any web browser
> *http://browsers.evolt.org*

Deja Vu
> *http://www.dejavu.org/emulator.htm*

Google Directory on Browser History
> *http://directory.google.com/Top/Computers/Software/Internet/Clients/ WWW/Browsers/History/?il=1*

Camino

If you're interested in some history, the original web pages for the Chimera project are still available on the Web. Camino's home page doesn't contain much, but you can find the essentials: news, downloads, links to documentation, and information about bugs. Don't forget to check out the Documentation section (especially the Tips and Tricks page), as it contains some good things to know.

Ars Technica has also published an interesting interview with Mike Pinkerton, the lead developer of Camino, that's worth reading if you'd like more information on the project.

Chimera
> *http://chimera.mozdev.org*

Camino's home page
> *http://www.mozilla.org/projects/camino/*

Camino Documentation
> *http://www.mozilla.org/projects/camino/docs/*

Camino Tips and Tricks
> *http://www.mozilla.org/products/camino/features/tipsTricks.html*

Ars Technica's "Interview with Camino Project head Mike Pinkerton"
> *http://arstechnica.com/columns/mac/mac-20040923.ars*

Opera

Opera's web site contains a lot to read and investigate. User help and support is very good; in particular, Opera provides an excellent, extensive overview of web browser security, including how you can configure Opera to be more secure (something that I wish more browser makers did). I mentioned plug-ins as an area in which users need help; not surprisingly, Opera's support pages have a special section on plug-ins and how to get them to work with the browser.

If you have any questions or problems with Opera, you should immediately check out Opera's support site. It really is excellent, with a thorough combination of documentation, tutorials, and a knowledge base—all searchable, of course.

If you want further help, you can try Opera's forums, where lively discussions on a variety of issues are available. If Usenet newsgroups are more your style, they're available too. If you just want the monthly news about the browser and the company, sign up for the Opera Newsletter.

If you want unofficial help, check out Opera7Wiki, where any user can contribute tips and tricks to the web site. There's a lot of good information there, including links to more Opera resources.

I covered some of the really interesting features that Opera offers, but there are more that I didn't mention; for the full list, see "Features in Opera." I think you'll be impressed by what you find there. A user has also posted his list of favorite features, which is an interesting counterpoint.

Opera's web site
  http://www.opera.com

Opera user help and support
  http://www.opera.com/support/

Opera security
  http://www.opera.com/support/tutorials/security/overview/

Opera and plug-ins
  http://www.opera.com/support/service/plugins/

Opera's forums
  http://my.opera.com/forums/

Opera on Usenet
  http://www.opera.com/newsgroups/

Opera Newsletter
  http://www.opera.com/mailinglists/

Opera7Wiki
  http://nontroppo.org/wiki/Opera7

Features in Opera
  http://www.opera.com/features/

Favorite features in Opera
  http://nontroppo.org/wiki/WhyOpera

Konqueror

Konqueror's home page is a good starting point, but you'll probably want to jump to information about its specific capabilities as a browser. If you're looking for the latest version of The Konqueror Handbook, you can find it online. The Konqueror FAQ contains solutions for various problems.

If you want to know more about Konqueror in general, Wikipedia has a nice page on the browser. David James has created a page comparing and contrasting Konqueror and Firefox; his site also includes an excellent collection of Konqueror tips.

If you want to set the home page for Konqueror, read the instructions in the FAQ. As I said, it's silly that it's necessary to read a help file to find out how to specify a home page, but that's the way it is.

You can find out more about Konqueror's lack of support for bookmarklets by reading the two bug reports in which the issue is discussed. The attitude of the Konqueror developer who refuses to implement bookmarklets is pretty much summarized in his own statement: "if you want it so much please submit a patch and convince the other konqueror developers to accept it. i won't do so as i have no interest whatsoever in bookmarklets...." As a result of this refusal, a new project has started to enable Konqueror to run bookmarklets. It's still early days, so we'll have to wait and see how successful the project is.

Konqueror's home page
   http://www.konqueror.org

Konqueror's features
   http://www.konqueror.org/features/browser.php

The Konqueror Handbook
   http://docs.kde.org/en/3.3/kdebase/konqueror/

The Konqueror FAQ
   http://www.konqueror.org/faq/

Wikipedia on Konqueror
   http://en.wikipedia.org/wiki/Konqueror

David James compares and contrasts Konqueror and Firefox
   http://david.jamesnet.ca/kde/fx_konq_compare.html

David James's Konqueror tips
   http://david.jamesnet.ca/kde/konqueror.html

How to set the home page for Konqueror
   http://www.konqueror.org/faq/
   #HowdoIsetmyhomepagethepageloadedonstartup

Konqueror and bookmarklets
   http://bugs.kde.org/show_bug.cgi?id=30302
   http://bugs.kde.org/show_bug.cgi?id=76423

A new project to enable bookmarklets in Konqueror
   http://konqlets.berlios.de

Safari

If you want to learn more about the problems in IE 5 for Mac, you have a few good options: a lengthy and well-documented list of bugs can be seen at MacEdition, while a good list of resources is at "Mac IE 5–problems with css rendering."

The home page for Safari can be found on Apple's web site. The page contains extensive information about Safari's features and a link to download the browser, but be aware that the latest version runs only on the latest version of Apple's operating system, which isn't a policy I agree with at all–Apple should make it available for earlier versions as well.

If you use a Mac, you should also use the excellent VersionTracker web site, which helps keep Mac users up to date with the latest versions of thousands of different software packages. This handy site will keep you apprised of any new releases.

Dave Hyatt is one of the lead developers of Safari, and his blog–Surfin' Safari–is required reading for those interested in the technical aspects of the browser. Since it's a blog, you can also subscribe to its RSS feed and keep up with it that way.

The always good Mac OS X Hints site also contains several tips and tricks for Safari.

IE 5 for Mac
> *http://www.macedition.com/cb/ie5macbugs/*
> *http://www.l-c-n.com/IE5tests/*

Safari's home page at Apple
> *http://www.apple.com/safari/*

VersionTracker on Safari
> *http://www.versiontracker.com/dyn/moreinfo/mac/17743*

Dave Hyatt's "Surfin' Safari"
> *http://weblogs.mozillazine.org/hyatt/*

Mac OS X Hints on Safari
> *http://www.macosxhints.com/search.*
> *php?query=safari&type=stories&mode=search&keyType=all*

OmniWeb

OmniWeb has a great web site, with lots of information about the browser, its features, and how to use it effectively. The writing on the site is cheeky and fun, which is always a plus.

Wikipedia also has a short page on OmniWeb that covers the basics. For updates, user comments, and more, see VersionTracker's page on Omni-Web.

For an excellent, thorough overview of OmniWeb 5, check out John Siracusa's review at Ars Technica. It contains one of my favorite tech review quotations ever: "Finding [this level of functionality] in a proper Mac OS X application from a respected developer with a proven track record is like finding a perfect 1/10,000th scale replica of the Eiffel Tower in a box of crackerjacks. Then the tower transforms into a tiny robot and makes you lunch."

OmniWeb's home page
   http://www.omnigroup.com/applications/omniweb/

Wikipedia on OmniWeb
   http://en.wikipedia.org/wiki/OmniWeb

VersionTracker
   http://www.versiontracker.com/dyn/moreinfo/macosx/3253

John Siracusa's OmniWeb review at Ars Technica
   http://arstechnica.com/reviews/apps/ow5.ars/1

Lynx

The home page for Lynx is pretty much bare, with just a link to download the software. To really find out about Lynx, you need to look elsewhere. A far better source of information, and the place I would go to first, is "Extremely Lynx."

Windows users interested in Lynx should visit CSANT.INFO (which also contains links to other sites about Windows and Lynx), while Mac users should look at MacLynx, which is irregularly maintained but available.

For a bit of background, Michael Grobe provides a personal look at the development of Lynx in "An Early History of Lynx: Multidimensional Collaboration."

Finally, there are several other good text-only browsers that compete with Lynx and are also worth looking at, including Links, ELinks, and w3m.

Lynx home page
> *http://lynx.browser.org*

"Extremely Lynx"
> *http://www.subir.com/lynx.html*

CSANT.INFO
> *http://csant.info/lynx/*

MacLynx
> *http://ccadams.org/se/lynx.html*

Michael Grobe's "An Early History of Lynx: Multidimensional Collaboration"
> *http://www.ku.edu/~grobe/early-lynx.html*

Links
> *http://en.wikipedia.org/wiki/Links*
> *http://artax.karlin.mff.cuni.cz/~mikulas/links/*

ELinks
> *http://www.elinks.or.cz*
> *http://en.wikipedia.org/wiki/ELinks*

w3m
> *http://www.w3m.org*
> *http://en.wikipedia.org/wiki/W3m*

B + ! FIREFOX OPTIONS

Back in Chapter 2, I went over the basic steps you should take to set up and configure Firefox. You have many options available to you when configuring Firefox, but I covered only the ones that are most important to change. In this appendix, I cover all the possibilities available to you when you choose Tools → Options.

When Firefox's Options window opens, you'll see five main buttons running down the lefthand side, with each button taking you to a set of configuration possibilities: General, Privacy, Web Features, Downloads, and Advanced. Let's look at all these in detail now.

General

General preferences are just that: as Figure B-1 shows, they allow you to change Firefox's overall look and behavior.

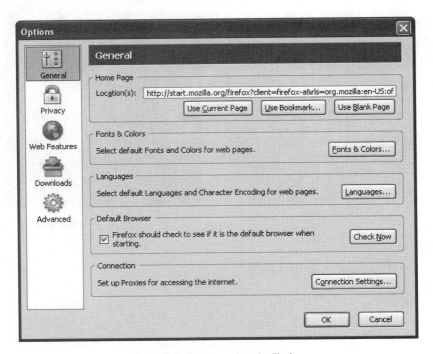

FIGURE B-1. General options for Firefox.

Your options on the General tab are:

Home Page

Sets your home page. This is covered in detail in Chapter 2.

Fonts & Colors

Controls how fonts appear. This is covered in detail in Chapter 2.

Languages

Specifies the default languages that Firefox uses. Since the Firefox download page offers you a choice of languages, you probably shouldn't have to change these; however, if you do, press the Languages button and make your choices. You can add as many languages as you want, and even place them in your order of preference.

A worldly browser

Don't worry about viewing a site in French, Spanish, or any other Western European language. Those should display just fine without any action on your part. In fact, most of the world's languages will "just work" in Firefox. You really need to change this setting only if you are experiencing a problem on a particular site. Wait until you discover an issue, then open this options screen, add the language you need, and see if that fixes things.

Default Browser

Determines whether Firefox should check to see if another browser has taken over as your operating system's default browser. This is covered in detail in Chapter 2.

Connection

Use this to configure a proxy, if you need one. A *proxy* is software that sits between your computer and the Internet, filtering all requests your computer makes. Companies often use proxies to keep their employees from accessing inappropriate web sites, but proxies can also be used to keep copies of frequently accessed web pages close at hand, which makes surfing the Web a lot faster.

If you need to configure your PC to use a proxy (most of you will not), you need to select the Connection Settings button and make your changes there. I can't really walk you through those settings, as the possibilities are endless. Ask your ISP or network administrator for the settings (if you even need them), and then enter the information as directed, or just try importing them from IE, as I discussed in Chapter 2.

If you do change your proxy settings, you may need to reset them when you connect to a different network (for example, when you switch between using your laptop at work and at home). In such cases, you may find it helpful to use multiple *profiles*, which are discussed in Chapter 2. Configure one profile to use a proxy server and the other to use none, and choose the appropriate profile when you start up Firefox.

Proxified!

It's possible that you're using a proxy without even knowing it. If you use a cellular network, or some hotspot or corporate networks, there's a good chance that all your web requests are going through a proxy that doesn't need browser configuration on your part (this is called a *transparent proxy*, since its operation is transparent to you). This proxy grabs web pages and images for you, shrinks them down to save bandwidth, and sends them back to your computer.

When you're done with the General options, you do not need to press OK; in fact, if you do, the Options window will close, and you'll have to reopen it to continue on with the Privacy options. Just press the Privacy button and continue.

Privacy

As I stated in Chapter 2, Firefox does a great job with its default settings for the Privacy options (shown in Figure B-2). However, you may still want to change things, depending on your level of paranoia (and remember, it's not paranoia if they really *are* out to get you).

Currently there are six areas in Privacy that you can alter: History, Saved Form Information, Saved Passwords, Download Manager History, Cookies, and Cache. These sometimes change—after all, Firefox is a product that is constantly being worked on and improved—so be prepared for some differences between what I say here and what you may see on your computer. Let's take a look at Firefox's Privacy options:

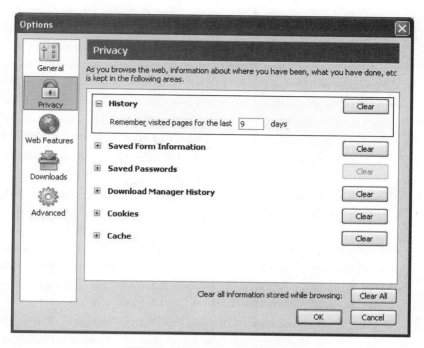

FIGURE B-2. Privacy options for Firefox.

History

This controls how many days Firefox remembers where you've been. The history can be useful if, for example, you'd like to go back to that web page you were looking at last Tuesday but can't remember the address for. To view a listing of your browsing history, select View → Sidebar → History. A sidebar will open on the lefthand side of Firefox, and you can look for the desired web page by date. This feature can be tremendously helpful, but, of course, it can also let people find out where you've been on the Web. By default, Firefox saves this information for nine days. Adjust this setting according to your comfort level; set it to zero days to disable History entirely. You can read more about the History Sidebar in Chapter 3.

Saved Form Information and Saved Passwords

Saved Form Information and Saved Passwords are both designed to act as time-savers. The former remembers what you've typed into form fields and helpfully offers to fill in those details in the future when you start working on another form, while the latter remembers login details on web pages you visit that require usernames and passwords. Of course, if you leave these options checked, anyone using your computer will be able to find out what you've been entering into forms and will also be able to get into sites that require you to enter your password. Note that unless you use a Master Password (discussed in a few paragraphs), all users of your machine will be able to view the passwords and will be able to sail right into sites for which you've already saved your passwords. (Are you starting to see that it's a good idea to use a Master Password?) If you're worried about these scenarios, make sure the boxes next to these options are unchecked.

If you want to see which sites have passwords saved, press the View Saved Passwords button so the Password Manager opens. The first tab—Passwords Saved—lists the sites for which you've saved passwords and the usernames for each site. If you realize that you either stored the wrong password for a site or no longer want a password saved for a site, select it in the list and press Remove. If you want to start completely from scratch, press Remove All.

If you press Show Passwords, the Password Manager will do just that: all your passwords will now be visible in a new, third column. This is obviously not a good idea from a security perspective, so you really should set a Master Password—Firefox will then prompt anyone who presses the Show Passwords button to type in the Master Password before it spills the beans. Once you view the passwords, the button changes from Show Passwords to Hide Passwords, but you don't really need to worry about clicking the button because Firefox will automatically hide this column again when you close the window.

Passwords Never Saved lists all the sites for which you've told Firefox not to save password information. If you find a site in here that you in fact want Firefox to store a password for, select it and press Remove; likewise, if you want to remove all those sites and start getting asked again about saving passwords, press Remove All.

Now, at this point, you may be thinking that the Saved Passwords feature sounds useful—and really, it is pretty handy—but it's not safe. If anyone can see and use your passwords, that's a problem. Fortunately, Firefox is already one step ahead of you. If you want to protect your passwords, press the Set Master Password button. You'll be prompted for a password that will act as the gatekeeper to all your other passwords. The first time you hit any site that has a stored password in Firefox, you will be prompted for the Master Password; enter it, and all passwords will be filled in for you automatically after that, for the remainder of your browsing session. In order to keep things safe, close Firefox when you're finished using it, so anyone else sitting down at your computer will be prompted for the (hopefully unknown) Master Password at the first password-protected site he visits. As a cool feature-within-a-feature, Firefox also provides you with a "password quality meter" that lets you know the strength of your password choice. Here's a hint: 12345 does not please the password quality meter!

Don't lose it!

Do not forget or lose your Master Password! It is unrecoverable, and if you lose it all the information you saved using it will be unrecoverable.

Download Manager History

Download Manager History logs everything you've downloaded using Firefox, including programs, PDFs, and any pictures on which you've right-clicked and then chosen Save Image As. Firefox includes a drop-down that lets you specify when you want to remove files from the Download Manager. Your choices are: "Upon successful download," "When Firefox exits," and "Manually." If you're extremely paranoid and don't want any record of your downloads left behind in that window, choose "Upon successful download"; if you're kind of paranoid, choose "When Firefox exits"; and if you either don't care, want to keep a record of everything you've downloaded, or just don't trust computers to do what they say they're going to do, choose "Manually." Of course, if you remove a file from the Download Manager, you'll lose your record of where you downloaded it from, so if you've forgotten the source it won't be so easy to re-download the file later. However, this isn't really a big concern, since you can usually use the History to find the site again.

Cookies

I know that a lot of people don't like cookies—they are used to track your movements on a particular web site, after all, and accepting a cookie means you are allowing a web site to write files onto your hard drive—but they can come in very handy when you visit a site that requires a login or one for which you want to remember your preferences. I allow *The New York Times* web site to set a cookie on my laptop so I don't have to log in every single time I want to read the news, for example, and I allow Google to set a cookie because I want my search results to be delivered to me in groups of 50 at a time, not 10.

However, not all cookies are wanted. A lot of web sites try to set cookies for no other reason than keeping track of visitors and the pages they view. For instance, as I look through the list of sites that have tried to place cookies on my computer (but were blocked), I find *ad.doubleclick.net* (a web mega-advertising company that has engaged in some shady practices in the past), *www.forbes.com* (I don't plan on buying archived articles, so why do I need a cookie from your site?), and *www.adobe.com* (I just want to download software from you, not let you track me!). Fortunately, Firefox makes it easy both to allow sites you approve of to set cookies on your machine and to block other sites from attempting to track you with cookies, as you can see in Figure B-3.

If you want to block all cookies on your computer by unchecking "Allow sites to set cookies," Firefox will let you do so. Your web experience is going to be severely limited in many ways, but you can do it—as with so much to do with Firefox, it's your choice.

I recommend checking the boxes next to "Allow sites to set cookies" *and* "for the originating web site only," and changing the setting in the Keep Cookies drop-down menu to, well, whatever you want. Here's my reasoning. First, you should enable cookies for the reasons I give in the "Cookies?!?" sidebar in this appendix: because some sites require cookies to really be functional. However, be aware that some web sites have banners and other ads on them, and in addition to the web page itself, these ads can set cookies as well. By checking "for the originating web site only," you prevent ads from ever even attempting to set cookies on your machine.

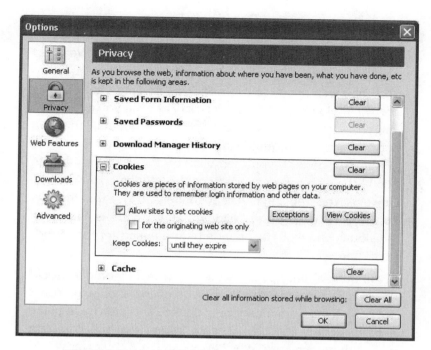

FIGURE B-3. Cookies: to accept or not to accept? That is the question.

How long you should keep cookies is, as I said, up to you. If you choose "until they expire," you'll be asked whether to accept a particular cookie and won't be bothered again until that cookie expires. Some cookies expire in a few hours; others, like Google's, don't expire for over 30 years! This setting, however, will be the least bothersome. If you're the kind of person that just wants to set your preferences and not have to think about cookies again, use "until they expire."

If you're more paranoid about cookies, you might want to use "until I close Firefox." With this setting, all cookies expire the moment you close your web browser. True, this is far more secure, but it also means that you'll have to log into *The New York Times* web site or My Yahoo! every single time you open up Firefox. It's not that big a deal, but some people might find it annoying.

Finally, if you're as paranoid as I am, pick "ask me every time." Every single time a web site tries to set a cookie on my machine, I get asked for permission. That way, I know what's going onto my computer and which web sites are tracking me. I do get asked about

Cookies?!?

What are cookies, and why do you need them? We need cookies because web servers—the computers that store and send web pages to users like you and me—are actually pretty simple things, with no memory at all. If you go to *http://www.widgets.com* and click on the link for "Products," the web server gets the request and obediently sends back the "Products" page. If you then click on the link for "Widgets 2000," the web server sends back the "Widgets 2000" page. However, the web server has absolutely no idea that the person who requested the "Widgets 2000" page is the same individual who just 10 seconds before asked for the "Products" page.

If you think about it, you can see how this ignorance would cause a real pickle when it came to online shopping. You'd put something in your shopping basket, and then try to place another item in the basket, only to find that the first item wasn't there anymore. Why? Because the web server would have no way of knowing that you were the same person who wanted the first item!

To get around this problem, Netscape unveiled cookies in 1994 with the release of Netscape Navigator 1.0. Basically, a cookie is a small text file on your computer's hard drive, placed there by a web site you are visiting that wishes to keep track of who you are as you go from page to page to page. A cookie, in and of itself, cannot identify you personally. Basically, it's just an identification number, such as "A9865T3459X" or some other gibberish. However, once a web site has set a cookie on your computer, it can query that cookie each time it receives a request for a web page, and thereby check whether you've been to the site before, or keep track of the pages you're visiting or the items you're purchasing.

cookies quite a lot as a result of that setting. Cookies are everywhere on the Web, and it sometimes seems like every other web site I visit attempts to set a cookie on my computer. Fortunately, you can reduce the number of times you'll be asked about cookies by paying attention when Firefox asks you about them, because it will remember which sites you've specified not to accept cookies from.

If you want to see the cookies that are on your computer, press View Cookies. A window will open listing all the sites that have placed cookies on your PC; to view the contents of a cookie, select it. You probably won't understand anything you see besides the expiration date, but even that can be interesting. Why, for example, does Google's cookie not expire until 2038? What's up with that?

You can remove a selected cookie by choosing it and then pressing Remove Cookie, or, if you're feeling particularly destructive, you can choose Remove All Cookies and de-cookify yourself completely. If you want to remove a cookie for a site and don't want to be bothered by that site ever again, make sure you check "Don't allow sites that set removed cookies to set future cookies." I leave that one unchecked, since I may change my mind in the future, but you may want to check it.

Finally, the Exceptions button opens a new window that lists your cookie policy for each web site that you've encountered. Each site is listed, and next to it are the words Allow and Block. If you realize you've made a mistake with a site, select it, press Remove Site, close the window, and then visit the site again, changing your answer to the question of whether to accept the cookie or not. If you want to start over from scratch, press Remove All Sites and be prepared for a barrage of cookie-related questions as you travel about the Web.

Cache

The last privacy setting is for your cache. Firefox uses a cache just like all other web browsers do: as a temporary storage location for pages you've visited. That way, when you hit the Back button or revisit a site you've been to recently, Firefox checks to see if the page you're returning to is in your cache, and if it is, it uses that stored copy instead of actually requesting the page again. Obviously, this can speed up your browsing experience. But don't worry: if the page has been updated, Firefox will get the latest version even if it's not the one in your cache. It verifies the page version by asking the web server the date and time at which the page was last modified and comparing that to the date and time at which your copy of the page was cached. If changes were made after you stored your copy, Firefox requests a new copy from the server.

By default, Firefox uses a cache of 50 MB; if your hard drive is small, you'll probably want to adjust that down. If you never want to use a cache and always want to request pages from the Web, set the disk space for the cache to zero. If you've been visiting pages that you don't want to appear in your cache, click on Clear to remove everything that Firefox is storing. There's one more option available on the Privacy screen: at the bottom of the window is a Clear All button. Pressing that will remove everything: cache contents, cookies, saved passwords, saved form information, and browsing history. If you want to leave as few tracks behind you as possible, press the Clear All button when you're done browsing—but be aware that you are sacrificing a lot of convenience by doing so.

Prying eyes

If you're using Firefox on a public machine—at an Internet café, for instance—I suggest that you definitely press Clear All when you're finished with the machine. That way, the next guy sitting down at the computer won't be able to use your information or track you. If you're surfing the Web at home, on the other hand, whether or not you'll want to clear all your stored info at the end of a session depends on the trust you have for the people with whom you live.

Now we've set up Privacy, so let's move on to Web Features.

Web Features

Firefox's Web Features options, which you can see in Figure B-4, take care of a lot of safety and annoyance issues that web users have to face.

Here are the options that you can configure:

Block Popup Windows

Let's start with Block Popup Windows, which you must be sure to check now. Right now. Set this book down, open Firefox, and make sure that you are blocking pop-up windows. Once you've done that, come back.

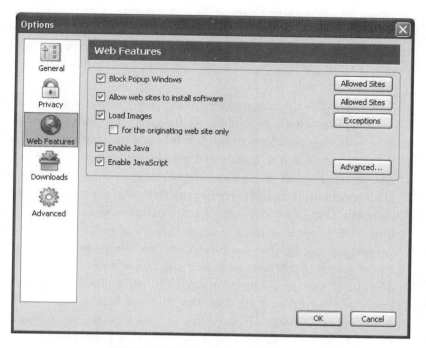

FIGURE B-4. Web Features options in Firefox.

Finished? OK, let's continue. What did you just do? Well, if you've ever used the Web for any length of time, you've undoubtedly been annoyed by a barrage of pop-up and pop-under advertisement windows. Introduced a few years ago, they rapidly became one of the most annoying things web users have to face. By checking the box next to Block Popup Windows, you just restored a measure of peace and quiet back to your web-browsing experience. If you want to test your now pop-up-less browser, head over to *http://www.gambling.com*, enjoy the unbelievably gaudy animated graphics, and then either hit the Back button or head on to another site. If you were a Windows user using Internet Explorer on anything but XP Service Pack 2 (you know, that update that fixed a huge number of security flaws but broke a few other things in the process), upon leaving the site you would find yourself faced with an explosion of pop-ups. We Firefox users, on the other hand, are faced with...nothing. No pop-ups, no pop-unders. Ah, bliss.

A couple of notes: first, Firefox blocks the pop-up windows that open when you enter or leave a web page. If you click on link once a page has loaded—let's say, to add an attachment in a web-based email program or to view a larger image in a new window—Firefox will not block it, because you requested the action. If you ask for it, you can still get it; if it was forced on you, Firefox blocks it. Now that makes sense!

Secondly, while the vast majority of the pop-up windows that open when you hit a web page are advertisements, not all of them are. Some web designers have decided to incorporate into their web sites the very feature that so many other people have grown to hate: pop-ups. In other words, these web designers want you to head over to *http://www.pretentious.com* intending to view that site's content, and then immediately cry out in joy when *another* window suddenly pops open with the real web site content in it. Brilliant. Normally, most people just say bye-bye to those sites, but every once in a while you're forced to grit your teeth and accommodate one because you absolutely must access its information. In cases like that, open this preference screen and click on the Allowed Sites button next to Block Popup Windows. In the Allowed Sites window, you can enter the URL of the site for which you want to allow pop-ups. Enter `www.pretentious.com`, or, if you want to allow any of the sites in the "pretentious" domain to open pop-ups when you visit them—such as too.pretentious.com, overly.pretentious.com, or snooty.pretentious.com—enter `.pretentious.com`, with the dot at the beginning, and then press OK. In addition, you may want to send an email to the site's webmaster, explaining to him that his web site is annoying…but that one is up to you.

If you add a site to the Allowed Sites list and then want to remove it later, just select it and press Remove Site; if you want to remove every site on the list, press Remove All Sites. Pretty easy.

Allow web sites to install software

You should leave "Allow web sites to install software" checked, or you will not be able to install any add-ons for Firefox. If you're really paranoid and you want to download each add-on to your hard drive and then manually install it, uncheck the box; most people, though, should leave it checked. Don't worry that you just opened yourself up to all of Internet Explorer's security holes, though—as discussed in Chapter 4, Firefox has many safeguards in place that protect you as you install software.

If you know of a site right now that you want to put on the whitelist of places that can install software, go ahead and press the Allowed Sites button next to this option. This window is just like the Allowed Sites window for pop-up windows, so you shouldn't have any problems.

Load Images

Images are one of the cornerstones of the Web, so you really should leave Load Images checked (unless you're on a painfully slow Internet connection or you are visually disabled and cannot view pictures). You may also want to check "for the originating web site only"—but on the other hand, you may not. The idea is that checking it will block a lot of ads, since many web sites have two kinds of images on them: those they serve and those served by third-party providers. For instance, news pictures on *The New York Times* web site will come from *www.nytimes.com*, but ads may come from *ads. nytimes.com*, or even *www.doubleclick.com*. If you checked "for the originating site only," you would see the news pictures on the site but not the ads.

Unfortunately, this can cause problems in two ways. First, not all ads come from third-party web sites, so you won't block everything (and AdBlock, discussed in Chapter 5, is a better way to block ads, believe me). Second, a web site may actually serve pictures from several sites, and those pictures may not be ads, so if you check this option you may well block images that you actually want to see. Since those problems exist, I don't recommend checking the "for the originating web site only" box.

Even if you are loading images, you can still block sites on a case-by-case basis. Just press Exceptions, and a window will open in which you can allow or deny sites the right to display images in your web browser. However, I wouldn't bother going this route—instead, take a look at sections "FlashBlock" and "Adblock" in Chapter 5, for tools that are both easier to use and far more powerful than these settings.

Enable Java

Enable Java should remain checked so you can view and use Java applets on web sites. Java is a programming language developed by Sun, and Java applets are programs written in that language that run inside your web browser. Java has been a very safe environment on the Web, with few of the security hazards that plague Microsoft's

ActiveX technology, so I encourage you to go ahead and allow it. Of course, you'll need to have Java installed for this to work (see Chapter 4 for details).

Java what?

Java and JavaScript have nothing whatsoever to do with each other, except a shared name. (Michael Jackson and Michael Caine also both share the same first name, but again, that's pretty much where the similarity ends.) To help reduce the confusion, Java-Script is now officially known as ECMAScript, but that name hasn't exactly caught on, so you'll still see references to JavaScript all over the place for some time to come.

Enable JavaScript

JavaScript is a bit more problematic than Java—many security holes over the years have been related to IE's handling of JavaScript. Firefox, however, hasn't had the same continual issues, and a lot of web sites require JavaScript to work effectively—heck, it was a necessity on several web sites I've created. Even so, don't just enable Java-Script without also pressing the Advanced button to the right of the feature and taking a look at the options in the window shown in Figure B-5.

FIGURE B-5. Use JavaScript, but set it up in a way that benefits you.

JavaScripts allow web developers to control web pages and how they behave. This can be a good thing, but rude or malicious developers can also use it to hijack your web experience. If you uncheck

"Move or resize existing windows," you'll never again hit a web site that suddenly causes your browser window to contort into a new set of dimensions unforeseen by you. If you uncheck "Raise or lower windows," you'll never again click on a link to find another window leaping up in front of yours.

Ever tried to right-click on a picture to save it to your hard drive, only to get a pop-up window informing you that right-clicking has been disabled? If you uncheck "Disable or replace context menus," web developers can't pull that trick, or any others involving the contextual menus that appear when you right-click in a web browser.

Next up, if you uncheck "Hide the status bar," and you open a small pop-up window by clicking a link on a web page, that window won't be able to open without a status bar in place (which the web site could be obscuring to hide valuable information).

A few years ago, a fad of streaming text in the status bar located at the bottom of the web browser window swept the world of web design. A lot of people–myself included–found this quite annoying. If you want to prevent this from happening, uncheck "Change status bar text." This will also ensure that the status bar is displaying the true destination of a hyperlink when you hover over it with your mouse.

The last advanced option for JavaScript is "Change images." I don't recommend unchecking the box for this option, because that would prevent rollovers from showing up in your web browser. Rollovers are often used for navigation on web pages: you see a row of buttons, say with white text on a blue background, but when your mouse passes, or *rolls*, over each button, that particular button changes in some way to indicate that your mouse is over it and it is clickable. Rollovers are not a bad thing, and some web sites are impossible to navigate if you have them blocked, so you should allow your web browser to change images using JavaScript.

Once you have JavaScript set up the way you want it, go ahead and choose OK to close the Advanced JavaScript Options window.

That's it for Web Features–the next section in this advanced tour of Firefox options is Downloads.

Downloads

One of the coolest features of the Web is that there's so much great stuff out there for you to grab and play with, try out, or use. As you can see in Figure B-6, Firefox allows you to control how acquiring that stuff works.

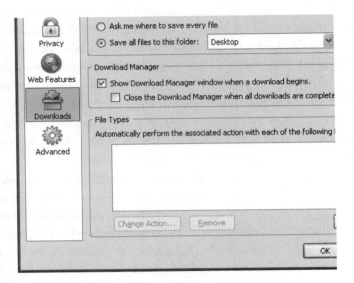

FIGURE B-6. Download options for Firefox.

Let's take a look at the full range of Firefox's Downloads options:

Download Folder

This determines where downloaded files go by default. It's covered in Chapter 2.

Download Manager

We looked at Firefox's Download Manager in Chapter 3. To set it up, check both "Show Download Manager window when a download begins" and "Close the Download Manager when all downloads are complete."

File Types

This section shows you what Firefox will do when it encounters files on the Web, either when you click on a link or when a type of multimedia is embedded in a web page. If you want to change what Firefox does when you click on a link for a certain kind of file type (e.g., .DOC, .MPG, .MP3, or .MOV), first select the file type from the list provided, press Choose Action, and then make your choice from the

Change Action window. Your choices are to open with a default application, open with a different application that you choose, or save the file to disk. Press OK to close the Change Action window, and your choice will now be used.

If you click the Plug-Ins button, a window will open indicating if a plug-in is available for a particular file type. You can prevent a particular plug-in from kicking in when it spots a particular kind of file by unchecking the file type. Firefox will then download the file instead of attempting to play it with a plug-in. When you're done, press OK to close the Plug-Ins window. I discussed plug-ins in more depth in Chapter 4.

Downloads are taken care of, so it's time to advance to the last section: Firefox's Advanced options.

Advanced

The Advanced settings tab, visible in Figure B-7, is where Firefox keeps all the more specialized goodies. They're not essential, but I guarantee you'll find at least one item in here that exactly solves a problem you've been having, or provides a feature that's just perfect for your needs.

Here are the sections you'll see on the Advanced tab:

Accessibility

Don't skip this section just because you think you don't need it! The second of the options offered here is something all Firefox users should consider.

The first choice—"Move system caret with focus/selection changes"— is not generally useful, unless you're using a screen reader or magnifier. If you enable "Move system caret," the small blinking up-and-down line (the caret) you're probably used to from word processors will now appear on your web page. This doesn't mean that you can type on the web page; instead, it indicates where the focus is; in other words, where you've clicked. Screen readers will use that focus to know which areas to read, and magnifiers will use that focus to know which areas to magnify. You can then move focus using either your mouse or the arrow keys on your keyboard, and the caret will move also.

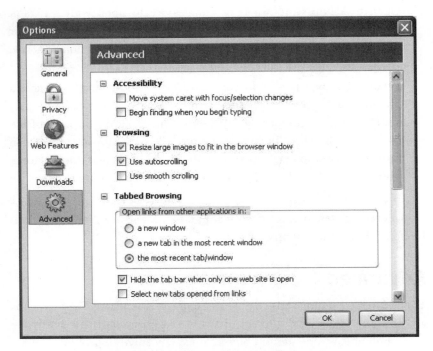

FIGURE B-7. Advanced options in Firefox.

Flip the switch

Another way to turn on that caret is to press F7 on your keyboard. Although the dialog box that opens refers to it there as Caret Browsing, it's the same thing. In fact, if I need to toggle between viewing the caret and turning it off, I just press F7 to see it, and then press F7 again to turn it off.

The second option under Accessibility, "Begin finding when you begin typing," is a great feature that invokes Firefox's Find feature (which I discussed in "Find in This Page and Find As You Type" in Chapter 5) the moment you begin typing something. With this feature enabled, you don't even have to press Ctrl+F to start searching a web page.

Browsing

The Browsing area of the Advanced options tab governs how Firefox presents web pages to you.

Checking "Resize large images to fit in the browser window" means that if you visit a web page containing a picture that is so large that it would require scrolling (either up and down or right and left) to view it all, Firefox will automatically shrink it and display the picture within the confines of your browser window. If you click on the picture, it will jump to its full size; click on it again to restore it to the smaller size.

Zoom, zoom, zoom

To test this feature, load this URL in your browser: *http://www. ibiblio.org/wm/paint/auth/vinci/joconde/joconde.jpg*. You should see a small Mona Lisa; when you move your mouse over her, you should see a small magnifying glass with a plus sign (+) in it. Go ahead and click on the image, and you'll see a really big Mona Lisa; click again and she returns to her smaller size.

If you have a mouse with a scroll wheel (and who doesn't, these days?), you may also want to check "Use autoscrolling." If you check this option, you can press down on the wheel and, while holding it, move the mouse up or down to scroll the web page you're viewing in the direction you're dragging the mouse. I find this behavior annoying, so I make sure this option isn't checked, but your tastes may vary.

Before discussing the third option, "Use smooth scrolling," let's review the many ways you can move up or down while you're viewing a web page:

- If you click on the scroll arrows at the top or bottom of the vertical scrollbar on the righthand side of your browser, you move the page up or down a few lines at time.

- If you click inside the vertical scrollbar, or use the PgUp or PgDn keys on your keyboard, you move up or down a screen at a time.

- If you press the spacebar, you advance down one screen at a time.

- Finally, if you click and hold the scrollbox in the vertical scrollbar, you can drag it up or down to move as much or as little at a time as you like.

If you do not check "Use smooth scrolling" and you use the first, second, or third of the methods listed above, your screen will jump as you move up and down. If you place a checkmark next to "Use smooth scrolling," instead of jumping, Firefox slides the screen up or down. It's hard to describe, and you will either love it or hate it, so I suggest finding a long web page with a lot of text and testing both settings, and then choosing accordingly.

Of course, "Use smooth scrolling" doesn't affect the fourth method listed above, since the amount of movement there is completely under your control.

Tabbed Browsing

Tabs are one of the coolest features Firefox has to offer, so it's not surprising that you get to exert control over how this feature works in the browser. Your Tabbed Browsing options are shown in Figure B-8.

The section-within-a-section labeled "Open links from other applications in" is designed for users who have made Firefox the default web browser on their Windows systems. Let's say a friend has sent you an email with a hyperlink in it. You click on it so you can view the referenced web page...but now what? If you've made Firefox your default web browser, the link will open in Firefox, but how, exactly? The choice is up to you.

Do you want a new window to open up, even if Firefox is already running? Pick "a new window." Do you want Firefox to use the window you already have open, and just open a new tab in that window? Choose "a new tab in the most recent window." Or maybe you want the new link to open in the active tab or window, replacing the current contents. If so, select "the most recent tab/window."

The next option under Tabbed Browsing is "Hide the tab bar when only one web site is open." As I discussed in Chapter 2, I don't think checking this option is a good idea—leaving the tab bar in place is a handy reminder to newbies that the option of opening multiple tabs exists, and it's not as though the bar takes up much browser real estate.

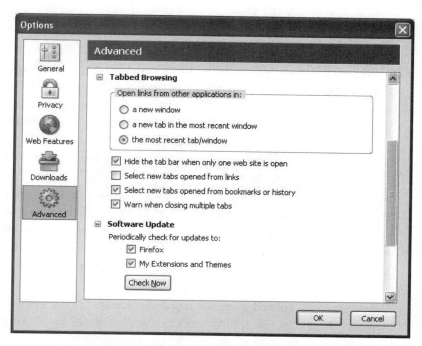

FIGURE B-8. Tabbed Browsing Advanced options in Firefox.

Whether to enable the "Select new tabs opened from links" option is completely a matter of personal choice, but let me make a case against changing it from its (unchecked) default setting. Normally, when you open a link in a new tab by right-clicking on it and selecting Open Link in New Tab (or by middle-clicking on a link, or by pressing Ctrl while clicking with the left mouse button), the new tab opens in the background. In other words, it opens next to any already open tabs, but Firefox keeps the tab you're currently viewing in focus.

If you check the box next to "Select new tabs opened from links," each new tab you open will immediately grab focus and become the tab you're viewing. This may make sense to you, but it would drive me completely insane. Let's say I'm reading Google News. I scan the page looking for interesting stories. Oh, there's one—so I right-click and choose Open Link in New Tab. There's another one—so I repeat the process. And another. And another. Now I still have Google News open in the tab I'm viewing, but I also have four other tabs open, each with pages I want to read, and each loaded in the background. When I'm ready to read them, I click on each tab in turn and read the stories. Easy, simple, and sane.

If I had "Select new tabs opened from links" checked, the process would instead have occurred like this: read Google News. Right-click on link and choose Open Link in New Tab. Gah! Now that tab has seized focus and is the one I'm seeing, not Google News. Click back on the Google News tab so the story I wanted to eventually read can continue loading in the background. Reorient myself to Google News, and continue reading. Another link looks good, so I right-click to load the link in a new tab. Gah! It did it again! The other tab jumps to the front! Back to Google News while the other tab loads. And so on. I find this process to be distracting and annoying. Tabs are supposed to enable you to better use your web browser, not force you to constantly jerk your mental focus from page to page—do yourself a favor, and leave "Select new tabs opened from links" unchecked.

"Select new tabs opened from bookmarks or history" is the same as the previous option, except that it causes a tab created by clicking on a bookmark or history selection to grab focus. This one I actually leave checked: if I chose the bookmark, I want to see it now, so I want that tab to have focus.

If it were up to me

I would have renamed these two options something like "Tabs opened from links grab focus" and "Tabs opened from bookmarks or history grab focus." I think that wording would make these options more obvious.

Finally, unless you like living on the edge, you should definitely leave "Warn when closing multiple tabs" checked. If it's not checked, you're going to run into the following situation sooner or later: you've got 10 tabs open that you've carefully selected for reading, research, or fun. You accidentally close the browser window instead of a single tab, by clicking on the X in the upper-right corner of the window instead of the X on the righthand side of the tab bar. Boom! The browser window closes like you told it to, and all your tabs are gone. Yes, you could recover them using the History Sidebar (covered in "Sidebars" in Chapter 3), but it's a pain. Better to check this box here, and be warned if you try to close a browser window that contains multiple tabs. It's saved my bacon, and it will yours. Don't uncheck it!

Software Update

The next section is Software Update, and it's a doozy. There is simply no good reason not to check the boxes next to both Firefox and My Extensions and Themes. By doing so, you enable Firefox to check every once in a while for updates to your browser and any extensions or themes you've installed. If you're feeling impatient, or just extra paranoid, go ahead and press Check Now, and Firefox will immediately inquire if there are any updates available. In both cases (i.e., Firefox checks periodically or you force a check), if any updates are found, a window appears asking you if you'd like to install them. Do it, and that's one less thing you have to worry about.

Security

The Security section is easy to talk about: don't you dare uncheck anything. All three options—Use SSL 2.0, Use SSL 3.0, and Use TLS 1.0—should be checked and remain checked. Ever been to a web site that used *https://* instead of *http://* in the address? Ever bought anything securely on the Web with a credit card? Then you've used *SSL* or *TLS*, technologies that encrypt the conversation between your web browser and the web server to which it's talking. If you turn off SSL or TLS, you won't be able to access and use secure sites anymore. Now why would you want to do that?

Certificates

Figure B-9 shows the options under Certificates, the next section in the Advanced tab.

Certificates help secure web sites prove to your web browser that they are who they say they are. I'd leave everything here alone, just the way that Firefox set it up for you. Change it only if you must, and in that case, you'll know enough to know what to change and how to change it—or your system administrator will. The vast majority of Firefox users will never, ever need to touch this section.

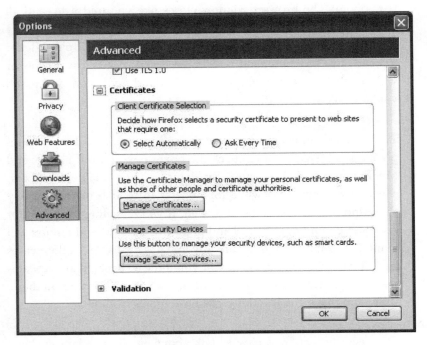

FIGURE B-9. Advanced options for Certificates in Firefox.

Something not look right?

Firefox developers have made it very clear that both the Certificates and Validation sections may change in future versions of the browser, so be prepared for differences between the screenshots presented here and what you see in front of you in Firefox.

Validation

Validation, pictured in Figure B-10, is the last section in the Advanced tab.

As with the Certificates section, most (nearly all) Firefox users shouldn't have to mess with the options here and can just leave these settings the way they are. Again, if you know enough to know that you need to change these settings, you should know enough to do so without causing a problem.

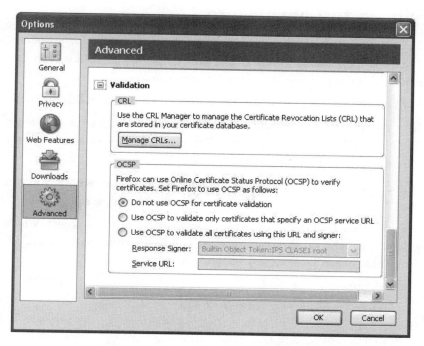

FIGURE B-10. Advanced options for Validation in Firefox.

That's it! You are now a Firefox options expert. Just write to O'Reilly and let them know, and you'll get a handsome embossed certificate proclaiming your advanced skill and knowledge!

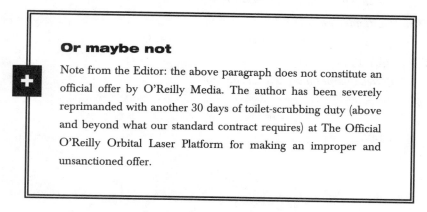

Or maybe not

Note from the Editor: the above paragraph does not constitute an official offer by O'Reilly Media. The author has been severely reprimanded with another 30 days of toilet-scrubbing duty (above and beyond what our standard contract requires) at The Official O'Reilly Orbital Laser Platform for making an improper and unsanctioned offer.

Where to Learn More

There's not a lot of documentation out there about Firefox's options. Your only real source of info at this time is the official Firefox web site, which provides an overview of the Options window.

For more on proxies, see Wikipedia's article (noted later in this section).

If you're interested in learning more about passwords, I wrote a column for SecurityFocus titled "Pass the Chocolate" that gives some tips for choosing a good password.

Wikipedia has a good piece that explains what cookies are, or you can read "The Unofficial Cookie FAQ," which, though old, is still good.

For more on JavaScript, see Wikipedia's article on the subject, which gets pretty technical in several places. The first section explains the differences between JavaScript, Java, and JScript.

Firefox's options
> *http://www.mozilla.org/support/firefox/options*

Wikipedia on proxies
> *http://en.wikipedia.org/wiki/Proxy_server*

"Pass the Chocolate"
> *http://www.securityfocus.com/columnists/245*

Wikipedia on cookies
> *http://en.wikipedia.org/wiki/HTTP_cookie*

"The Unofficial Cookie FAQ"
> *http://www.cookiecentral.com/faq/*

Wikipedia on JavaScript
> *http://en.wikipedia.org/wiki/JavaScript*

Index

We'd like to hear your suggestions for improving our indexes. Send email to *index@oreilly.com*.

About the Author

Scott Granneman is a consultant, educator, and author. As a consultant for Bryan Consulting, he works with small- and medium-sized businesses and nonprofits to bring them the beneficial uses of technology. In particular, as the lead architect of the Bryan Consulting Content Management System (CMS), he envisions, designs, and helps develop new extensions for the CMS that benefit all of the company's clients.

As an educator, Scott has taught thousands of people of all ages—from preteens to senior citizens—on a wide variety of topics, including technology, education, and literature. As his focus has shifted in recent years to Linux and other open source technologies, he has worked to bring knowledge of these powerful new directions in software to people at all levels of technical skill. He currently works as an adjunct professor at Washington University in St. Louis, Missouri, teaching courses about technology.

As an author, Scott has written articles about computer and Internet security and privacy for SecurityFocus, the largest community of security professionals on the Internet, and *Linux Magazine*. He currently writes as a monthly columnist for SecurityFocus, with op/ed pieces that focus on general topics of security, for *Linux Magazine*, with a column focusing on new and interesting Linux software, and as a professional blogger on The Open Source Weblog. He is currently working on a book about the Knoppix Live CD version of the Linux operating system.

Colophon

Our look is the result of reader comments, our own experimentation, and feedback from distribution channels. Distinctive covers complement our distinctive approach to technical topics, breathing personality and life into potentially dry subjects.

Mary Brady was the production editor and proofreader for *Don't Click on the Blue E!* Rachel Wheeler was the copyeditor. Philip Dangler and Claire Cloutier provided quality control. Lucie Haskins wrote the index. Lydia Onofrei provided production assistance.

Scott Idleman/Blink designed the cover of this book. The cover image is a photograph of a red fox (*Vulpes vulpes*) from Getty Images (Photographer/Artist: Peter Lilja). Karen Montgomery produced the cover layout with Adobe InDesign CS using Berthold Akzidenz Grotesk font.

Marcia Friedman designed the interior layout. This book was converted by Andrew Savikas to FrameMaker 5.5.6 with a format conversion tool created by Erik Ray, Jason McIntosh, Neil Walls, and Mike Sierra that uses Perl and XML technologies. The text font is Berthold Baskerville; the heading font is Adobe Helvetica Neue; and the code font is Lucas-Font's TheSans Mono Condensed. The illustrations that appear in the book were produced by Robert Romano, Jessamyn Read, and Lesley Borash using Macromedia FreeHand MX and Adobe Photoshop 7.

Related Titles Available from O'Reilly

Windows Users

Access Cookbook, *2nd Edition*

Access Database Design & Programming, *3rd Edition*

Excel Hacks

Excel Pocket Guide

Outlook 2000 in a Nutshell

Outlook Pocket Guide

PC Annoyances

Windows XP Annoyances

Windows XP Hacks

Windows XP Home Edition:
The Missing Manual

Windows XP in a Nutshell

Windows XP Pocket Guide

Windows XP Power User

Windows XP Pro:
The Missing Manual

Windows XP Unwired

Word Hacks

Word Pocket Guide, *2nd Edition*

Keep in touch with O'Reilly

1. Download examples from our books

To find example files for a book, go to:

www.oreilly.com/catalog

select the book, and follow the "Examples" link.

2. Register your O'Reilly books

Register your book at *register.oreilly.com*

Why register your books? Once you've registered your O'Reilly books you can:

- Win O'Reilly books, T-shirts or discount coupons in our monthly drawing.
- Get special offers available only to registered O'Reilly customers.
- Get catalogs announcing new books (US and UK only).
- Get email notification of new editions of the O'Reilly books you own.

3. Join our email lists

Sign up to get topic-specific email announcements of new books and conferences, special offers, and O'Reilly Network technology newsletters at:

elists.oreilly.com

It's easy to customize your free elists subscription so you'll get exactly the O'Reilly news you want.

4. Get the latest news, tips, and tools

http://www.oreilly.com

- "Top 100 Sites on the Web"—PC Magazine
- CIO Magazine's Web Business 50 Awards

Our web site contains a library of comprehensive product information (including book excerpts and tables of contents), downloadable software, background articles, interviews with technology leaders, links to relevant sites, book cover art, and more.

5. Work for O'Reilly

Check out our web site for current employment opportunities:

jobs.oreilly.com

6. Contact us

O'Reilly & Associates
1005 Gravenstein Hwy North
Sebastopol, CA 95472 USA

TEL: 707-827-7000 or 800-998-9938
(6am to 5pm PST)

FAX: 707-829-0104

order@oreilly.com
For answers to problems regarding your order or our products.
To place a book order online, visit:

www.oreilly.com/order_new

catalog@oreilly.com
To request a copy of our latest catalog.

booktech@oreilly.com
For book content technical questions or corrections.

corporate@oreilly.com
For educational, library, government, and corporate sales.

proposals@oreilly.com
To submit new book proposals to our editors and product managers.

international@oreilly.com
For information about our international distributors or translation queries. For a list of our distributors outside of North America check out:

international.oreilly.com/distributors.html

adoption@oreilly.com
For information about academic use of O'Reilly books, visit:

academic.oreilly.com

O'REILLY®

Our books are available at most retail and online bookstores.
To order direct: 1-800-998-9938 • *order@oreilly.com* • *www.oreilly.com*
Online editions of most O'Reilly titles are available by subscription at *safari.oreilly.com*